THE THEORY AND PRACTICE OF HISTORICAL MARTIAL ARTS

Guy Windsor

www.spada.press

(c) 2018 Guy Windsor

www.guywindsor.com

ISBN 978-952-7157-28-2 The Theory and Practice of Historical Martial Arts (hardback)

ISBN 978-952-7157-29-9 The Theory and Practice of Historical Martial Arts (paperback)

ISBN 978-952-7157-30-5 The Theory and Practice of Historical Martial Arts (PDF)

ISBN 978-952-7157-31-2 The Theory and Practice of Historical Martial Arts (EPUB)

ISBN 978-952-7157-32-9 The Theory and Practice of Historical Martial Arts (MOBI)

Book design by Zebedee Design

Cover Artwork by Curtis Fee

For my wife Michaela

Love, always.

TABLE OF CONTENTS

Introduction   7

THEORY   17
The Seven Principles of Mastery   19
Fencing Theory   37
How to Recreate Historical Martial Arts from Historical Sources   67
    What Counts as a Source?   68
    How to Choose a Source That's Right For You   73
    An Overview of Popular Sources From Between 1300 and 1800   75
    How to Use Translations   83
    How to Approach Your Chosen Source   86
    Principles of Drill Design   96
    Create Your Cornerstone Drill   102
    Syllabus Design   110
Ethics   118

PRACTICE   129
Safety   131
Equipment   136
Choosing a Sword   142
    Types of Sword   150
Handling the Sword   166
Skill Development   176
Judgement   188
How to Start a HMA Club   190
How to Teach a Basic Class   197
How to Teach an Individual Lesson   227

Tournaments 232
   Training for Tournaments 235
   Preparing for Tournaments 238
   How to Use Tournaments in Your Training 239

ATTRIBUTE TRAINING: HEALTH, STRENGTH, SPEED 243
Sleep 245
Nutrition 248
Physical training 265
   Flexibility Training 267
   Strength Training 269
   Speed Training 274
Training for Foresight 283
Training for Boldness 287
   Fear Practice 291
   Fear Management 293
Meditation 295
Breathing 298
Why Do We Do This? 329
Bibliography 335

Acknowledgements 341
About the Author 343

INTRODUCTION

I think it all began at the fencing club at Edinburgh University in 1992, when Charlie Napier ran down the fencing strip at me. His foil was held across his body, with the point way back behind him. I extended my arm, and he ran his body onto my point as his foil flicked around, the blade bending in a graceful arc and tapping me harmlessly on the shoulder. Both lights went off, and the president called the hit. For Charlie. Because he started moving forwards first: he had priority, and his suicidal approach took precedence over my safe, careful and lethal response. I'd been fencing for five years at school, but there we had always followed a much stricter interpretation of the International Fencing Federation's (FIE) rules, leading to a much more classical and cautious style of play.

But when Charlie got given point after point, I realised that the modern sport of fencing was completely unrealistic and had practically nothing in common with its martial roots any more. A little while later I was at a local competition and got talking to a beginner fencer, Paul, who had taken up the sport a few weeks earlier and was already becoming disillusioned with it. We got together in Holyrood Park under Salisbury Crags, and with épées and fencing masks set about trying to kill each other in a realistic manner. Proper hits. No suicidal running about. Treat the swords like they are sharp, and bugger the modern rules.

My grandpa had been a fencer, but he died when I was only thirteen. I'd had a couple of lessons off him, but nothing serious. The next time I went down to London to see my granny, I dug through Grandpa's books and found Alfred Hutton's *The Sword and the Centuries*. In it, Hutton refers to dozens of old books written *in the days when swords were used for real*. This set me off on a quest to find some of these books, and I set to work figuring out how swordfighting should be done. It has always been obvious to me that people who fought for real are more likely to know how to fight than us modern folk trying to figure it out from scratch. And one day, in the National Library of Scotland, I found Donald McBane's *The Expert Sword-Man's Companion*. This glorious little book begins with 70 pages or so of autobiography (and what a life he led! Duelling, gambling, whoring and soldiering his way across Europe under Marlborough at the turn of the eighteenth century), which was followed by a very practical treatise on sword fighting and a set of instructions for gunnery. Before long my friends and I had also tracked down George Silver's *Paradoxes of Defence* from 1599, and some really poor photocopies of some medieval sources, such as I.33 and the Novati facsimile of *Il Fior di Battaglia*. By the beginning of 1994, we realised we had to create a formal society for studying these arts (we didn't even have a name for what we were doing – I think we came up with the term "historical swordsmanship" around then). This was mostly so we could get other people to come along, because we were getting bored fencing just with each other.

We came across battle re-enactment and were extremely excited to meet other sword enthusiasts – until we realised that they were not interested in the historical swordfighting methods that we were obsessed by. Their interest was broader, and encompassed the clothing, uniforms, battle formations and all that; the actual combat styles were completely unhistorical, invented solely as a way to allow steel-on-steel action in the safest possible way. I regret to say that, being young and foolish, we occasionally behaved rather badly and put our historical techniques to work on unsuspecting re-enactors.

Unbeknownst to us, other groups with interests closer to our own were springing up across the world: the Chicago Swordplay Guild, for one; and the Historical Armed Combat Association in Texas, for another. The internet was only just becoming a thing, so we had no way to find these people until it was actually possible to "search the World Wide Web" in the mid nineties. The Swordplay Symposium International, held at Livermore, California in 2000, was the first convention dedicated to Historical Martial Arts, and Paul went to it. Then all of a sudden, word got around, and we were no longer just a little group of oddballs in Edinburgh; we were at the forefront of a growing international movement. The rest, as they say, is history.

You might be asking who am I to be teaching you this material, and you should ask this question of every expert and the author of every book, treatise, source or reference you come across. Let's face it: not every author really ought to be writing books, and not everyone who claims to know things about swords actually does – and this is just as true today as it was hundreds of years ago. I would say it's especially important when you're considering modern experts (like me).

I've been researching historical source material since about 1993. I have a degree in English literature from Edinburgh University, so I know how to read books and write about them. I graduated in 1996. I founded The Dawn Duellists Society in Edinburgh in 1994. It is still going strong today. I founded The School of European Swordsmanship in 2001. It's still going and it has branches all over the world. My first book, *The Swordsman's Companion*, came out in 2004. I've written and published eight books since then and my training syllabus is online for all to see. I've also created *Audatia: the Medieval Combat Card Game*, which accurately represents medieval Italian longsword fencing.

All that this means is that it is easy for you to judge one way or the other whether my opinion and my approach, my way of doing things, is worth anything. So have a look at my videos and read some of my books (like this one), and decide for yourself whether or not you think I know what I'm talking about. It's perfectly all right if you think I don't.

It's really important that you can clearly identify the authority behind whatever it is you're practising. You might practise your art because this is what your teacher tells you to do. That's fine. You might practise it because this is how it was written down in this particular book hundreds of years ago. That's also fine. Or you might practise it this way because you can win tournaments with it. That's fine too. So long as you are absolutely clear what your authority is, you can practise authentically. I hope that after studying this book you'll be able to use a historical source as your authority, and then have other people who have read the same source look at what you've come up with and say "do you know what? You're probably right."

The theory and practice of Historical Martial Arts is a huge and varied topic, so I will break it up into manageable chunks. The first division is inspired by Ridolfo Capoferro's *Gran Simulacro dell'Arte e dell'Uso della Scherma*, or the "Great Representation of the Art and the Use of Fencing." Or indeed, the Theory (art) and Practice (use) of fencing.

Over the last twenty years there has been a huge revival of interest in the martial arts of the past. This ranges from medieval knightly combat to World War Two sentry-killing combatives, and from the self defence of Victorian gentlemen to the cavalry charges of the Hakkapeliitta (the Finnish light cavalry fighting for Gustavus Adolphus during the Thirty Years War, 1618–48). Bare knuckle boxing, knife fighting, swordsmanship, mounted combat, wrestling, military tactics, and black-powder musketry: we have everything, and I have tried an awful lot of it since the very early days of the movement, beginning in 1992. Since 2001, I have been researching and teaching historical swordsmanship, specifically medieval and renaissance Italian swordsmanship, as my full-time job, and I have watched with glee as the field gets wider and wider, and deeper and deeper. Before we dive in though, let's define some terms.

Historical. In my view, a historical martial art is one based on historical research. It's that simple. A historical martial artist can point to the page in the source text that describes what they are doing, or can explain why what they are doing is different from the book. The largest single section of this book covers *how* to choose a source and develop a working training system from it. I'm aware that practitioners of some very old martial arts that have survived in an unbroken lineage (such as some Japanese *koryu*) refer to their arts as "historical", but I am using the term exclusively to mean "based on historical research".

The majority of historical martial arts currently practised are based on a European source. There are useful historical martial arts sources from many cultures and periods which are written in sufficient detail that you can actually recreate the arts they represent, but a very large proportion of these sources are European and, as far as I am aware, the idea to start recreating these arts began in Europe and the United States, and so naturally focussed on the European sources. The European martial arts revival of the last twenty years is also in part a reaction to the massive success and popularity of Asian arts in the West. There is nothing wrong with those arts – I have spent many years training in Chinese and Japanese arts – but they are not my focus, though when we look back, we find that at a similar level of technology (say, comparing Europe in 1500 to Japan in 1800) the martial arts are remarkably similar.

Martial. To be worth studying, a martial art must actually work in the context in which it is intended to do so. It is necessary to evaluate the martial quality of the sources, and of the practices that you develop from those sources. In this book I'll take you through that process in some depth.

Art. An art, historically speaking, was defined as natural human actions developed into a system so they can be studied and taught. Fighting is natural. Martial arts are systems that improve on natural fighting, but are very firmly based on it. Art is always a product of the culture it springs from and, while aesthetics are not our primary goal, they are nonetheless an intrinsic part of the arts we practise. A good martial art is efficient, effective and aesthetic. Fighting skill is efficient and effective; a martial artist's practice takes fighting skill a step further, into the realms of artistry.

So what about HEMA? The acronym stands for Historical European Martial Arts, and for a long time that is what most people have called my art. However, the field has grown so large, and has wandered into areas that I find uninteresting (such as creating a modern sword sport), that I'd rather not use it here. Also, and far more disturbingly, the term has been co-opted by fascists, white supremacists, and similar scum, who use it to hark back to the mythical 'good old days' of whites-only Europe (which never existed). I despise that kind of bigotry with my entire being, and I'd rather abandon the tainted label and call my art something different.

This has been a very challenging book to write, so much so that I broke it up into pieces, took them in a haphazard order, and published six of the pieces as separate booklets: instalments 1–6 of *The Swordsman's Quick Guide*. I also developed several online courses to address these principles, particularly my course "Recreate Historical Swordsmanship from Historical Sources" (see swordschool.teachable.com). The work I did on that course forms the basis of the section of this book that covers working with the sources. The overall structure of this book looks like this:

Part 1: Theory
The seven principles of mastery. This is the most general theory of how to get good at anything, and as such belongs at the beginning. If you follow these guidelines, you will find everything else in this book much easier to master.

Fencing theory. This covers the overall structure of fencing systems, and explains all of the main components.

How to recreate historical swordsmanship from historical sources. This covers basic historical theory, and teaches you how to choose a source that suits your needs and interests, and how to work your way through it to create technical and tactical drills; in short, to develop a working martial practice. This section is adapted from material in my online course.

Ethics. I believe it is essential to consider the ethical dimension of the arts you practice, especially when they are based on violent death. This section asks some questions and gives some sample answers, and – most importantly, I think – encourages you to think about things you may have taken for granted.

Part 2: Practice

Safety. This is the basis of all training with weapons. You can't practice if you're broken or dead, so we begin with the principles of safety.

Equipment. To train, you will need weapons and protective gear. In this section I describe the equipment you will need, and we consider where to get it and how to prioritise your purchases. This includes *Choosing a Sword*.

Skill development. This chapter describes how you can develop from training using set drills, through increasing levels of complexity, to freeplay or sparring with your partners.

How to start a training group. There isn't yet a HEMA club in every town in the world. There will be! This chapter outlines the differences between the varying kinds of groups and schools, and the principles behind starting and running a successful training club.

How to teach a basic class. One of the biggest barriers to starting a club is the lack of qualified, experienced instructors. In this chapter I show you how to get started without one by becoming an instructor yourself.

Tournaments. Tournaments are a big part of the modern HEMA scene. In this chapter I outline what they are good for, what they are bad at, and how you can train to win them if you want to.

Physical training. How to develop flexibility, strength and speed, and also how to develop the aptitudes of foresight and boldness. This section includes thoughts on sleep, nutrition, breathing training, and meditation.

It is impossible to cover every technical detail of every HMA practice in a single book. Or even in an entire library. So what I have done here is distil the principles behind good research, good training and good practice to help guide your specific efforts. While this book should be quite readable to a layperson and it has some interesting ideas for advanced practitioners and instructors, I've written it for beginners, with an emphasis on getting you started in sound practice based on clear theory. Wherever I am outlining a skill (such as mindfulness, choosing a good source to work from, or analysing fencing theory), I have included some practical exercises. If your interest in HMA is entirely theoretical, feel free to skip them, but if you intend to be a practitioner, I encourage you to give them a go.

Also, this is a reference resource: it is not a step-by-step guide. I encourage you to skip any section that is not immediately interesting to you. Use the table of contents and pick out whatever piques your fancy. Within each chapter, do try not to skip because they tend to be built up into coherent arguments, but I have not designed this book such that one chapter absolutely depends on the one before it. Where you do need to have some specific prior knowledge, I'll point to the bit you need to read first.

Age and Disability

The majority of HMA practitioners use weapons of some kind: most commonly swords. Weapons are the great equaliser, and the whole point of using one is that it makes it possible for smaller, weaker people to defeat bigger, stronger ones. As George Silver wrote in *Paradoxes of Defence* in 1599:

> "I speak not against Maisters of Defence indeed, they are to be honoured, nor against the Science, it is noble, and in mine opinion to be preferred next to Divinitie; for as Divinitie preserveth the soul from hell and the devil, so doth this noble Science defend the bodie from wounds & slaughter. And moreover, the exercising of weapons putteth away aches, griefs, and diseases, it increaseth strength, and sharpneth the wits. It giveth a perfect judgement, it expelleth melancholy, cholericke and evil conceits, it keepeth a man in breath, perfect health, and long life. It is unto him that hath the perfection thereof, a most friendly and comfortable companion when he is alone, having but only his weapon about him. It putteth him out of fear, & in the wars and places of most danger, it maketh him bold, hardie and valiant."

One of the most famous British military heroes of the Napoleonic era is Lord Nelson, one of the greatest admirals in history. He was also blind in one eye and missing an arm. The most celebrated British fighter pilot of the Second World War was without doubt Douglas Bader, holder of the DFC and the DSO. When he was shot down, he escaped so many times from German prison camps that they sent him to Colditz. All this is impressive even if you didn't know that he had lost both his legs before the war!

My point is simple. There is a long tradition of warriors achieving great things regardless of injury, disability or other impediment. I don't mean to diminish the difficulty that you may face if you are disabled in some way, but in my opinion, the worse your starting point, the greater honour you may attain through your accomplishments. The best student I ever had was a little girl I never met. Her neurological problems were so severe that she became ready to learn to walk at the age of nine. But being the size of a normal nine-year-old, falling down really hurt so she was too frightened to learn. She was being cared for by one of my students who used our falling training to teach her to fall without hurting herself, *and she learned to walk*.

Best. Student. Ever.

If you have some kind of disability, the most qualified person to figure out what you can and can't do is you. I know people who fight in full armour with a peg-leg, who out-wrestle me but are blind, who are in a wheelchair but can fence beautifully. Of course, in a "real fight" it's better to have both legs, be able to see, and not be stuck in a chair. But nobody trains these arts for the sake of winning real fights on the mean streets of Ipswich, so the point is not "who can I beat?" The point is "how good can I become?" And the answer to that, regardless of your disabilities, age, lack of fitness, being overweight, or any other damn thing, is "better than I was yesterday."

And that is enough.

THEORY

THE SEVEN PRINCIPLES OF
MASTERY

I am a swordsman. That means that I tend to approach all problems using the principles of swordsmanship training, so this chapter is about how to pursue your goals in life using these principles. It encapsulates everything I have learned from training martial arts over the last thirty years, and from teaching martial arts over the last fifteen years to hundreds of very different students with all kinds of physical and intellectual imperfections. I've never seen a perfect person, and am not interested in doing so; it is much more interesting to help a person in whatever state they happen to be in to become more fully realised, more fully themselves. Usually, the hook is the sword. Almost all of my students come to me at first because they want to learn sword fighting. But swordsmanship is really just a metaphor for the struggle of life, and their desire to be a good swordsman is thwarted far more by the physical and emotional baggage they bring with them than by any lack of technical or tactical training.

So here is the core of what I do to be able to accomplish my goals, in swordsmanship and in life. There are three internal principles to cover how you think, and four external principles to govern how you act.

The internal principles are:

1. Mindfulness.
2. Flow.
3. Adopt useful beliefs.

The external principles are:

1. No injuries.
2. The Pareto Principle: 80% of outcomes come from 20% of inputs
3. Run a diagnostic, fix the weakest link, and run the diagnostic again.
4. Distinguish between knowledge and skill.

Nobody gets all of these right all the time. Principles are abstract, perfect ideas; we are real, imperfect people. So don't beat yourself up if these seem hard to reach. I will describe each principle in turn, and where necessary I'll give you one exercise for each that will help you embody the principle better. With practice and patience, you'll find them easier and easier to apply.

Let us begin with the internal principles.

Three Internal Principles

These three internal principles are orders of magnitude more important than the four external ones. This is because they govern how you do everything, and why. I go into all of them in more detail in my book *Swordfighting for Writers, Game Designers, and Martial Artists*.

1. Mindfulness

Mindfulness is simply placing your attention where it will do most good. That's it. And it is really, really hard to do, especially when the world is so full of distract – . . . that's a pretty sword . . .

You get the point. The ability to focus, to pay attention, is perhaps the most important life skill you can develop.

There is absolutely nothing wrong with gathering together with some swordy friends and having a bash. Neither is there anything wrong with playing around with some aspects of swordsmanship. I would actually go so far as to say that not all practice should be mindful, because you can become too goal oriented: it's the journey that matters, not the destination. But to really improve your skills in any area, mindful practice is without doubt the most efficient approach.

If you're not sure what skill you're trying to develop, it's not mindful practice. If it does not demand the absolute limit of your concentration and physical skill, it's not mindful practice. If it does not generate measurable improvement, it's not mindful practice. If it's not tiring, frustrating or painful, it's probably not mindful practice. If your practice highlights your every weakness and makes you strengthen it, efficiently and deeply, then it is – must be – mindful.

Mindfulness exercise

The main type of exercise I use to develop the skill of mindfulness is meditation. This comes in lots of forms, each targeted to specific aspects of controlling your mind. You will find more detailed information about meditation on pages 295–297 but here is one simple exercise to get you started. I use this a lot.

The idea is just to pay attention to your breath. Your breath is pretty boring (until you learn to see it differently) and so your mind will wander. That's okay. The exercise is *to return your wandering attention to your breath*. Not to be good at it already.

- Sit comfortably, or lie down
- Set a timer to two minutes, or more. Start easy though. I use between five and fifteen minutes
- Notice your breath coming in and out. Do not interfere with it; just focus on it
- Count each inhalation
- When you get to 10 inhalations, start again at 0
- Pay attention to your breath. As your mind wanders, bring it gently back to your breath
- If your mind wanders and you lose track of the count, don't worry; just return your attention to your breath, and start again from 0
- Keep going until the timer beeps. Smile, and get up.

2. *Flow*

The optimal mental state in which to train is called "the flow state," most famously defined by Mihaly Csikszentmihalyi in his 1990 book *Flow*. Buy it and read it. You won't regret it. This book made me realise that the thing I was really trying to teach most of my students was how to develop an autotelic personality, which means a person who is able to set their own goals. Now that may not sound like much, but actually it is pretty rare. A truly autotelic personality can find meaning and purpose in any situation. It is the one best predictor of mental health and success in any field.

The key defining feature of an autotelic personality is how much time they spend in a flow state; that optimum band of attention in which the thing you are doing is challenging enough to be interesting, but not so challenging that it becomes frustrating. And the key insight is that how you approach the material is the thing that determines how challenging it is.

For instance, if you are trying to master some ghastly engineering maths and failing miserably, a normal person will quit in disgust and frustration. But an autotelic person will find ways to break the maths down into manageable chunks, go back to more basic exercises on which the unattainable maths is based, and plug away at it cheerfully until it all becomes clear.

In short, the thing you are aiming at should be only just out of reach; and by managing the complexity of the material, you enable the flow state – which enables learning.

It is much easier to develop an autotelic personality if you have a supportive and similarly motivated social network. Training partners and colleagues who share your goals and attitude make creating a flow-inducing environment much easier. The thing to look for is a group or school that emphasises process over outcome.

The most common problem I have had in my career choices to date is putting outcome before process. When I went to university to get my degree, I was more interested in training martial arts than in studying English literature. Although I got my degree, I didn't get that much out of it at the time. I wanted the outcome, not the process. As a swordsmanship instructor I am a much better reader than I ever was as a literature student. Then when I went to be a cabinetmaker, again I was more interested in having made the furniture than in actually making it. Sure, I enjoyed parts of the process very much. But I did not have that dedication to perfection in process that marks a really good cabinetmaker. Ironically, now that I do it for a hobby, I enjoy the process of it a lot more. Teaching swordsmanship is the only thing I have ever done where I have truly been more concerned with process than with outcome, which is why I am a much better swordsmanship instructor than I ever was a cabinetmaker. While I am deeply dissatisfied with the outcome (i.e. my current level), I am actually quite pleased with how far I have come: the process so far.

Because I am interested in the process, my mind can be on what I am actually doing, not what I am doing it for; and so flow is easy to attain. The flow state allows you to bring order to consciousness, as opposed to the entropic chaos that it will default to otherwise. And within that order, there is beauty, truth, and meaning.

Flow exercise

I am sure that there is at least one activity you do in which the flow state comes naturally. Perhaps it's playing a computer game, or fencing, or kicking a ball about with your kids. It doesn't matter what you are doing to get into it; just identify the activity in which you are most likely to lose track of time.

While you are doing it, you won't be thinking about flow or mental states at all (if you are, it ain't flowing!). But before you start, notice that you are about to go into the flow state; and when you're done, notice that you were in the flow. Then consider what it was about the activity that led you to enter the flow state. It was probably absorbing for all sorts of reasons.

Then identify the activity you want to be able to be in the flow state for. Training swordsmanship, for instance, or statistical analysis, or changing diapers. What can you do to alter the target activity in which flow is hard, to make it more like the first one, in which flow is natural? Would adding game elements help? Or is there some ritual you do that gets you into the state?

Josh Waitzkin has a section on building triggers in his excellent book *The Art of Learning*, which you might find useful. In short, you create a ritual that you do before the naturally flow-inducing activity, so your body and mind associate the ritual with the mental state that the activity enables. Then when that association is firmly created, you can use the same ritual before any other activity to induce the desired state of mind.

3. Adopt Useful Beliefs

Your beliefs, especially those you are not aware of, hugely influence the effectiveness of everything you do. Annoyingly successful people are often gifted with an inherent belief in the possibility of their own success, or cursed by an inherent belief in their inadequacy, which forces them to strive ridiculously hard.

If you want your training to be successful, it is more important that your beliefs serve your interests than that they are objectively true. For instance, hard work does not guarantee success. But believing that it does makes it more likely that you will work hard, and therefore makes your success more likely.

Useful beliefs that I have adopted include:

- Swordsmanship training is necessary for many people if they are to live a worthwhile life.
- The growth mindset (which I also think is objectively true).
- Every problem can be trained past. (Which I know is not objectively true, but I don't care.)
- My happiness is not the point.

Swordsmanship training is necessary

This may be true for many people. Whether I can prove it or not, it's the reason I can justify devoting my life to the study of my art. I believe that swords can act as the hook that fishes people out of mundane, meaningless, pointless lives, and into their best selves. I've seen it happen, and it makes the hard times worthwhile.

The growth mindset

This just means that you must abandon any idea of inherent talent, or lack of it. The only thing that matters is your attitude to training. Believe that improvement is possible, and you will, by following these principles, inevitably improve.

I highly recommend reading Carol Dweck's book *Mindset: The New Psychology of Success,* and will summarise her findings here. Readers of my blog and my book *Swordfighting for Writers, Game Designers, and Martial Artists* will already know my views on this. The rest of this section is abridged from there.

In short, Dweck's work in psychology has demonstrated that belief in fixed traits (such as talent) leads to the "fixed mindset." This creates all sorts of problems, which are solvable by switching to a "growth mindset" – a belief that things can be learned.

For fixed mindset people, achievements are a reflection of innate traits. And it's bullshit. For growth mindset people, achievements are the outcomes of processes like training.

So why do people continue to believe in talent? For two fundamental reasons:

1. We tend to praise attributes over effort and ascribe results to innate factors, rather than processes. It's the outcome-over-process problem all over again. So kids grow up believing that some people are just naturally gifted, which is partly true but wholly inaccurate, and wildly counterproductive

2. Attributing success to talent gives us an excuse to fail. "He did well because he's a natural; therefore my failure is not my fault. I am just not naturally good at it."

The best tool you can use to develop a growth mindset is to mindfully edit your internal monologue, and the way you speak to others. For instance, if something is hard to do, the phrase "this is very hard, I'm no good at it" will develop a fixed mindset; but saying "this is very hard, I'm not good at it yet" will, by just the addition of that one word, help you develop a growth mindset. Even better would be "this is very hard, so I will work hard to master it." Acknowledging weakness can help you grow strong, but identifying yourself as inherently weak will keep you so.

Every problem can be trained past

You can be a great swordsman. I believe this as an article of faith. Nobody has a truly accurate self image, and it is far more common for people to think that they are worse than they really are, than it is for them to think the reverse.

I've had students with all sorts of disabilities come through my salle over the years, and every one of them, in my eyes, had the ability to be a great swordsman. So what if you only have one arm, or legs that don't work? I really don't care. It just makes things harder – not impossible.

Are you overweight? If so, which is more useful: to believe that your weight is genetically pre-determined, or that it's a result of your diet? Both of these beliefs are partly true. But one empowers you to shift some flab, and the other condemns you to powerless submission to chocolate and burgers. Choose your beliefs wisely.

My happiness is not the point

About a decade ago, before I met my wife, I was going through a really shit time. I was questioning the point of my swordsmanship career and was miserable after the demise of a long-term relationship, and it was just crap. I'm sure you've been somewhere like it, or worse.

A friend of mine who knows me well, and who is deeply

sceptical of the meditation stuff I do, challenged me to put it to use. "It's a technology. Use it. If it works, keep it. If it doesn't, discard it." So I did. And it led to an epiphany of sorts. I acquired a moment of clarity and, in the silence, I realised that *my happiness is not the point*. I don't do swordsmanship to be happy. Or rich, or respected, or any other damn thing. I do it because I believe it is fundamentally worthwhile. Given that my happiness or otherwise is not the point, it doesn't actually matter whether I'm happy or not. I get it done anyway.

I think this insight above all others led me to the state of being in which real happiness became possible. A few months later this woman showed up at my housewarming party and never left. I got a lot happier.

"Does it make me happy?" is a fundamentally stupid question – perhaps the only stupid question. "Is it worthwhile?" is a much better question. My happiness is not the point.

Examine your beliefs

The most difficult skill to master is honesty. It is so, so easy to delude yourself about what you are really doing, and how good you are at it. So I suggest regularly examining your beliefs and seeing if they help you achieve your goals. If any of them do not, change them. One of the most profound insights of psychology was the discovery that depressed people tend to have a *more* accurate view of how much control they truly have over the world around them. Healthy people are *necessarily* a bit deluded on this score. So, an unreasonably positive belief in how much control you have over your life is necessary to be mentally healthy.

This is a contentious statement that not all psychologists will agree with, so let me provide some sources. This theory of mental health is called Depressive Realism, and its key sources are: Alloy and Abramson (1979), Dobson and Franche (1989), and – most famously – Daniel Gilbert in his *Stumbling Upon Happiness:*

"What gets us through life, evidently, is just the right amount of delusion – enough to fool us into feeling relatively good about ourselves (. . . we all believe ourselves to be above average; 90 percent of drivers certainly do), but not so much as to exceed our own credulity. If we were to experience the world exactly as it is, we'd be too depressed to get out of bed in the morning."

I am very committed to the truth of the Art of Arms. As my regular readers know, I put truth above all other things when it comes to my interpretations of historical sources, and so on. I routinely admit mistakes and change my interpretations accordingly. But I require my beliefs to be *useful* more than I require them to be *true*. Which is also why I do not usually make authority statements about my beliefs. You will not hear me state outright that any belief for which I do not have a body of supporting evidence is objectively true. This is because I edit the content of my mind to suit my overall life goals. And I suggest you do the same.

Adopting useful beliefs exercise

Most people cannot simply choose what they believe, because their beliefs form a deep and important layer of protection for their psyche. A militant atheist *cannot* believe in God, because it would attack their very identity to do so. And it is very common for major changes in beliefs (such as a religious person losing their faith) to come with all sorts of psychological issues. Most beliefs are adopted because they simply feel right, and that feeling is deeply comforting.

Once you have identified something that you wish to include in your life (such as swordsmanship), identify a belief that would help you to do that (such as "swordsmanship is good for me"). Here are the steps:

- Define the belief clearly. "Swordsmanship training is good for me"

- Define the reasons why: swords are cool, it's healthy, it's fun, and so on
- Attribute every good thing that happens to that thing. "I had a good day at work today; must be because of the training I did yesterday"
- Whenever the subject comes up, say to yourself "swordsmanship training is good for me"
- Think of the behaviours that someone who truly believed would do. Then model them. In any situation, ask yourself "what would someone who truly believed that swordsmanship training is good for them do right now?" And then do that thing
- Lower the barriers to training: do some footwork exercises that need no equipment or partner; keep a sword or stick handy in the living room and do six lunges every time you come into the room or leave it; as well as finding a group, studying the books, and so on.

One simple trick I use to train more is to change how I define training. When I'm feeling lazy or overworked and need to take some time off, training swordsmanship is a great way to relax. When I'm feeling harried and I really need to get some real work done, well, training is work. Better get to it then.

Four External Principles
1. No Injuries
This is number one: you cannot afford time off training for stupid injuries. Life's too short. Whatever training you are doing must, must, must leave you healthier than when you started. You will not win Olympic gold medals this way, but you won't end up a cripple either. The path to sporting glory is littered with the shattered bodies and minds of the unlucky many who broke themselves on the way. Don't join them.

Every time I find myself teaching a group I don't know, I tell them that the class will be successful from my point of view if everyone finishes class healthier than they started it. Most injuries in training occur either during tournament (highly competitive) freeplay, or are self-inflicted during things like warm-ups. In my school (and other classes) we have a zero tolerance policy on macho bullshit. If any exercise doesn't suit you, for any reason, you can sit it out or do some other exercise. If you are sitting it out, a good instructor will ask you why, and they will help you develop alternatives or work up to the exercise in easy stages. But they will never pressure you to do something that might injure you.

This is also true of work-related injuries, like forearm problems from typing, or the ghastly effects of sitting all day. By avoiding the things that will hurt you, you will naturally seek out the things that are good for you. Hungry? Avoid sugar, avoid processed foods, and lo! There's a fresh salmon salad. Tired? Sleep is better than barbiturates, no?

This requires good risk assessment skills (I recommend *Against the Gods: The Remarkable Story of Risk,* by Peter Bernstein) and the courage to take risks that truly serve your overall aims. A safe life is not worth living, but foolish risk-taking will not make your life meaningful.

No injuries exercise
This is a tough one to incorporate into an exercise, because it's more about avoiding unnecessary risk than it is about doing any particular thing. Try adopting these key habits:

Before any new activity, do a risk/reward calculation. How risky is it, and how rewarding?

Practice saying no to training suggestions: even safe ones. Most people do stupidly risky things due to peer pressure. Being able to say no to your peers is perhaps the most important skill in reducing injury rates. If this is hard, make it a habit to decline at least one suggestion every session, until it's easy.

2. *The Pareto Principle*

The Pareto Principle derives from the work of Italian economist Vilfredo Pareto, done in the late 1800s. (So it's historical and Italian, which is fitting from my perspective at least!) It states that 80% of outcomes come from 20% of causes. In our case, 80% of skill comes from 20% of the training.

I've found that this principle applies to most areas of life. For instance, 20% of my students log 80% of the training time. Also, 20% of my readers produce 80% of the useful feedback. I use 20% of the techniques I know approximately 80% of the time. The numbers are not exact, of course; in most cases it's closer to 95–5.

The key for our purposes here is to identify the areas in which you want to develop sufficient skill to accomplish your goals, but have no deep interest in the subject for its own sake. Examples for me include strength training, learning the basics of setting up a website and driving a car. Then in those areas, ruthlessly apply the Pareto principle. Identify the 20% of essential knowledge, and acquire it. This minimises the time spent. I'm a good enough driver, but I can't do good handbrake turns. I set up my own website, and it's okay. Any masterful web developer would do it better, but I don't want to spend years learning to code just to make it a little bit better. And I can add strength to any part of my body quickly; right now I'm strong enough for everything I want to do. The question you should ask yourself: "is what I am about to do the most effective way to reach my goal?"

I am not interested in training for the sake of training. I am interested in training for the sake of accomplishing other goals: mastery of swordsmanship, health, and so on. So I only do the few small things that make big differences. In the areas of my real interest, such as martial arts, I go deep into the realm of diminishing returns, and pour effort into areas that give only tiny, *tiny* benefits, because I have already plucked all the low hanging fruit and am loving the process of stripping the whole damn tree down to its bare twigs.

Pareto Principle exercise

Go through the activities that make up your training time. It helps to keep a thorough log to start with, so you can get an accurate idea of what you are actually doing when you think you're training. Then, rigorously assess each activity according to the following criteria:

• What is this activity supposed to accomplish? if you don't know what it's for, drop it from your training
• Does it actually do that? Can you test the outcomes of this activity?
• Is there a better way to accomplish the same end?
• Is that end actually useful?

You will probably find that 80% of your outcomes are coming from only 20% of your activities; so cut the 80% of your activities that do not currently serve your goals, and devote the extra time to those activities that you have demonstrated are most useful.

Remember though that "fun" is a legitimate training goal, so don't be too hasty to bin activities that do not directly make you better; their purpose may be to keep you actively training, rather than to improve your skills directly.

3. Run a Diagnostic

At every stage of training, you are either running a diagnostic to find out what you should focus on, or working on fixing the one weakest link. It is a cycle that goes: diagnosis, fix, diagnosis, fix . . . ad infinitum. This means that you are only trying to fix one thing at any given moment, and you have both a method in place for identifying what that one thing you should be fixing is and a method for evaluating whether your attempted fixes are working. You should always be absolutely clear what the thing you are doing is for, be that "developing the reach of my lunge," "strengthening my lower back," or just "having fun."

Key points

Do one thing at a time. Whatever you are doing, whatever you are focussing on, everything else can slide. If you have decided that you need to work on a particular parry, then – in any drill or exercise that includes it, be it set drill or freeplay – success is defined only by how well you did that parry.

You remember that which you are ready to learn. In other words, if you can't remember it, you can't train it. So memorising the overall shape and content of the material allows you to run through it in your head, and pick the weakest link. This means that every time you train or show up to class, you should have a clear idea what it is you should be working on; and if you don't know, you should have a clear method in place for figuring out what you should be working on.

Run a diagnostic exercise

Choose one drill or exercise that you know well enough to remember it clearly.

1. Practice it at a pace and level that generates error
2. Articulate the error in the clearest possible terms. This becomes your goal
3. Select the training tools that you think will most efficiently address your goal. Apply them with rigour
4. Test to see whether your goal has been reached. Do this by returning to the original set-up in which the error occurred
5. If yes, return to step #1 to find a new error. If no, either select new tools or apply the same ones better.

For best results, you need to distinguish between knowledge and skill, and between breadth and depth.

4. Distinguish Between Knowledge and Skill

Knowing how to do a particular technique is not the same thing as being able to do it. Training begins with knowledge: learning the things you need to know. From there, you must develop the skills to apply that knowledge. The specific steps with which I take my students from knowing something in theory to being able to do it in practice are covered in the chapter "Skill Development," p. 176.

In lieu of a separate exercise in distinguishing between knowledge and skill, let's just take a simple concrete example: a disarm against a forehand attack with the dagger (such as Fiore's first play, first master). We might start with a very basic set-up in which your partner gently strikes, and you try to intercept their hand and turn it to make the disarm. All 100% co-operative. If you can do that, you "know" the technique. But could you do it against someone attacking hard and fast? Or by surprise? Or from a different angle? Or with multiple blows, not just the one? Probably not. So knowledge is required, but it's just the beginning of building up skills.

I think of this as building pyramids. We lay a couple of blocks (techniques or concepts) to create a base. We then set a block on top (more advanced skill in applying the techniques). The next block can go either to widen the base (add a new technique), or to add height (build more skill). You need both, and if you keep the pyramid analogy in mind you will know whether your base needs widening or your pyramid is looking a bit flat and should be built up.

The wider the base, the higher we can build. But (and this is important):

Skill beats Knowledge
The point of the knowledge is to guide your development of skill. It is better to be a specialist in your area of expertise, but no true expert has a very limited skill set. Take brain surgeons, for example. They all train as general doctors first, then as surgeons, and then as specialised surgeons. This means that they have a sufficiently broad base of knowledge on which to build

their skills. Without that breadth, they would be unable to improvise when things go wrong.

To bring this back to martial arts: in a fight, things are always going wrong. You are vulnerable to anything you've never trained against, so you need breadth. But you cannot successfully defend yourself without high-level skills, so you need depth. At any moment in your training you should be very clear about whether you are trying to acquire breadth or depth, because drills tend to give you one or the other.

And Finally . . .

You may have noticed that the organisation of these principles follows a pattern that has been around for at least a thousand years. It's a group of seven things (seven days of the week, seven deadly sins, seven brides for seven brothers – the list is endless), further divided into a group of three (a trinity) and a group of four (a quaternity).

In medieval education, the seven liberal arts (the subjects that all free people should study) were the three "soft" sciences (logic, rhetoric and grammar) and the four "hard" sciences (arithmetic, geometry, music and astronomy). Christianity is largely based on the Trinity (father, son and holy ghost) and the four gospels. Medieval medicine is all about balancing the four humours. I'm sure you can think of a dozen other trinities and quaternities, and I'd be surprised if whatever martial art you study (you do study one, right?) doesn't have something like it.

Three times four is twelve, so there we have another excellent number into which things may be organised: twelve months of the year, twelve longsword guards, twelve apostles, twelve days of Christmas, and so on.

Chinese culture, and hence Chinese martial arts, tends to organise information into fives and eights, such as the five elements (fire, earth, wood, metal and water) and the eight trigrams of Taoist cosmology (usually referred to as *Bagua*). Is it any wonder that traditional T'ai Chi forms use "thirteen postures"?

My point is that these seven principles I have identified are not absolute. It is a very useful and powerful structure, especially for Westerners, but please don't confuse it for gospel or be limited by it. If I were Chinese, I'd probably make it eight principles. If I had wanted a longer list, I probably would've come up with twelve.

Once you have worked through my seven principles, think about them, argue about them, change them according to your experience, add to them, subtract from them, and above all, make them your own. They are a tool I have developed to help you achieve your goals.

FENCING THEORY

You know, then, that all the liberal arts are comprised of theory
and practice. Likewise is it so for this one, and both theory and
practice must be considered. The theory of the art of fencing
teaches with reason the ways to defend oneself and harm the
enemy. The practice, then, is that which one acquires from
familiarity with its operation, that is, by long use and continuous
practice.

> – Dall'Agocchie, 1572 (translated by Jherek Swanger)

As the quotation above suggests, fencing theory is the intellectual,
abstract structure that fencers use to describe, define, and explain
their art. For modern sport fencers, the fencing theory that their
art is based on has been refined and defined and described to
the nth degree; it can be simply learned from a book (I
recommend the British Academy of Fencing's documentation for
this).

For historical fencers the situation is very different. Many
historical sources don't discuss theory at all: they just describe
a list of guards and techniques. Others describe the theory of
their art in such metaphorical or culturally specific terms that it
is very hard to understand what they are actually trying to say.
The purpose of this chapter is to give you the mental tools to
analyse the fencing theory of any style.

It would be tempting to be very deterministic about this. I've
been swinging swords for a very long time, and I have my own
views about what is and is not vital in terms of fencing theory.
But this book is about the theory and practice of *historical*

European martial arts, not of "Windsor-style-swording" (whatever that may be). So I will restrain myself and lay out the underlying principles of fencing theory in general, so you can apply them to whatever art you are practicing.

Fencing theory is not a new idea. At the bottom of the first page of the earliest fencing treatise we have, *Royal Armouries MS I.33*, there is the phrase: "Notandum quod ars dimicatoria sic describitur: Dimicatio est diversarum plagarum ordinatio, et dividitur in septem partes vt hic." Jeffrey Forgeng translates it as: "Note that the art of combat is described as follows: Combat is the organising of various blows, and it is divided into seven parts as here." (Forgeng 2013, page 47.) In his first translation, he translated "dimicatio" as "fencing" (Forgeng 2003), and so we had the immortal line "fencing is the ordering of blows." This ordering is strictly theoretical; it is the mental structure that allows you to bring order and reason to the chaos of combat.

Every fencing system has a theory behind it. In some cases, the practice of the art is based on the theory: somebody figures out a new system and tries to apply it. But as I see it, more often the theory is an attempt to explain what is going on after the fact: "this stuff seems to work. I wonder why?" The point of all this is to be able to figure out what went wrong so you can fix it, or to figure out what is working so you can do it again. Fencing theory, like cosmology, religion, fashion and manners, is very culture-specific. The notion of what makes a good sword, or the winning conditions of a swordfight, are largely culturally determined.

Fencing theory changes from period to period, style to style, and era to era. There is no one consistent theory of fencing that binds it all together. This is true of all sorts of ways of organising information. Let's take road maps as an example. We are all familiar with how they work. Streets have names, and the buildings along them usually have numbers indicating where on the street you can find them. Take 277 Tawana Close, Gaborone, for example.

In America, they pay a lot of attention to crossroads as well (though they call them intersections), so you can find the right bit of the street. "The restaurant is on Madison and 47th" means that it's on Madison avenue near where 47th street crosses it. The blocks don't have names. They are just space.

But streets don't usually have names in Japan. Blocks have names or numbers, and streets are the unnamed spaces between them. And the buildings in the blocks are numbered according to when they were built, not where they sit along the (unnamed) street. Does this mean that the Japanese are perennially lost, and their postal system doesn't work? No. But it does mean that the ways in which we divide things up so we can understand their structures vary hugely from culture to culture. We do not live in the same culture that spawned the arts we study: cultures change enormously over time. I would argue that modern Japan probably has more in common with modern Manhattan than modern Manhattan does with medieval Milan.

It is possible to use terminology and theory from one style to explain another, but it is a risky business, because the assumptions and goals of the two styles in question might be very different. I learned this the hard way: my background in sports fencing led me to start my longsword training by treating it as basically a big fencing sabre. I broke a finger before I realised that this was a bad approach!

I think, in general, fencing theories contain and define the following components:

- **Doctrine**: the idea behind the art. What is the best way to win a sword fight? What is the best kind of sword fight?
- **Strategy**: the end state that you aim for in a fight. For example: stab him in the face, disarm him, throw him to the ground, or score five points before he does
- **Tactics**: the choice of specific techniques that will lead to your strategic goal
- **Time**: the timing of your actions relative to those of your

opponent. Many styles define actions in terms of the number of motions they require, and distinguish between acting before, during or after your opponent's motion

- **Measure**: the distance between the two fencers. Any fencing action has a specific measure in which it works best, and most styles distinguish between being able to hit without stepping, or with a single footwork action, or requiring more than one step. Many also include grappling measure.
- **Postures**: the static positions that are defined in the art. Even in arts where there is no standing still, there is usually at least one "on guard" position defined somewhere
- **Actions**: movements of the sword or body: cuts, thrusts, parries, lunges, passing steps, turns, steps, and even backflips. **Combinations**: specific actions strung together in sequence, usually for tactical reasons. Common combinations often get given names and are thought of as "a technique," such as the *punta falsa*, the *krumphau*, the *scannatura*, or the one-two
- **Mechanics**: very few historical fencing sources discuss mechanics in any detail, but most give at least some indication of *how* an action should be done
- **Additional elements**: many sources or styles also include other elements, such as virtues, philosophy, or even astrology.

It is my intention that having studied this chapter, you will be able to determine and describe the fencing theory behind whatever swordsmanship style you favour, and be able to state definitively which elements are historical (i.e. derived directly from the source) and which you have had to interpolate, extrapolate, or import from other systems.

You may have noticed that I have just invented a meta-theory of fencing: a theory about how fencing theory works in general. And if you have a deep background in martial arts or fencing, you may very well disagree with my analysis of the components. I'd be very interested to hear from you if so!

When you approach a treatise or system, you can ask yourself what the doctrine, strategy, tactics, postures, actions and combinations are, note where these are clearly stated in the text, and (more interestingly perhaps) note where they are missing and have to be interpolated from the evidence. For example, very few texts clearly state their doctrine; but if you have a source that shows no wrestling nor thrusts but shows lots of cuts, and in most cases the defender gets killed, you could hypothesise that the doctrine is "attacking with cuts is best." Of course, it's usually much more complicated, because most sources show lots of different blows being used to win, and show both successful defences and successful attacks. It may take years of immersion in the system before you develop a confident idea about its underlying doctrine. So let's take a closer look.

Doctrine, Strategy, Tactics

Martial arts are usually about systematically increasing your likelihood of surviving combat and achieving your goals (though this is not always true, and is very much culturally dependent). The layperson tends to see martial arts as sets of kicks, punches, weapon strikes and so on. But the specific techniques of a given art are in some respects its least important factor. Much more critical are the goals of the art in question, because these are at the heart of why the art is as it is. And it's also why the popular image of a martial arts master being incapable of giving a straight answer to a straight question is so prevalent. Yes, there is some Yoda-esque stuff which is just true and irreducible; some questions to which the only honest answer can appear to be mumbo-jumbo or deliberate avoidance of the topic. But by and large, it has been my experience that many martial artists don't know what their art is for, nor why they do things in a particular way. Let me quote from *The Medieval Longsword*:

"Every martial art, from T'ai Chi Chuan to the nuclear deterrent, is based on a doctrine: an idea of how combat works. The actions and tactics of a given art reflect the conscious and unconscious assumptions of its founder. If we compare two

41

combat sports, boxing and Greco-Roman wrestling, we can see a basically similar situation: two antagonists, without weapons, in a controlled environment, with a specified fighting area and a referee. But they are acting in completely different ways. One pair punches each other, the other rolls around on the ground. In both cases, if the fighters switched tactics, they would be barred from competition. The source of these different approaches is in the minds of the founders of the sports: what constitutes the best way for two fighters to determine who is better? The rules of the contest are then developed to encourage the desired fighting behaviour, and the techniques most likely to achieve victory are then determined by those rules. So, to contrast these sports, we have:

	Wrestling	**Boxing**
Doctrine	Grapples and throws are best.	Hitting with hands is best.
Strategy	Immobilise opponent.	Damage opponent with punches.
Tactics	Choose best throws and locks.	Combinations of strikes.

There is no way to say which is better; both work well in their contexts. But which is better for you? Much depends on your nature and your body type. This process is exactly the same in a lethal environment. There is no one "best" way for a gun to be carried – or even one "best" gun to carry. (For an in-depth discussion of doctrine, strategy and tactics, see Forrest E. Morgan, *Living the Martial Way*).

In *Meditations on Violence* (p. 7) Rory Miller suggests that martial arts have many conflicting possible goals or ideals: self defence, the duel, sport, combat (i.e. military), assault, spiritual growth and fitness. To this list I would add display (such as stage combat). Knowing which one your art is adapted for is critically important, because that is the only thing it is likely to be efficient at delivering.

There are few things sadder than seeing someone whose art is optimised for spiritual growth trying to spar with someone whose art is optimised for sparring.

Most of the swordsmanship sources I study assume that you know the context in which you will fight. I go into Fiore's contexts in some detail in *The Medieval Longsword* but, in short, the arts I study are mostly adapted for success in the duel: two people fighting at an agreed time and place, with agreed weapons, to death or incapacity, and doing so for social advancement. It is well to remember that the context determines the goals, and thus also the doctrine, strategy, and tactics; and the context is almost entirely cultural. Combat is a *social* activity, and is more bound by cultural restrictions than one would think. While the explicit rules are vitally important, the implicit rules are often just as critical, though harder to establish.

Time

Fencing time is measured by the actions of the fencers, rather than in minutes and seconds. (In modern electrified fencing there are exceptions to this, but not otherwise.) Fencing time is generally concerned with three things:

• Speed: how quickly an action or actions are done
• Timing: how actions are done relative to each other
• Initiation: which bit of the sword/swordsman moves first.

Speed

Let's start with speed. Every action has a beginning and an end: we measure the speed of the action by the time it takes to get from one to the other. The speed must be sufficient for the action to arrive in time (e.g. your strike before your opponent's parry), and sufficient for the action to strike with enough force to do the necessary damage. Given that swords are sharp and so don't need much force behind them to do amazing damage, in general speed is more important when it comes to arriving "in time." This is determined by the opponent's actions. I cover speed in more detail in the **Mechanics** section below.

Timing: number of motions

Every motion done in measure is a "tempo" (to use the Italian term). I'll discuss measure below. For now, you are "in measure" if you can strike with a single action. Motions done out of measure don't count, because they are neither a threat nor an opportunity.

The number of motions a given fencing action requires is important to know, and in general we distinguish between one, two, and more than two.

Single time

Examples of single-time actions include:

- A simple blow
- A counterattack, in which you parry and strike in a single motion
- A counterattack, in which you avoid and strike in a single motion.

Two-time (due tempi)

Examples of due tempi actions include:

- A parry (which takes one motion) followed by a riposte (which takes one more)
- A beat attack, where you hit their sword out of the way and then strike
- A feint followed by a real strike.

In general, defences done in two tempi are easier to do, but easier to counter. Defences done in a single motion are harder to do safely, but harder to counter.

More than two tempi

Any sequence or combination that takes more than two motions tends to be broken up into its component parts, or to get clumped together into a named "technique." For example: beat their blade away, feint, and when they parry, disengage and strike; that's at least three, maybe four motions if you count the disengage and strike as separate actions.

Timing: relative to the opponent

Any counter to the opponent's action must occur at the correct moment during that action. For example, my opponent tries to hit me on the head. I want to knock his blow aside and hit him. If I parry before he strikes, my action fails. If I try to parry after he strikes, he's already hit me. If I parry during his strike, it may work. We can in theory divide his strike into an infinite number of tiny units of time, but in practice we can act against his blow at the following times:

- Before it starts – we can prevent it ever happening
- During its movement towards us
- After it has passed the target (this requires us to have avoided the blow).

So far so good; we can act before, during and after the opponent's motion. The "during" bit can be further divided, and some fencing systems take this to extraordinary lengths. But let's keep things reasonably simple: we can act against their blow at the beginning, middle or end of the motion.

In general, we can counterattack during the beginning or middle of his blow, or we can parry during the middle or end. If you try to counterattack at the end of the blow, you're likely to get hit; if you try to parry at the beginning of his blow, he'll see it and avoid it too easily.

Initiation

Time also refers to the initiation of an action: which bit moves first? George Silver was, as far as I know, the first to write definitively on this subject, and he explains the following true (i.e. correct) timings in his *Paradoxes of Defence* (1599):

* The time of the hand
* The time of the hand and body
* The time of the hand, body and foot
* The time of the hand, body and feet.

What this means is that the hand (i.e. the sword) moves first. Depending on your measure, you may also need to move your body and/or feet; if so, the movement goes hand, then body, then one foot, and then the other. The sword should always move first. Specifically, the point of the sword should move first. This is always true in swordplay, but not always true in other parts of the fight, such as when grappling. If you have gripped your opponent's arms, you might then step behind them and turn your body (hips) to throw them, adding momentum with your hands; the initiation is then foot-body-hand. But it should be obvious that if you step into measure without creating a threat with your sword (by moving or keeping it forwards), your opponent could hit you.

Who moves first is often used as the organising principle behind an entire treatise; the terms "Agent" and "Patient" are a sign of this. The "Agent" acts first, and the "Patient" waits for the Agent to do so. This is common in English martial arts, and also in most sixteenth-century Italian sources. Other styles might not define who moves first but rather who *attacks* first, and so assign the roles "attacker" and "defender."

Tempo

Let me sum up with a brief discussion of tempo. It's an Italian word that is used to mean many things, but most commonly time, timing and rhythm. I think the best place to begin a study of tempo is Angelo Viggiani's *Lo Schermo*, from 1575. In it, he discusses tempo in terms of Aristotle's *Physics*, books 7 and 8. Briefly put, time is measured by movement. When a body is at rest, we have no way to perceive time. But as it moves, we can track it in space and time. Every movement begins with a period of rest, measures a period of time, and then ends in another period of rest. So every blow begins in a guard and ends in a guard, and by measuring the blows we measure fencing time. One tempo is therefore one unit of fencing time: the time it takes to make one action. In real time (if there is such a thing – we measure it mostly by the vibration of atoms, or the *click-click* movements of the cogwheels in a clock, rather than the *swish-slash-ching* of sword blows), a fencing action may take fractions of a second or several seconds to complete. That doesn't matter, because our actions must be in proportion to those of the opponent. Our blow arrives if it strikes *before the parry*, not if it takes a specific number of milliseconds. And specific fencing actions or techniques may take more than one tempo. The most common example of this is to contrast the defences "parry and riposte," in which one tempo is used for defending and a second for striking back, and "counterattack," in which the defence and the striking back both happen during the same single motion.

Tempo, then, is the study of time as measured by fencing actions. And as those actions happen in response to one another, it is common for a rhythm to build up. That rhythm is also described as the tempo of the fight.

Measure

All fencing actions have their proper measure: the distance at which they are supposed to work. Many sources don't discuss measure at all, but in later Italian fencing theory (specifically that of the early seventeenth-century rapier masters), measure is determined as simply the distance between the point of your sword and the target area on your opponent's body. This works wonderfully with a rapier, which is normally held pointing forwards, but is less perfect when using a longsword, because the point may be to the side or even behind you. The position of the sword determines the length of the strike itself: how far the sword point has to travel from where it is to where it is going. The position of your feet and weight relative to the target determine how far you need to step during that motion of the sword to strike. With the longsword we take both the motion of the sword and the footwork into account when determining measure, but as a general rule measure is described according to what the feet have to do to accomplish your goal. As you approach your opponent, you are either:

- **Out of measure**, which means it will take more than one step to strike
- **In wide measure**, which means you can hit with your longest attack using a single foot movement. Most historical systems include the pass, which is the longest strike; but many emphasise the lunge and think of lunging measure as the beginning of wide measure
- **In close measure:** you can hit without stepping
- **In grappling measure**: if you can reach your opponent's arms or body with your hand, you can grapple.

At any given time, your opponent will also be in one or other of these measures. Depending on the angle of approach, your reach, and the lengths of your swords, one of you may well be in (for instance) wide measure, while the other is out of measure. The ideal position to be in is such that you can strike without needing to step, while your opponent has to step to strike. Silver calls this "gaining the place." It is usually achieved through geometry: by stepping offline, especially towards your opponent's back, you can arrive at a place where you can reach them and they can't reach you.

Various masters at different times in fencing history have

defined these measures a little differently or more precisely. However, in general, it is enough to know when you and your opponent can strike without stepping, need a single step, or need more than one step. For example, in chapter IV of *Gran Simulacro*, Capoferro defines the following measures:

> "The measure is a just distance from the point of my sword to the body of my adversary in which I can strike him, according to which all the actions of my sword and defence are given direction.
>
> The wide measure is, when with the increase of the right foot, I can strike the adversary, and this measure is the first narrow one.
>
> The fixed foot narrow measure is that in which, by only pushing my body and legs forward, I can strike the adversary.
>
> The narrowest measure is when the adversary strikes at wide measure, and I can strike him in his advanced and uncovered arm, either that of the dagger or that of the sword, with my left foot back, followed by the right while striking."
>
> (Translation: William Wilson and Jherek Swanger.)

In summary: he defines three measures, each measured according to the distance of your point from your opponent's body. The widest is when you need a lunge to strike, the next is when you can strike by moving your body (I call this a "lean"), and finally the shortest measure is when you only need to extend your arm. Oddly, though the rest of the book has dozens of examples of attacking with a pass, Capoferro doesn't include the measure of striking with the pass here.

Just as time is determined by the relation between our actions and those of our opponent, not by minutes and seconds, so measure is determined by the possibility to strike, not by feet and inches (or, god forbid, centimetres and metres).

The anchor point for judging measure is the fixed foot. If you lunge, moving only your front foot, it's the position of your back foot that determines whether your lunge will reach the target. If you're striking with a pass, it's the position of the front foot that determines how far forward you can go with one passing step. This is why it is very important which foot is forwards when considering guards.

Guards

Postures, guards and wards are all the same thing: a static position that is either a "ready position" you take after drawing the sword and getting to the edge of wide measure, and/or a way of defining the beginning, middle and end of the blows. As a general rule, in early fencing sources – say pre-1550 – there are a lot of guard positions shown. This is because almost every motion you make is done from guard to guard. Only a few parries are described in the same way by the end of the eighteenth century (such as the parry from *tierce* to *carte*, where both *tierce* and *carte* are previously defined as guards). The lunge position is not described as a guard in the way that extended positions – such as Fiore's *posta longa* or Liechtenauer's *langenort* – are. So in your system there may be positions that you need to know but which are not defined as static positions in the text.

The primary tactical considerations of a guard are:

- The position of the sword: chambered to strike? Point in line? Closing one line or another?
- The position of the feet: if your right foot is forwards, you can lunge with the right foot or pass forwards with the left.
- The position of the weight: on the front back foot, or in the middle. On the front foot makes the pass forwards easier; on the back foot makes the lunge or pass back easier; in the middle lets you hedge your bets.

Actions

Any movement you make for a tactical or strategic reason is considered a fencing action. They are most commonly attacks or defences of some kind, but they can also be feints, provocations, invitations, actions in countertime, and so on. Any movement will have a stylistically and mechanically "correct" execution, and will fit within the theoretical framework in a specific way.

Most sources distinguish in some way between the following types of action with the blade.

- Cuts: strikes with the edge
- Thrusts: strikes with the point
- Offensive actions: cuts or thrusts done to the opponent in order to strike
- Defensive actions: actions made to defend yourself against your opponent's offensive action
- Attacks: cuts or thrusts done when you have the initiative, or are the first to move
- Preparations: actions done to create an opening in which to strike (such as beating the opponent's sword aside), or to draw them out of their guard
- Invitations: actions giving the appearance of an opening, to encourage your opponent to attack
- Feints: cuts or thrusts done towards the opponent in order to generate a reaction
- Parries: actions done to defend against an attack without simultaneously striking
- Ripostes: cuts or thrusts done after a successful parry
- Avoidances: getting out of the way of an offensive action
- Counterattacks: defences that combine defence (parry or avoidance) with offence (cut or thrust) in a single motion
- Entering: moving from one range to a closer range (such as from a measure where you can only strike with the sword to grappling range)
- Actions done in opposition: you close the line of your opponent's weapon.
- Actions done by angulation: you angle around your opponent's weapon

- Actions on the blade: you do something to change the blade relationship, such as a disengage, cutover, bind, glissade, coupé, transport, croisé, and so on.

Classical fencers will be wondering why actions in countertime, actions in second intention, and other such things are missing from this list. Allow me a moment of fencing nerdery: a feint is done differently from an attack in second intention. The feint will usually fall short if the defender doesn't parry, but the attack in second intention is done the same way as a real attack; the only difference is in the mind of the attacker. So the action itself is the same. Likewise, a feint that draws a counterattack instead of a parry requires the feinter to respond (usually) by parrying the counterattack in countertime, but that parry in countertime is not really a different action to a parry done against a simple attack; it's what came before it that changes how it is classified. Don't get me wrong, I love classical fencing terminology as much as the next man. But the purpose of this book is not to cover classical fencing theory in detail, but to outline how fencing theory in general works.

A single blow, such as a simple downwards strike, can be an attack, counterattack, parry, riposte, preparation, invitation, or feint; and done in opposition, angulation, or as an action on the blade. We tend to think of these kinds of distinctions as being quite modern; indeed, the list above is adapted from my modern sport fencing foil training. But these distinctions go way back. In *I.33* for instance, the *obsessio* is an action that threatens the opponent, forcing them to bind your sword; using our definitions above, it is a preparation. In the Liechtenauer sources from the fourteenth century, meanwhile, there is a great deal of emphasis on counterattacking, and on who has the initiative (*vor*); actions like the *duplieren* are clearly angulated, and actions like the *zornhau* are clearly counterattacks done with opposition.

Many sources, especially the earlier ones, also include wrestling, pommel strikes, and parries or strikes with a second weapon such as a dagger or buckler. From a tactical perspective, this makes no difference. For example, if I attack you with a dagger thrust, you can do this to me:

You, enjoying yourself

Me, having a bad day

(Seventh play of the ninth master of the dagger, *Getty MS.*)

In all likelihood, I attacked, and you parried and stuffed my hand between my legs (I do this with a groin strike, but please don't). This throw then occupies the same tactical space in the system as a riposte: it's an offensive action done after a parry. The point of having this catalogue of definitions is to enable you to determine what the tactical function of any action may be. That is: what it is for, how it works, and how it can be countered. This absolutely does not mean that you should describe the fencing actions in the source using modern terminology, but it is very useful to have this framework to see where the actions in the source might fit.

While we're on the subject of terminology, let's look at the naming of a single blow – a forehand horizontal strike, for example. Fabris would describe it as a *mandritto tondo*. But Fiore would call it a *mandritto mezano*. German medieval sources would call it a *mittelhau*. Roworth, writing in 1798, would call it a "cut 5"; and in modern sabre fencing the angle of the blow isn't usually described – just the target, so it would probably be a "cut cheek" or "cut chest." My point is that blows can be classified according to their angle or target, and they can be named or numbered. So it is unwise to import naming conventions from one system to another. Viggiani's famous Tree of Blows is a lovely example of a complete naming system, with every blow determined by whether it strikes with point, true edge, or false edge; whether it comes from the forehand or backhand side; and the angle it's striking through.

Tree of Blows

Hierarchy of Actions

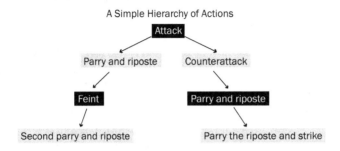

A Simple Hierarchy of Actions

"The hierarchy of actions" is a fancy way of saying "the list of what counters what." This is important, because every technique will have its own specific circumstances in which it will work. Parries are useless unless the opponent attacks, for instance. In the chart above, against a generic attack, the defender can either parry and riposte, or counterattack. If he parries, the attacker could have countered it with a feint and struck on the other side; if the attacker feints and strikes on the other side, the defender could do a second parry. This list is not exhaustive: the parry-riposte could be beaten by an angulated attack, by a second attack that pre-empts the riposte, by parrying the riposte and counter-riposting, by counterattacking into the riposte . . . the list goes on. But once we get more specific, we find that the optimal responses do tend to become more limited.

Put another way, the hierarchy of actions tells you what your opponent must be doing in order for a particular technique of yours to work. Let's take a famous rapier source as an example style: Ridolfo Capoferro's *Gran Simulacro*. In it, he mentions a lot of theoretical points, including the length your sword should be relative to your own body, how to deal with people who circle round you, and so on. But he doesn't explicitly give us a hierarchy of actions, so I worked one out. This is simplified and condensed for a general reader; Capoferroists will no doubt be much more specific.

Attack (cut or thrust)	Parry riposte in a single time, or parry riposte in two actions, or avoid and counterattack.
Parry riposte in a single time	Feint, parry riposte in two actions.
Disengage	Counter-disengage, or attack closing the line (parry and riposte in one motion).
Counter-disengage	Re-disengage or attack.
Stringering	Counter-stringering, or attack, or disengage-attack, or disengage beat attack.
Counter-stringering	Same as you'd do for stringering.
Beat attack	Deceive beat (disengage in time), or attack after beat, or parry in two actions.
Parry	Feint-disengage.
Counterattack	Parry, riposte.

Having a simple and consistent way to conceptualise the many different techniques – and to classify them according to their tactical use (or place in the hierarchy of actions) – makes it much easier to learn them in the first place, and to apply them in fencing.

Combinations

All fencing systems, indeed all martial arts that I've ever come across, include combinations of actions as part of their core technical repertoire. The parry-riposte is perhaps the most common in swordsmanship, but there are usually all sorts of sequences shown in which you do something, and to which your opponent reacts (or fails to) – thus creating an opening to hit them.

Here's one example from Fiore:

> "I show that I am coming with great force to strike the player with a middle blow in the head. And immediately that he makes the cover I strike his sword lightly. And immediately turn my sword to the other side, grabbing my sword with my left hand about at the middle. And I place the thrust immediately in the throat or in the chest . . ."

This is the eighteenth play of the second master of the *zogho largo*, known as the *punta falsa*, and so in its basic form is done as a riposte after you successfully parry the opponent's attack (as shown by the preceding master).

As a drill, it looks like this:

1. attacker strikes *mandritto fendente*;
2. you parry from the right into *frontale*, beating the attacker's sword wide;
3. you keep the motion going to strike a *mandritto mezano*, leaving your hands high and to the left;
4. attacker parries with *frontale*;
5. you strike lightly on their sword and turn your sword hand over, turning your sword around the midpoint;
6. reach for the middle of your sword with your left hand; and
7. thrust them in the mask, with an *accrescere* if needed.

In modern fencing terms, this would be a riposte by feint-disengage. But this is a good example of how modern fencing terms do not fit precisely. If this was a sabre bout and your parry touched my feint, I would lose priority, and if you riposted and hit me as I hit you, the point would be yours. If my action was successful and yours was not, it would be classed as a reprise of the riposte. But the intent of the *punta falsa* is absolutely to feint, as is clear from the description. You strike the parry deliberately. And of course you're not allowed to grab your blade with your left hand in modern fencing. So while having a set of modern terms to describe actions can be helpful, it can also be very misleading: use with caution!

I especially enjoy combinations with fancy names: in English longsword (according to Paul Wagner), one combination (from the *Ledall* MS) is called "the tumbling chase."

I know that some readers will want to know what this tumbling chase is, so here is the modernised transcription by Stevie Thurston. You can find the whole thing on wiktenauer.com.

The Sixth Chase; called "The Tumbling Chase": Two Double Rounds forward, with as many backward; all upon the left foot lithely delivered. Then tumble forward as round as a ball: that is to say; with a down-right stroke set forward the right foot, bringing the sword over your head void back the left foot, with another down-right stroke followed with the right leg. Then bring back the same foot with a back-thrust, set in the left foot and smite back a quarter.

It's as well to remember though that any combination is usually relying on a specific set of reactions from the opponent; the *punta falsa* in the example above won't work if the opponent doesn't parry, or manages to counterattack instead of parrying.

Mechanics

We can see from simply looking at the pictures in a range of old fencing books that the idea of the best guard, best movement, and best mechanics changes wildly from style to style, weapon to weapon, and period to period. To perform any art correctly, you must be able to reproduce its movement aesthetic, and understand why every action is done the way it is. So let's start by looking at what all martial arts have in common.

Structure and Grounding

This is the beginning of martial arts. Good structure is literally the foundation upon which all martial skill is based, and is the fundamental skill behind great feats of apparently magical ability. In short, it is as simple as making sure that for whatever you want to do, every bone in your body (there are over 200) is in exactly the right place, and every muscle (there are over 600) has exactly the right degree of tension. This takes some practice, but it is easy to acquire major technical improvement with relatively little work by minimising – as far as possible – the unnecessary tension that inhibits your movement.

No matter what your structure, it will be stable in some directions and unstable in others, with a specific pattern of strength and weakness. Martial skill comes from making sure that you move from a strong position that does not inhibit your movement, and then through a succession of equally supported positions into your final position; and all with no resistance from unnecessary tension, so the work being done by your muscles is all available for creating the movement. And this movement is directed into your opponent's structure in a way that fully exploits the pattern of strength and weakness in his position.

Let us take a simple example: stand with your feet apart, pointed in the same direction as you are facing. Have a friend gently press from the side against one shoulder. You should find it easy enough to direct that pressure into the ground through the opposite foot. Then have him apply the same gentle pressure into the centre of your chest, directly across the line between your feet. Given you have no leg in that direction, you will either fall, or be forced to take a step to support yourself. In other words, you have to change your structure to adapt to the pressure. The ability to route incoming pressure safely into the ground is called grounding, and the path through your skeleton from the point of contact to the ground is called the groundpath. Grounding and groundpaths are the primary way that most martial artists think of structure.

Human beings are essentially bipods: as any photographer could tell you, bipods are inherently unstable, which is why cameras are used with tripods. Imagine your opponent as a tripod: where would the third leg go? Any pressure in the direction of the imaginary third leg will be much more effective at destabilising him than pressure directed into either one of his actual legs. Likewise, as you move, you should be aware of your changing lines of strength and weakness. It is usually correct to strike with your groundpath directed into the line of your opponent's weakness.

One of the hallmarks of good structure, good grounding, in a martial arts position is that it allows the techniques that are supposed to work from there to flow easily from it. I consider structure and flow as the fundamental elements of basic training.

Flow

Flow describes your freedom of movement at any time. Good technique should flow effortlessly from and through your perfectly structured guard positions. If your actions fail to flow, you should fix your structure. If your structure is wrong, you probably moved into it wrong: you failed to flow. Anything sticky, awkward or stuck is wrong. Things that flow well might be right. This is the physical parallel to the mental flow state I discussed in The Seven Principles of Mastery.

In my experience, most students benefit from focussing on flow first, and then structure. You can destroy your opponent by breaking their structure or by interrupting their flow. If you successfully maintain your structure and flow, you cannot fail. Nothing breaks structure and interrupts flow quite like a sword to the head!

The Sword: divisions, crossings and binds

The sword introduces a whole new set of structures and focuses the fight on one primary aspect: the weapon. Unarmed combat is in practise much more complex than a sword fight, because there are more weapons involved from the outset.

Almost every swordsmanship treatise I have encountered divides the blade into at least two parts: the strong (the part closest to the handle) and the weak (the part further away). Some writers go further (such as Girard Thibault, who divides it into twelve!). In one of the four surviving manuscripts of *Il Fior di Battaglia* (the *Morgan MS*, M.383, folio 6r), Fiore divides the blade into three parts. They are:

- *Tutta spada*: the full of the sword: the first third of the blade, nearest the hilt
- *Meza spada*: the middle third of the sword
- *Punta di spada*: the point or tip of the sword.

We need not be mathematically exact about these divisions: if contact is made near the tip, it's at the *punta*; if its near the hilt, it's at the *tutta*; and if it's near the middle, it's at the *meza*. He describes these three divisions in the mounted combat section of the *Morgan* manuscript only, but in all the manuscripts he explicitly divides the longsword techniques into sections by where and how the crossing occurs. Fiore states that the *tutta* "withstands a little," the *meza* "withstands less," and the *punta* "withstands nothing." This effectively describes what happens when the swords meet. The further away the point of contact is from the hand, the less pressure you can withstand.

61

The development of enclosed hilts, which offer a lot more protection to the sword hand, changed the way parries were done. In medieval sources with simple cross-hilted swords, the parry is almost always described and shown done middle to middle. But by the end of the sixteenth century, when enclosed hilts were the norm, the sources usually tell us to parry closer to the hilt to gain a leverage advantage. Let's take a closer look at blade relationship.

Blade Relationship

When the swords meet, they will do so either at the middles, the weaks or the strongs; or some combination thereof, such as your strong against your opponent's weak. In a perfect world, there is no bind: if you attack, your strike lands, smashing through any parry that might be attempted; if you defend, your parry beats aside the incoming sword and you can strike immediately. In the real world all sorts of things can go wrong, and it is of course possible to avoid the blades meeting altogether.

The three critical variables to the blade relationship are:

- Which parts of the blades are in contact (e.g. middle to middle, middle to weak, weak to strong, etc.).
- How close your opponent's blade is to you, and yours to them
- How much pressure is being exerted on the point of contact.

It is generally impossible to notice these consciously when actually fencing, but they do determine more than anything else which technique will be most effective after the blades have met. Many sources are explicit about where the crossing should be, and some discuss leverage in detail. But whether they do or not, the laws of physics do not change. If your technique is failing, it may be because the crossing you are working from is not correct for the technique.

Speed and Power Generation

Power generation is a combination of structure and flow. Most sword styles use the sword as a labour saving device; you don't have to hit as hard as possible, because the blade gets the job done for you. This is the whole point of having a sharp sword: it takes much less energy to do much more damage. Most unarmed striking arts emphasise power more than fencers need to. But armed or not, power is still a requirement. In short, the key elements of power generation are:

- A supported structure
- Efficient movement
- Acceleration
- Speed.

These four elements are dependent on each other: if your structure is properly supported, you need less tension to hold it. So your action doesn't need to include a preparation phase of relaxation making it more efficient, which allows you to accelerate faster; so the blade is moving faster when it arrives, and so hits harder. It's worth having a more detailed look at speed.

Speed serves two functions in swordsmanship: damage and timing.

Damage first: the speed of the sword determines how hard it hits. $E=mv2$, so the energy available for damaging the target is proportional to the striking mass and to the square of its velocity. Double the mass of the sword and you double the impact; double the speed and you quadruple the impact. Of course, this assumes that to make the sword go faster you haven't made the motion less efficient, so that energy is wasted on impact. There is a huge difference in practice between the amount of energy technically available, and the amount actually delivered into the target.

I believe that the sword should act as a labour saving device. Its function is to destroy certain types of target, and it should require less effort to do so with the sword than without. So there is limited virtue in simply making the sword go faster and faster to hit harder and harder; at some point there is sufficient energy to do the desired damage, so additional speed is wasted effort.

Timing: as I mentioned above, the purpose of speed is to ensure that your strike arrives before your opponent's parry, and your parry arrives before his strike. It is therefore proportional to the motions of your opponent. The key skill here is to be able to adjust the acceleration of the weapon, rather than attain a specific top speed. There is a lovely section on this in Karl Friday's excellent book *Legacies of the Sword*, on pages 74–5. The graphs showing the different rates of power applied to the weapon by beginners versus experts are especially good.

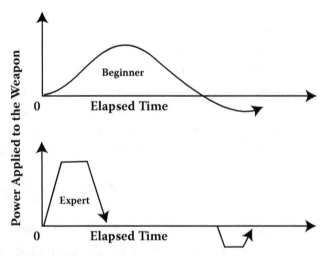

The key point is that the expert can accelerate the weapon quickly. The total force exerted is actually a lot less, but the weapon is moving fast enough when it needs to be. The key to this kind of skill is to eliminate inefficiencies in the starting position, minimise the tension in the muscles about to act, and develop perfect mechanics for the strike itself.

The easiest way to reduce the time in which an action is done is to make the action shorter. So, a great deal of speed training, training to do an action in less time, is to eliminate any extraneous motion – to pare the movement down to its absolute minimum: to take a beginner's marathon and create an expert's 100 metres. There are several ways to do this from the obvious (select a starting point that is closer to the end point) to the more sophisticated (tuning the path taken between those two points). In general, the sword hand should move in a straight line from A to B. But sometimes it's the middle of the blade that does that, and sometimes it's other parts of the weapon or wielder.

In practice, it is useful to be able to adjust the path and the rate of acceleration at various points on the path for best effect. To simply hit hard, make sure the sword is at maximum velocity at the moment of impact. To make the hit more likely to land, though, adjust the acceleration pattern and the path taken to best fit the tactical circumstances. Easier said than done. It is always slower to lift a heavy weight than a light one. So speed training is also about reducing unnecessary tension, making the action as smooth and efficient as possible, and expending the least possible force to get the job done.

Additional Theoretical Elements

Recall my example of the Japanese road maps. In addition to the guards, blows, techniques, mechanics, timing, measure and so forth that the system you study does define, there may well be all sorts of elements that the author chooses to include as if they were fencing theory, but which we would not think of as such – Fiore's four virtues, for example. In the *segno* page of the *Getty MS*, f32r, Fiore illustrates the four virtues a swordsman must possess. They are:

- **Fortitudo:** strength. This is represented by an elephant with a tower on its back. Strength is not simply muscle power, but – as the image suggests – comes from correct structure
- **Presteza**: speed. This is represented by a tiger holding an arrow. We think of this as flow, not least because the image of the arrow in the sky (representing lightning) and the

tiger being named after the swift-flowing Tigris River both suggest it

- **Avvisamento**: foresight. This is represented by a lynx holding dividers – symbols of good eyesight and accurate measurement. This refers to judgment of time and measure
- **Ardimento**: boldness, or courage. This is represented by a lion holding a heart: symbols of lion-hearted valour.

These are explicitly virtues, and therefore intrinsic elements of the swordsman's character and way of being. How do they fit into the theory of fencing that his book represents?

I think we can probably agree that boldness is a commonly required virtue in any combat art. But how many sources explicitly describe it?

The question then is what else does your source or art describe that does not fit into any of the categories I have included here? There's bound to be something.

HOW TO RECREATE HISTORICAL MARTIAL ARTS FROM HISTORICAL SOURCES

This section is about how to recreate Historical Martial Arts (HMA) from historical sources, and its purpose is to give you the skills and confidence to work directly with historical sources.

For many people, historical fencing manuals are somewhat intimidating. They are obviously fabulous and glorious and beautiful and full of extremely cool sword fighting stuff. But sometimes they're written in a foreign language, sometimes the pictures are difficult to interpret, and sometimes it's all just a bit complicated. If you don't have a solid academic background, it can be really hard just to approach them. So what I'm going to do in this section of the book is to give you the necessary skills and the necessary confidence, so that when you find a book that interests you, your initial reaction is: "you know what? I can do that."

We will cover:

- How to choose a source from the many available
- How to work with translations. Working with translations can be a little bit tricky because of course you're always dealing with somebody's opinion on what somebody else has said. Chinese whispers can set up if you're not careful, so we'll go over that

- How to approach the source itself
- How to extract the core techniques and plays
- How to construct basic drills from those plays so that you have something to actually practice
- How to identify the system that's represented in the source, once you've practiced some of those drills.

What Counts as a Source?

Let's take a step back and look at an idea: how do we know what we think we know? This branch of philosophy is called epistemology. We know what we think we know from our own experience or by reference to authority. Sources of authority include books, teachers, friends or videos – that kind of thing. As historical swordsmen, we rely on historical sources for our authority. These historical sources are usually books. This is an act of faith. We believe that the swordsmen of old knew what they were doing. We believe that their books represent the truth of the art of swordsmanship far better than we could recreate it by ourselves in our modern context.

The process of recreating a historical swordsmanship style starts with the book. From the book we get to your interpretation of the book. Your interpretation leads to your practice. Your practice leads to your experience, and your experience will feed back into the book. As you recreate the art that is represented by the book and as you practise that in the real world, it will colour how you read the book. But if it ever comes down to a question of "my experience is this but the book says that," we go with the book. That is what it means to be a historical swordsman.

It is necessary to distinguish between primary sources and secondary sources. Primary sources are your focus of study, and in our context they are books written from first-hand knowledge. Swordfighting treatises written by actual swordsmen are our best primary sources, but other primary sources include eyewitness accounts of sword fights.

Secondary sources are books written about other books. These can be analyses or commentaries related to the focus of study.

Let's take a concrete example of this. Here is a primary source:

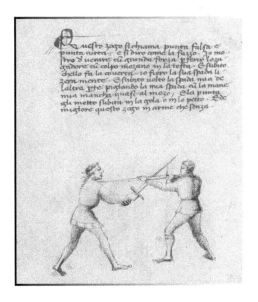

This is a page from Fiore dei Liberi's fantastic *Il Fior di Battaglia*. This illustration shows a technique called the *punta falsa* and its counter. It is a historical technique in a historical book (our primary source). I wrote a book which includes an analysis of that play, and you can see in the picture below that the little figures are doing things that look a lot like the *punta falsa*. But this is a secondary source.

This is a book that I have written to help people interpret the primary source. Fiore is the primary source. Windsor is the secondary source.

In the future somebody might get the bright idea to recreate historical swordsmanship as it was at the beginning of the twenty-first century. They might then take my book (which I consider a secondary source) as their primary source. The primary source is your focus of study, and the secondary sources are those books which help you analyse your focus of study.

The critical point is that primary sources are produced at the time in question. Here we have a picture of two smallsword practitioners, but it comes from Alfred Hutton's *The Sword and the Centuries* from 1901.

The picture, as Hutton says, is taken from Angelo's *The School of Fencing*, 1787. Depending on the question you want to answer, Hutton could be a primary source or a secondary source. If your question is "what was swordsmanship like in the late eighteenth century?", Angelo is your primary source and Hutton is your secondary source. But if your question is "what did people think about eighteenth-century swordsmanship in the early twentieth century?", Hutton is your primary source and Angelo is actually irrelevant, unless you want to compare or evaluate how accurate Hutton's interpretations may have been.

For our purposes, a good primary source of historical swordsmanship is a book that was written by a knowledgeable author, and which was intended to describe a contemporary swordsmanship system. The three things to look for are:

• Does the author know what he's talking about?
• Does the book describe enough theory and technique to be useful?
• When was the book written?

Let's take these one at a time.

Was it written by a knowledgeable author? The best way to judge this is by the reputation of the author in his own lifetime, and in the decades afterwards. Salvatore Fabris was fencing master to the King of Denmark. In Fiore's home town of Premariacco, the main street is still named after him. Dozens of German fencing treatises from the 1400s and 1500s refer to Johannes Liechtenauer. All of these are good indications that the author was well respected by people living in a swordfighting culture. Not every excellent author gets that kind of recognition, but be wary of authors whose work is significantly at odds with other masters of the time, who seem to have left no mark on history, and/or whose work seems not to have spread.

Does it describe enough theory and technique to be useful? Some sources, such as the manuscript known as *I.33*, have very little theory but lots and lots of techniques, which are described and illustrated. Others, like George Silver's *Paradoxes of Defence*, describe lots of theory and very few actual techniques. Some others are so cryptic that while they describe lots of techniques, it's impossible to know whether you have actually recreated them as intended (such as the Ledall manuscript, one of the earliest English sources). On balance, I'd take a book with lots of techniques over one with lots of theory, because it is much easier to reproduce techniques and work out the theory from them than it is to reproduce theory and work out techniques from it.

The period in which your source was written is extremely important. The closer it was to the period in which the weapons were actually used, the more likely it is to be accurate. Eighteenth-century ideas of how medieval knights might have fought are generally valueless, even though the writer may be living in a sword culture. I will cover this in more detail in the later section on historical context (p. 94).

How to Choose a Source That's Right For You

Before you commit to the long and challenging process of interpreting a source, it's worth taking some time to carefully choose the right source. The four main reasons to choose a particular source over others are:

- its period (the time it was written)
- the weapons that it covers
- the language that it's written in, and
- the available support.

Let's take things one at a time.

Period – when the book was written is quite important. Somebody interested in armoured combat and jousting has different needs from a historical source than someone who wants to be a musketeer. Establishing the period that you're interested in will narrow the field and help you to choose a source that will serve your needs.

Weaponry is also something to consider. What weapons does this source cover? If you are particularly interested in a kind of weapon, like sword and buckler for instance, you may be more interested in that than in the period itself, and this may be your main criteria for choosing a source. That said, you should take into account whether these weapons were commonly used in the period that the source was written in, and the availability of the equipment. Let's take scythes for an example. There are one or two sources that include scythes . . .

From P.H. Mair, 1542.

. . . but they are not commonly used for fighting in any period, because they're not terribly easy to fight with and they are actually quite hard to make.

Language matters because if you can't read the book, you can't study it. Not every interesting historical source has been translated into English, so you should look into what translations are available if the source is not in your own language or a language you can read. The culture from which the system comes is also important, as we saw in the Fencing Theory chapter, and we'll look into it in more detail later.

Lastly, you need to consider the available **support**. What books have been written about this source or style? What books are available about this period? Who else is working on this topic and are there videos, blogs or other materials available? All of this boils down to: do you want to blaze your own new trail, or do you want to work on more commonly known material? Both are good. There's nothing wrong with deciding to pick something because nobody else has ever studied it (or at least published on it), but it is a lot more difficult to get a coherent system out of that sort of book than it is to get one out of a book which lots of other people are also working on.

An Overview of Popular Sources From Between 1300 and 1800

The History of Fencing, by William Gaugler, was published in 1998. This 500 page book overlooks everything written before the 1500s, and glosses over the 250 years between Marozzo (1536) and Bremond (1782) in a mere 75 pages. He then writes over 200 pages on the nineteenth century, and another 150 on the twentieth century! This is understandable given that he was a classical fencing master, and indeed he is unusual in according any respect at all to the older forms of swordplay. But it's worth noting that his interest in fencing really kicks off at the point when the sword was no longer commonly used in earnest – exactly the point at which my interest wanes. So I will confine myself here to noting the most popular sources in the current HMA world, from their beginnings in the 1300s up to the end of the 1700s. For a comprehensive study of what happened after that, please refer to Gaugler – there's plenty of HMA from the 1800s and early 1900s.

This list is by no means exhaustive, but I have tried to include the major sources of all the major styles. Many of these books were hugely influential, and were produced in several editions.

This section of the book was the one that drew the most fire from my beloved beta readers; everyone wanted their own favourite treatise included. Please bear in mind that this is absolutely not a comprehensive list, and if you are an experienced HMA practitioner and I've left out a source you feel is vitally important, feel free to get a pen and write it into your copy; by all means email me the details and I'll add it into future editions. One obvious gap is that I have left out all Eastern European sources, the Dutch sources, and I have not even begun to consider sources from outside Europe, though bear in mind that they do exist.

The majority of these sources up to about 1700 can be found for free online at wiktenauer.com, which is a fabulous treasure trove of fencing treatises.

The Fourteenth Century

1320s: Our earliest source is the *Royal Armouries MS I.33*, which dates to about 1320 (according to the latest scholarship). This is a beautifully illustrated manuscript detailing lessons in sword and buckler combat between a priest and his scholar. It takes the form of a series of lessons in which the priest trains the scholar in his own method, explicitly contrasted to that of the "common fencer". This was translated and published by Jeffrey Forgeng in 2003 as *The Medieval Art of Swordsmanship: A Facsimile & Translation of Europe's Oldest Personal Combat Treatise, Royal Armouries MS I.33 (Royal Armouries Monograph)*, and again in 2013 in the companion volume of the truly extraordinary *Extraordinary Editions* version.

1389: *Ms. 3227a* (Germanisches Nationalmuseum, Nuremberg) is a hausbuch (a sort of domestic almanac) that has sections on all sorts of things (such as fireworks, alchemy and astrology), including several on swordsmanship, the most important of these being a record of the *merkeverse* (mnemonic verses) of Johannes Liechtenauer. It is the earliest reference we have for the Liechtenauer school of longsword combat, which spawned a plethora of illustrated glossa (commentaries on a text) in the following century.

There are no other manuals definitively dated to the 1300s, though it is likely that the bulk of Fiore dei Liberi's treatise was written at the end of the 1300s.

The Fifteenth Century

1410: *Il Fior di Battaglia*: the work of the Friulian master Fiore dei Liberi, which exists in four known manuscripts. This is a complete system for all the knightly weapons (sword, dagger, spear and pollax), on foot and on horseback, and in armour and without. This is one of my primary sources and will be discussed in detail in the following section.

Ca. 1430: *Gladiatoria, MS KK5013* (Kunsthistorisches Museum, Vienna) a treatise of knightly combat with spears, longswords and daggers in armour, and a section on wrestling.

The majority of sources from the 1400s are German in language and origin, and are almost all essentially glossa on Liechtenauer's verses. There are at least 40 manuscripts to choose from here, and another 50 or so from the following century. The most studied of these include:

1443 (and later copies from 1446 and 1459): Talhoffer's *Fechtbuch, MS Chart.A.558* (Universitäts – und Forschungsbibliothek Erfurt/Gotha, Gotha, Germany). This was published in translation by Mark Rector as *Medieval Combat: A Fifteenth-Century Manual of Swordfighting and Close-Quarter Combat* in 2000. This is a treatise of knightly combat with all sorts of weapons in and out of armour, and includes an array of judicial duelling techniques, including duelling with shields and duels of men against women.

1452: *Codex Danzig, Cod.44.A.8* (Biblioteca dell'Accademia Nazionale dei Lincei e Corsiniana, Rome) is a treatise that includes but is not limited to glossa on Liechtenauer's verses, and has sections by the following authors: Peter von Danzig zum Ingolstadt, Martin Huntfeltz, Jud Lew, Johannes Liechtenauer, Andre Liegniczer, and Ott Jud. This has been published in English by Christian Tobler in his *In Saint George's Name*, Freelance Academy Press, 2010.

1470 (and two slightly later versions): Paulus Kal's *Fechtbuch Cgm 1507* (Bayerische Staatsbibliothek, Munich). This is again a wide-reaching treatise with sections on all the knightly arms and some judicial combat.

1478: *Kunst des Messerfechtens,* by Johannes Lecküchner. This is a huge manuscript covering fighting with a messer (a falchion) in great depth.

1482–7: *De Arte Gladiatoria Dimicandi* (Biblioteca Nazionale, Rome) by Philippo Vadi, from Pisa. This book is a detailed discussion of swordsmanship theory, and contains illustrated plays with all the knightly weapons (sword, axe, spear and dagger).

There is also one fifteenth-century treatise in French on the use of the pollax: *Le Jeu de la Hache, MS Français 1996,* (Bibliotheque Nationale Francaise, Paris). Its exact date is unknown.

The Sixteenth Century

The 1500s saw an explosion of swordsmanship treatises, driven by the twin engines of social change (the rise of the merchant classes, who demanded and could afford both training in the art of the sword and books on their art) and the printing press: almost all swordsmanship texts from here on are printed. The most important works of this period are as follows.

Ca. 1500: *Anonimo Bolognese (MSS Ravenna M-345/M-346).* This manuscript is often thought of as the foundation of the Bolognese school.

1509: *Exercitiorum Atque Artis Militaris Collectanea* by Pedro Monte, in Latin, published in Milan. Unusually, the original draft seems to have survived; it is in Spanish, and is at the Escorial. This work surveys the martial arts of the time, and as Sydney Anglo writes in *The Martial Arts of Renaissance Europe*:

> "No master was more comprehensive than Pedro Monte in 1509. He not only deals with wrestling, dagger fighting, the use of long and short lance, two-handed sword and the single-sword on its own or in combination with various types of shield and buckler and cape; he also discusses the various types of pole arm such as the partisan, the ronca, spetum, and halberd. He examines in detail fencing and wrestling on horseback, along with various types of mounted lance combat; treats physical exercises such as running, jumping, and vaulting; provides a little encyclopedia of contemporary arms and armour; and finally places the entire corpus of material within a broader context of the art of war."

Monte is also interesting because he probably knew of Vadi; he is mentioned (in glowing terms) in Castiglione's *Libro del Cortegiano,* which was based on the court of Guidobaldo da Montefeltro, to whom Vadi's treatise is dedicated.

1531: *Opera Nova* (Venice, unknown publisher, 1531) by Antonio Manciolino (published in translation in 2010 by Tom Leoni as *The Complete Renaissance Swordsman*). This is a thorough and readable description of the style of swordsmanship commonly referred to as Bolognese (as most of its author exponents hail from there). It is also the earliest printed source for this particular style.

1536: *Opera Nova* (Modena, unknown publisher, 1536) by Achille Marozzo, republished in 1546, 1550, 1568 and 1615. This is a very comprehensive description of the Bolognese style, and is thought to have been very influential in its time, as witness its many editions.

1540s: *Opus Amplissimum de Arte Athletica (MSS Dresd.C.93/C.94)* by Paulus Hector Mair. Mair was an avid collector of treatises, and subsidized his work by embezzling funds from the city of Ausburg, for which he was hanged in 1579. I do not recommend you follow his example, but we should be grateful for his dedication.

1553: *Trattato di Scientia d'Arme, con vn Dialogo di Filosofia*, by Camillo Agrippa (Rome, Antonio Blado, 1553). This was the famous architect's attempt to use geometry and reason to create a system of swordsmanship from first principles. Its influence is a matter of debate. It has been published in translation by Dr Ken Mondschein as *Fencing: A Renaissance Treatise*.

1569: *De la Filosofia de las Armas y de su Destreza y la Aggression y Defensa Cristiana*, by Jerónimo Sánchez de Carranza. This is an in-depth fencing manual. It presented a new system of rapier fencing based on science and geometry, which he called *la Verdadera Destreza* ("the True Skill") in contrast to the *esgrima vulgar* ("vulgar fencing") taught by other masters.

1570: *Ragione di adoprar sicuramente l'Arme* by Giacomo di Grassi (Venice, Giordano Ziletti, 1570). This work has the distinction of being the first Italian swordsmanship treatise to be translated into English. This was done in 1594 by "I. G.", an anonymous "gentleman".

1570: *Gründtliche Beschreibung der Kunst des Fechtens* (*A Foundational Description of the Art of Fencing*) by Joachim Meyer (Strasburg, self-published – at ruinous cost – 1570). It was republished in 1590, 1600, 1610 and 1660, and published in translation by Jeffrey Forgeng in *The Art of Combat: A German Martial Arts Treatise of 1570.* This covers not only the longsword, but also the rapier (a long single-handed sword much like a rapier, though the method of use is quite different from the Italian), and the dusack (a single-edged military-type sword), as well as dagger, wrestling, and polearms.

1572: *Dell'Arte di Scrima Libri Tre* by Giovanni dall'Agocchie. This covers much more than just fencing, and is one of the more commonly studied of the Bolognese sources.

1573: *Traicté contenant les secrets du premier livre sur l'éspée seule*, by Henri Sainct Didier. This is the earliest printed source written in French, and covers the use of the sword alone.

1575: *Lo Schermo*, by Angelo Viggiani (Venice, Giorgio Angelieri, 1575). This book is the Rosetta Stone of Italian fencing theory. It details the function of the guards and the Aristotelean basis for the theory of tempo, and goes into detail regarding matters of mechanics that shine a necessary light on the earlier works – especially Fiore. I take pride in the fact that it is now available in translation; at my urging, Jherek Swanger has edited his previous free translation of part 3 and published it as *The Fencing Method of Angelo Viggiani: Lo Schermo, Part III.*

1595: *His Practice,* by Vincentio Saviolo. This is the first fencing book originally published in English, and details an unusual fencing style, probably influenced by both Spanish and Italian forms. It was edited and published by Jared Kirby in 2013 as *A Gentleman's Guide to Duelling.*

1599: *Paradoxes of Defence*, by George Silver (London, Edward Blount, 1599). This is not the earliest work in English, but it is by far the most influential, and has a wide following of exponents.

It concerns itself with two main themes: the utter wretchedness of all Italian fencing and fencers, and the solid English principles on which swordsmanship is, or should be, based. Taking it with his unpublished manuscript *Brief Instructions upon my Paradoxes of Defence* (*Sloane MS No.376*, which was discovered and edited by Cyril Matthey in 1898), we have a detailed and complete theory of fencing based on principles such as the four grounds (judgment, distance, time and place). Most famously though he details the True Times, determining what part of the body should move first: time of the hand; time of the hand and body; time of the hand, body and foot; and time of the hand, body and feet. His work has been republished and annotated in several places, notably Paul Wagner's *Master of Defence* (2003) and Stephen Hand's *English Swordsmanship* (2006).

The late 1500s saw the emergence of treatises on the longer, thinner rapier (despised by Silver). Perhaps the first of these was Giacomo di Grassi's *Ragione*, which led up to the "big three" rapier treatises: Fabris, Giganti and Capoferro.

From the early seventeenth century onwards, there was an explosion of fencing treatises, especially in France.

The Seventeenth Century
1600: *Libro de las Grandeza de la Espada*, by Luis Pacheco de Narváez. This is a continuation of the Verdadera Destreza school, founded by Carranza.

1606: Salvator Fabris published his monumental *Lo Schermo, overo Scienza d'Arme* (published in translation by Tom Leoni in 2005 as *The Art of Dueling: Salvator Fabris' rapier fencing treatise of 1606*). This was so successful it was republished in 1622, 1624, 1672, 1676 and 1713. It is a very thorough and clear explanation of the art of fencing.

1606: Nicoletto Giganti published *Schola overo Teatro* (translated by Tom Leoni as *Venetian Rapier, Nicoletto Giganti's 1606 Rapier Fencing Curriculum*, 2010), which is a much simpler exposition of the art. Leoni calls it a curriculum, and that is close to the truth.

Giganti spends much less time on theory, and presents the material in a logical order. A second book published in 1608 by Giganti, thought lost for centuries, was discovered in the summer of 2012 by Piermarco Terminiello, who published it in translation in 2013 as *The 'Lost' Second Book of Nicoletto Giganti (1608)*.

1610: Ridolfo Capoferro published *Il Gran Simulacro dell'Arte e dell'Uso della Scherma* (*The Great Representation of the Art and the Use of Fencing*). It is perhaps the most famous fencing treatise ever written, and in its time went through many editions. For such a famous work, we know almost nothing about the author save that which he tells us himself: he was 52 at the time of writing, and he came from Cagli, in Italy. There are at least three modern translations available.

1628: *L'Academie de l'Espee* by Gérard Thibault d'Anvers. It's one of the largest and most expensive fencing books ever written, lavishly illustrated, and represents a version of La Verdadera Destreza.

1640: *La Scherma,* by Francesco Fernando Alfieri, who also wrote books on signal flags and the pike.

1672: *Nueva ciencia, y Filosofía de la destreza de las armas,* by Luis Pacheco de Narváez, written in 1632 but not published until after his death.

1674: *Klare Onderrichtinge der Voortreffelijke Worstel-Konst* (*Clear Education in the Magnificent Art of Wrestling*) by Nicolaes Petter.

1686: *Le Maistre d'armes* by Sieur de Liancour. One of the foundational texts of the French school of fencing.

1686: *Regole della Scherma,* by Francesco Antonio Marcelli. This is a very detailed and complete method of rapier fencing.

1696: *La Spada Maestra,* by Bondì di Mazo (published in translation by Matteo Butera, Francesco Lanza, Jherek Swanger, and Reinier van Noort in 2016 as *The Spada Maestra*). This is a short, clear book that covers rapier fencing. It is perhaps the last "proper" rapier manual.

1696: *L'art en fait d'armes,* by Jean-François Labat. This treatise perhaps marks the beginning of the dominance of the French school of fencing.

The Eighteenth Century

1707: *A New Short and Easy Method of Fencing*, by Sir William Hope. Hope wrote several books before this one, including the *Scot's Fencing Master* in 1687.

1728: *The Expert Sword-man's Companion*, by the legendary soldier, whoremonger and duellist Donald McBane. There are three modern transcription editions to choose from, the most recent being Jared Kirby's of 2017. One of the few fencing books that is also a cracking good read.

1736: *Traite des Armes*, by P. J. F. Girard, published in translation by Philip Crawley in 2014 as *The Art of the Smallsword*. This is a comprehensive and excellent book which (in the original) also includes instructions on military drill, such as lighting and throwing a grenade!

1767: *L'École des armes*, by Domenico Angelo. The most famous smallsword book of them all, by the founder of the Angelo fencing dynasty. Published in translation by his son, Harry, in 1787.

How to use Translations

If you can't read the language of the book that you're interested in, you are going to have to rely on translations. There's nothing wrong with that unless you are teaching historical swordsmanship for a living. In my opinion, if this is your job then you really need to be able to read the sources on which you're presenting your interpretations in the original language. There really is no substitute for it. But for most people there is absolutely nothing wrong with using a reliable translation from which to recreate your system. The question is: what makes a reliable translation? The problem is that you can't know whether or not it's reliable if you can't check it against the original.

Let's take an example: the translation of Giganti's second book from 1608, published in 2013. There is no transcription of the original Italian, and there's no copy of the original Italian available anywhere in any format. I know the reputation of the people who produced it, Piermarco Terminiello and Joshua Pendragon, and it has a foreword by Tobias Capwell no less. So there's every reason to believe that this is a very good translation, accurate and consistent and all that sort of thing. But until I can check it against the original, I can't actually trust it.

So what do you do if the original isn't available? How do you know whether it's trustworthy or not? The first thing is the reputation of the people who did the translation, and the second thing is how the book reads. Just because the translation was done in period doesn't mean it's accurate. For example the first translation of di Grassi's 1570 book was published in 1594, and it is far from perfect.

Sometimes you have more than one translation to choose from. So how do you compare them? Let's use Ridolfo Capoferro's *Gran Simulacro* as an example. The first publicly available translation was done by Jherek Swanger and William Wilson, in 1999. *Italian Rapier Combat*, edited by Jared Kirby, was the first commercial translation to come out (in 2004), and Tom Leoni's *Ridolfo Capoferro's The Art and Practice of Fencing* was published in 2011. Let's compare an excerpt from each, such as the text at plate six.

From Swanger and Wilson: "There are two reasons (it seems to me) for which it is necessary to draw close to the adversary: the first is to stringer the sword in order to seek measure and tempo; the other is to draw close to the body of the adversary in order to seek only measure; which closings are best considered in the straight line; and because there are two causes of closing there must also be two occasions: the first occasion, of stringering the sword in order to seek measure and tempo, is when the said adversary lies in an oblique line, because the adversary lying with the sword in *quarta* which is aimed on an oblique line at your left side . . ."

From *Italian Rapier Combat* (Kirby): "There are two motives (it seems to me) for which it is necessary to *stringere* the adversary.

First, to *stringere* the sword in order to seek the *misura* and the *tempo*. The other, to *stringere* the body of the adversary to only seek the *misura*. These very good *stringimenti* are considered in the straight line. It is because there are two motives to *stringimenti* that there shall also be two occasions. The first occasion, to *stringimento* with the sword, is in order to seek *misura* and *tempo* when said adversary is found in an oblique line. For when you find the adversary with the sword in *quarta* such that it looks to the oblique line to your left side . . ."

From *Ridolfo Capoferro's The Art and Practice of Fencing* (Leoni): "I see two reasons to press the opponent. The first is to gain his sword in order to seek the measure and the tempo. The second is to advance against him just to gain the measure. Both these actions can be performed in a straight line.

These two reasons in turn pertain to two different situations. Gaining the opponent's sword to seek the measure and tempo should be done when the opponent is in *quarta* with his sword angled towards your left . . ."

Swanger and Wilson were careful to preserve as much as possible of Capoferro's phrasing and sentence structure; Kirby goes a step further in that direction, and leaves quite a few words in the original Italian in a way that is not necessarily as useful for the modern reader (especially where it says "to *stringimento*," which is like saying "to stringering"). Leoni has rewritten the text quite extensively into clear and easy to follow English, adding paragraph breaks and punctuation as needed.

If you are working on a treatise that has more than one translation, you should buy all of them and then compare them. As you're working through them you will get a sense of which book is better for your purposes. I would also advise you to seriously consider learning the language that the primary source is written in, and also seriously consider writing your own translation.

Some years ago a student of mine did this on her blog: she rewrote Capoferro in completely modern English. The bit that really stood out for me was in the dedication "To the most serene Lord Don Francesco Maria Feltrio della Rovere, Sixth Duke of Urbino." She put it like this: "Yo, Duke, here I wrote this thing." So to get a clearer idea of which bits you think you understand and which you really don't, rewrite the whole book in your own words (and in your own language, obviously). My student Ilkka Hartikainen taught himself Italian to read the Bolognese sources; my student Chris Blakey is currently teaching himself Latin to do his own translation of *I.33*. If they can do it, so can you!

To sum up, when using translations:

* check the reputation of the translator
* if possible check it against the original language and get a second opinion if you can; and
* if there's more than one translation, buy them all and particularly look for places where they clearly disagree.

Also, even if you can't read the original language, do consider writing what is effectively your own translation or your own rewording of the existing translations to represent your understanding of what's actually going on in the text. Be as colloquial and amusing as you like!

How to Approach Your Chosen Source

At this stage you have chosen your source. I hope you've chosen well. The first thing to do is to create a readable version of the text. If you happen to have chosen something that was printed in English and is nice and clear, you can skip this bit. If, however, there are any difficulties – if it's written in a language you can't read fluently – you need to find a translation or create your own. If it's written in manuscript form, you may have difficulty reading the handwriting. You need to find a transcription or create a transcription of your own.

Whatever format it's in, I would strongly recommend that you get started on creating a machine-readable version of the text. It will make searching for things later much, much easier. You could use OCR (Optical Character Recognition) and get machines to do that work for you, but there is really no substitute to writing the book out yourself. This sounds horrible. It sounds like vastly more work than you'll ever need to do. But what we're trying to do is get this book that exists in a physical or electronic form outside of your body into a matrix of information that exists in your brain so that you can easily refer to it. Typing it out is a great way to do that. As with every great big task, it's best to break it down into chunks. It is well worth your time to write out the book section by section.

Maybe spend twenty minutes on it every day for a while until the book is done, so that you have not only a machine-readable version of the text but you've actually gone through the whole thing using a method that is much less passive than simply reading it. As you go, write summaries of each section and note down any details that catch your attention. I like to get all the notes onto one great big piece of paper, so that I can see it all at once and patterns can leap out at me.

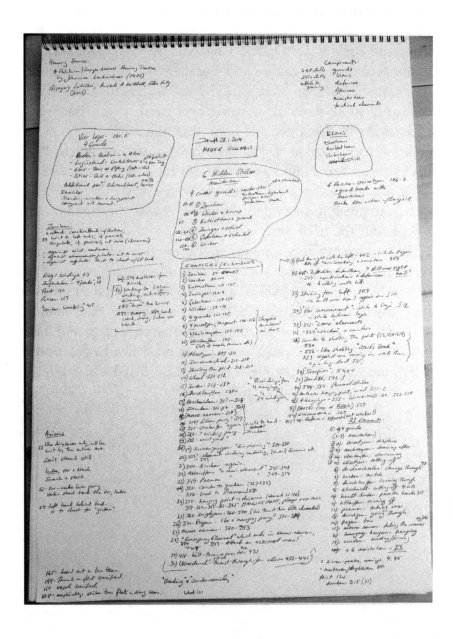

These are my notes for Lecküchner's treatise. I'm working from a translation (I don't read German). I started out with a huge piece of paper (It's A2 I think) because it's such a big book, and I started out by noting the following details with relevant page numbers:

- The date
- Details of the source
- Guards
- Blows
- Specific techniques, especially named techniques
- General axioms: anything that seems like it's applicable outside its specific context. For example, if the writer says "and when I'm attacked, I always step to the left", that may apply to this one particular play but it may also apply to every single play.

With a smaller, simpler book, you can just write an annotated table of contents, as you can see in my notes on Giganti. I just went through the book writing down what was happening on every page.

You might find it useful to review the "Fencing Theory" chapter to get an overview of the things you should be looking for in the book.

Martial Context

We have to place our source into the context in which it has been created. The three main contexts we need to concern ourselves with are the martial context, the historical context and the fencing context. From the point of view of creating the technical drills that are your first practical step in recreating the art, the first and most important context is the martial. That's because it determines what is going to work. Obviously the sort of techniques you might use to murder somebody in a dark alley are going to be quite different from the sort of techniques you'd use to win a fencing tournament. Those will also be different to the sort of techniques you might use to fight in a line of battle with a hundred of your friends.

The first step is to determine the martial context of the source that you have chosen. Most fencing sources tend to deal with the duel and, if you are reading it closely, you'll probably find all sorts of clues to the assumptions on the part of the writer. For example, he might only ever show techniques against one opponent, or perhaps he describes saluting the spectators.

Possible contexts include:

- Judicial combat
- Civilian duelling
- Police-type actions
- Tournaments where the main goal is to enhance your reputation
- Tournaments fought for prizes
- Fitness (some of the latest sources explicitly describe the healthy benefits of vigorous activity)
- Warfare
- Self-defence
- Murder.

I've never come across a book that has all of these in one, but you never know.

Fencing Context

No system exists in a complete vacuum. There's always something that came before it, whether it's recorded or not, and there's always something that came after it, whether it's any use or not. No source represents the entirety of world martial arts at any given time, so there are always other styles being practised at the same time. If you imagine this as a cross with your source in the middle, at the bottom we have the art that came before it, at the top we have the art that came after it, and either side we have styles that were practiced at the same time in the same area, or in different parts of the world (you can arrange this cross however makes sense to you – some people prefer the timeline to go left to right, not down to up).

The context is only really applicable when it can have some sort of bearing on the source that you're looking at. For example, you may have a contemporary source from Japan, but if there was no connection between the person who wrote the source that you're working on and the people who were writing the source in Japan at the same time, then the Japanese source is irrelevant in terms of the context. In a perfect world, you have this beautiful cross as you can see here, where I've chosen Marozzo as a primary source:

Fiore came before him, Capoferro after him, and Durer (from 1512) and Mair (from the 1540s) are approximately contemporary – at least within twenty years or so. Knowing that Marozzo existed in this context means we can see what happened in Italian swordsmanship after Marozzo; what happened in Italian swordsmanship before Marozzo; and what was going on in Germany a bit before and a bit after him, which gives you a better sense of what may be going on within the book itself. Not least because sometimes there are mysterious bits of a treatise which can be solved by reference to an earlier, later or contemporary source, especially if it comes from the same culture.

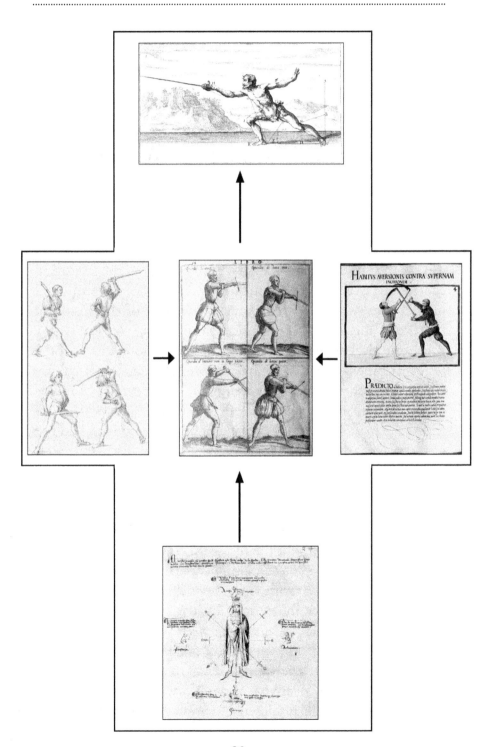

We could of course add Manciolino and any of the Bolognese sources – even Agrippa.

Once you have sketched out this fencing context cross, you can add to it as you come across new material. Eventually instead of having a cross with your source in the middle and one before it, one or two after it, and one or two on either side, you'll have this great big forest of fencing sources that you are at least tolerably familiar with. This will give you a deep understanding of the context of your primary source.

Historical Context

From the point of view of recreating the system as a set of technical and tactical principles and practices, the historical context isn't terribly relevant. You can become a pretty good martial artist without really having any idea of the historical context of the art that you practise. However, you can't be a good historical swordsman without having a good grasp of the history of the source; there are all sorts of elements of culture which are embedded in or represented by the system. All sorts of choices are being made based on cultural factors that can supersede martial factors. You have to be aware of them because it's a particularly common factor when you're discussing your art with other martial artists. When you agree, there's no problem; but when you don't agree, very often there is a good historical reason for your arts to be different. The difference will usually lie in one of these three contexts.

So how do you find out the historical context of your source? Most people are more interested in people than they are in facts, so I would suggest starting with a good historical biography of a famous person from the period. That will usually give you all sorts of background for what's going on. If you're doing fifteenth-century German stuff, the biography of Maximilian might be a good starting point. It's perfectly all right to pick something that's relatively accessible, relatively straightforward. It doesn't have to be some eighteen-inch thick finely printed thing with a million footnotes. You just need to start becoming familiar with the people and the culture of the time.

Next, find a general historical overview of your period. Anything that covers a 50 year window around your source would be perfect. It should give you an idea of what wars were going on, who was murdering whom, and political instabilities – that kind of thing.

When you've done that, have a look to see if you can find one thing that will affect your reading of your source based on your historical research.

Another factor to take into consideration is the role of the weapon that you're dealing with in this period. Was it an agricultural implement that became a popular sport weapon of the aristocracy, for instance? Or was it a general side arm that most people of a certain class would carry? Was it a weapon specifically developed for judicial combat, or some other context? Use your historical research to answer the question of "what was the role of this weapon in this time and place?" This will be very important in establishing the martial context, and it will give you all sorts of insights on why the techniques that you're going to be looking at will be as they are.

To summarise, there are three contexts to take into account: the martial context, the fencing context, and the historical context. Of all of these, the most important is the martial context. The next most important is the fencing context. From both a martial arts perspective and the perspective of recreating the art, the historical context is third on the list. Of course, for a fencing historian or a re-enactor, these priorities will change. My bias is probably clear from the topics I've chosen to write books about, such as medieval Italian martial arts (*Armizare*) and Renaissance Italian rapier.

Principles of Drill Design

Most martial arts have a foundation of a few core drills. When I build a syllabus, I like to create a single cornerstone drill from which all the others can be developed. To do this, you must first know what drills are for and how they are constructed. What follows are the principles of creating drills, which I have used to develop my syllabi for the last fifteen years.

1. Put first things first. This is important because in every drill there's a certain amount of assumed knowledge. When you're creating your drills, you have to start with the assumed knowledge being zero. If your drill has an attack and a defence in it, you must make sure that the attack is taught first, possibly in a separate drill. So put first things first and make sure that the drill doesn't depend on any knowledge that the students do not yet have.

2. Every drill should teach one thing. There is a primary purpose to every drill you create. Of course, there may be many secondary purposes and the drill can be practised for all sorts of purposes, but in its essence the drill should have one primary purpose. For instance, it might represent a particular play from a specific treatise in a trainable and accessible way, or it might develop the student's ability to deceive with feints. Those are two completely separate types of drills. The classic rookie mistake when creating drills is to try to cram too much stuff in. If your drill successfully teaches one thing, it is a good drill. If it successfully teaches two things at once, it's an impossible drill.

3. Distinguish between breadth and depth. Breadth is knowing many things. A drill that has you go through all nine masters of the dagger from *Il Fior di Battaglia* teaches breadth. Depth is being able to do those things under pressure, such as taking one of those masters and using his defence against resistant opponents. In their basic form, the drills you create will

emphasise either breadth or depth. These are not entirely mutually exclusive, but you should be clear at the outset whether your drill is intended to teach a series of things to expand the student's knowledge, or to teach the ability to do a particular thing better than they could do it before.

4. Lastly, we should distinguish between technical and tactical. A technical drill tells you how to do something. A tactical drill tells you when to do it and why. These are fundamentally different problems. For example, if I got hit in the head because I didn't know that I should have parried, I'd need a tactical drill to teach me that the parry is the correct response in this circumstance. If I parried but my parry failed because it wasn't good enough, I need a technical drill to teach me how to parry better. In every drill that you create, you should distinguish between technical and tactical. In their basic form, every drill should be either a technical drill or a tactical drill. At the basic level of the syllabus, every drill is a technical drill because your students don't yet know the techniques on which the system is built.

To recap, the principles of drill design are:

- Put first things first
- Teach one thing
- Distinguish between breadth and depth
- Distinguish between technical and tactical
- Drills can be solo or done in pairs, and can sometimes be done in multiple opponent situations
- Every solo drill at this stage is a technical drill. Every pair drill can be either technical or tactical. So we must distinguish between drills which are intended to be trained alone, and drills which are intended to be trained in pairs. In general, a handling drill which makes you flip the sword around in all sorts of funny ways is a technical drill, but has no tactical application and so shouldn't be done with a partner. The drills

you're going to come up with will emphasise either technique, tactics, or attributes. Here's a convenient Venn diagram I've put together for you to illustrate the different kinds of drill:

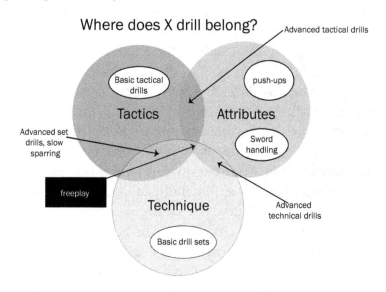

- Technical drills are the base of most martial arts systems. Your syllabus will be founded on technical drills that teach the student the fundamental actions of the system
- Tactical drills develop the student's ability to choose the right action: they teach you when you should do what. Any drill that includes choice is a tactical drill
- Attribute training develops attributes like strength, speed, timing, weapons handling, judgment of measure, or tactical awareness. A push-up is an attribute training drill; a footwork line drill is an attribute training drill too.

Let's take a straight punch as an example. Weight training that develops arm strength and improves your punch is attribute training. Technical practice, such as on the heavy bag, improves your punching technique (something that bench presses do not do). Training on the striking mitts with a coach teaching you when to use your straight punch is tactical training.

At the more advanced level, drills do tend to work on more than one of these factors. For example, if your technical drill is being trained hard and fast for the purpose of developing the attribute of speed, we can call it an advanced technical drill.

The drill in which you train tactics, technique, and attributes all at once is freeplay. As you would expect, anything that does more than one thing at a time tends to be not terribly efficient at doing any one of those things, but in a fight you must be able to apply your solid technique with speed and strength, and at the right time. It is necessary that you have the opportunity to practise all of these things together at some point.

When you are creating a drill, you need to think to yourself where it would fit in the previous diagram. Is it purely a tactical drill that relies on a certain assumed technical knowledge? Is it purely an attribute drill which requires no knowledge or technique? Is it a technical drill which can be done slowly and calmly, and without any sense of tactics at all while the students are learning the basic choreography?

One critical thing to mention regarding drill design is this: every drill has a dollop of bullshit built in. It has to. The important thing is that you should know what that dollop is. The real thing is the only bullshit-free scenario in martial arts. If you're an MMA fighter, that's the ring on fight night. If you're a soldier, that's being in the presence of the enemy. And if you are a swordsman, that is someone trying to take your head off with a blade. But the real thing must be prepared for, so we have drills, exercises and training. Problems only arise when we mistake one scenario (a training drill) for another (the real thing). To properly understand any drill, you must have a clear idea of exactly how it deviates from reality. I call this spotting the bullshit.

Let us take a simple example, a drill that is usually included in day one of our Fiore beginners' course: the basic execution of Fiore's first play of the dagger. This technique is a disarm, done against the common overhand blow.

In its basic set-up, the drill goes like this:

"Both players start left foot forwards, hands down, in a proper guard position. This is very artificial, and is intended only to create a consistent starting point for beginners.
Disarm and counter:
Attacker and defender both in *porta di ferro*, left foot forwards.
Attacker passes to strike with a *fendente*. Aim it at the mask!
Defender intercepts attacker's wrist with his left hand, and
Turns it to the left, creating a leverage disarm with the dagger against the back of his wrist.
Defender collects dagger and strikes."

(Quoted from *Mastering the Art of Arms vol 1: the Medieval Dagger*, page 51.)

There is nothing wrong with this, as a starting point. But it has at least the following dollops of bullshit in it:

- The attacker is not trying to kill you
- The weapon is not sharp
- The roles are pre-set: attacker and defender
- You can't run away or call the cops
- You have to wait for the attack
- You are wearing protective gear that will allow the attacker to make contact, but which would not work against a real dagger (we tried this with a mask on a dummy: the mask failed against all medieval weaponry)
- The line of the attack is pre-selected
- Your defence is pre-selected
- The attacker is not allowed to counter or continue
- The attack is done with little force
- The attack is done slowly.

I am sure that you can think of other dollops, but eleven is enough to be going on with. So, how do we deal with this? How can we eliminate the bullshit without killing students?

To start with, #1 cannot be trained outside of the real scenario.

Don't even try. It is this one element that really makes the difference between those that have done it for real and those that haven't. (I haven't and don't intend to.) Regarding combat sports, you haven't done it until you've been in the ring or competed in a serious tournament. Fortunately, those are much more survivable environments, so anybody who trains seriously enough can get there and do that art "for real". This is one of the big attractions of combat sports, I think: the real environment is available. I will never forget my first fencing competition. It was an eye-opener, to say the least!

So, if my drill above is so full of bullshit, why do we do it?

It does:

- Teach core mechanical principles, such as grounding, finding lines of weakness, etc.
- Teach core tactical principles, such as controlling the weapon before you strike, timing, and control of distance
- Give beginners a chance to reconstruct a technique from the book, given the source of our art
- Serve as a perfectly good starting point. Just as a child learning to read sounding out the individual letters and creating the words is not really reading yet, we don't say that they should just recognise the words straight away. This level of practice is a necessary step on the way to expertise.

But be aware that this drill does NOT:

- Teach a survival skill
- Teach situational awareness
- Teach decision making or judgment
- Teach the ability to execute the action under pressure.

But given our list of eleven dollops of bullshit, we can map a route through training to systematically eliminate each of them (except for the first). For instance, by applying the "who moves first" multiplier we can eliminate point #5, so the "defender" is not required to wait but can enter or move away, gaining some control. By allowing degrees of freedom for one or other student, we can eliminate #7, #8 and/or #9. By applying the rule of Cs (see page 183 for the definition of this rule and how to use it) you can increase the intensity in a systematic way, so eliminating #10 and #11.

It is very important to not eliminate all the bullshit all at once. Especially when eliminating #2 by practising with sharps, you should absolutely keep all sorts of other bullshit present to avoid serious injury.

So, by carefully considering all the ways in which a set drill is not a real fight, you can design variations to the basic version to systematically clean up some of the bullshit. You will need lots of different drills, each with a different bullshit profile, to make sure that you are training in all of the attributes of the "real" technique.

Now that we have got that out of the way, the first step in creating your syllabus is to design what I call the "cornerstone drill."

Create Your Cornerstone Drill

My cornerstone drills (I have one for every sword style I teach) are always a four step drill in which everything that is vital to the system is represented in some way. The four steps are usually an attack countered by a defence, which is countered by a counter to the defence, which is countered by a counter to the counter to the defence.

The four steps:

- Attack
- Defence
- Counter to the defence
- Counter to the counter.

The critical thing about the cornerstone drill is it must be representative of the system as a whole. If there are all sorts of sneaky little techniques that occur once in the system and in a very specific context, they may be interesting and important, but you'll get onto those later. Your cornerstone drill should be primarily technical. To begin with it will be trained slowly and carefully, not developing any particular attributes. Furthermore, while it represents a set of tactical preferences, it is not a tactical drill because it doesn't include options at this stage.

Before you do any actual physical practice, you must read and understand the Safety chapter, which is on page 131. You may also find the Equipment chapter useful, p.136.

With your cornerstone, you want something that represents as closely as possible the fundamental tactical and technical preferences of the system that you are trying to represent. This is quite a tall order and there will be lots of little side quests as you progress through creating your cornerstone drill. If it makes you feel any better, the cornerstone drill that is the foundation of my Fiore syllabus in my school took, I think, eleven years to get to its current and hopefully final incarnation. So don't worry if you don't get it absolutely perfect first time – you're in good company. As long as you have a clear idea of what you're trying to accomplish, you should find getting there a lot quicker than the eleven years it seemed to take me.

The six steps to creating your cornerstone drill are:

- Create a solo technical drill. Start by choosing an attack that is commonly used in your system
- Create the drill that is the defence against that specific attack.
- Take that defence out and create a drill in which you practise it solo
- Put them back together and explain (to yourself and any students present) the tactics behind it. This gives you an idea of how drills in general are constructed
- Add the attacker's counter to the defence and explain (to

yourself and any students present) the tactics behind it
- Add the defender's counter to the attacker's counter to the defence.

There are therefore six steps overall to create a four step drill. The two extra steps are a solo practice of step #1 (the attack), and a solo practice of the second step of the drill (the defence).

Step #1: The Attack

Begin with one or two basic actions from your source, such as an *oberhau*, a kick, a *mandritto fendente*, or a lunge in *quarta* and recover. Then create a standardised way in which to practise it. You need a standard starting position, which is followed by the movement and then followed by however you recover from it.

For instance, it could be: I start in *posta di donna*, I cut *mandritto fendente* with a pass, I end in *dente di zengiaro*, and I pass back. Or: I stand in on guard in *terza*, I extend in *quarta*, I lunge and I recover.

Then you need to explain – at least to yourself, but ideally write it down with as much detail as possible – why you've chosen each part of that drill. So why *posta di donna*? Why *quarta*?

Then identify any prerequisite knowledge. Suddenly you'll realize that well, okay, your students don't know *posta di donna* yet, or they don't know how to hold a sword properly; or, if your drill includes ninja assassin techniques, they don't know their backflips yet (it is a truth universally acknowledged that you've got to be able to do backflips to be a ninja assassin).

Your first side quest on the way to creating the cornerstone drill will be to note down that these elements will have to be trained either in their own separate drills or as part of the drill that you are trying to create. There is already all sorts of room for adding breadth, so on your second side quest you could repeat this exercise for every single common strike in the system: *mandritto fendente, roverso fendente, mandritto sottano, roverso sottano,* different lunges and passes, and so forth. You'll notice if you have a look in my syllabus for the longsword that we have the "cutting drill" and the "syllabus form," which do all that. We also have it in the rapier footwork form, which contains all of the footwork actions that are commonly used in Capoferro's system.

Don't go off on these side quests just yet because we're still working on the cornerstone drill. Just note that you'll need to expand in these directions later.

Step #2: The Defence

Choose a counter to the action that you've just trained. Ideally choose one directly from the source. For example, against a *mandritto fendente*, you could parry from *tutta porta di ferro*. Or against the lunge in *quarta*, you could counterattack also in *quarta*. (I don't know how ninja assassins defend against a back flip.) Then set up the drill so that you know what everyone is doing and why, and you should notice at this stage that most of the plays we find in most of the sources are usually a simple defence against a simple attack.

However, they are often preceded by implied or stated actions. Let's take plate seven from Capoferro as an example.

The text (in William Wilson's and Jherek Swanger's translation) reads:

> By way of clarification of the following figures, I say that D having the figure marked C stringered on the inside, the same C disengages in order to give a thrust to the chest of figure D. D strikes him with a thrust in the left eye with a fixed foot or an increase of pace as the figure shows.
>
> But yet I say that if C had been a shrewd person, when he disengaged he would have disengaged by way of a feint, with his body somewhat held back, and D approaching confidently in order to attack C, C would have parried the enemy's sword to the outside with the false or the true edge, giving him a *mandritto* to the face or an *imbroccata* to the chest, and in such a conclusion would retire into a low *quarta*.

The action begins with your opponent standing on guard in *terza*, and you approach them in *quarta*. If they do nothing, you will just hit them. However, as you approach them in *quarta*, they disengage, find your sword, and stab you through the chest in *seconda*. That is the attack that is stated in the text and shown in the picture, being done by the figure on the left.

But as you approach them, you stringer them in *quarta* and they disengage to strike in *seconda*. You parry and strike in a single motion, stabbing them through the left eye in *seconda*. That is the actual play that the plate shows. That presupposes that you know how to *stringere* in *quarta* and that your opponent knows how to attack by disengage. The cornerstone drill that we use for our rapier training is this one from plate seven, but it must be preceded by exercises on how to *stringere* and exercises on how to attack by disengage – because without those there is no way to set up the situation that occurs on plate seven.

Step #3: Solo Training

In most circumstances it's a good idea to extract the defender's part of the drill and practice it solo so you have a nice start, middle, and end. For example, if you're doing a parry from *tutta porta di ferro* against a *mandritto fendente* coming from *posta di donna*, you should practice the parry movement by itself – particularly if this is in a very basic class. Being able to do the movement correctly makes doing the action a lot easier, but having somebody actually trying to hit you in the head while you're trying to do your movement makes everything more complicated. It's a good idea, particularly at the basic level, to extract the defender's action and practice it as a movement in its own right.

Step #4: Reassemble the Drill

Explain to yourself or to the students what exactly is going on – the tactical rationale for making the defence the way you're doing it. It's not enough for you as the syllabus designer to just repeat it slavishly from the book. It's not a bad start, but it's not sufficient. You need to understand why every action is as it is, and for that you are going to need to have a pretty solid idea as to why this particular defence should be done in this particular context. If you're new to this, don't worry. This level of information or level of expertise will develop over time.

Step #5: Add the Attacker's Counter

Having put the drill back together, now add the next step: the attacker's counter to the defence. Ideally source it from the book. For instance, in the plate seven example above, Capoferro is kind enough to state that if C had been a clever person, he would have disengaged by way of a feint and, D coming to strike, C would parry and riposte. That's ideal. Likewise, Fiore gives us a counter that is good "against all the plays that come before it", which is to yield and pommel strike. We use that for step three of our First Drill. (You can find the play on f.44v of the *Getty MS.*)

107

Now explain the tactics behind the attacker's continuation.

If your book doesn't have a specific counter to that defence in the context of that defence being made (in other words, as an actual continuation of that defence), you're going to have to find it from somewhere else in the book. If your book doesn't have attacker's continuations against defences, we have to wonder whether that book is actually fit for purpose: you do need to have a solid grasp of all the parts of fencing in your chosen system, and ideally you need to get those from a historical source before you end up making stuff up. You are going to need to be able to continue fencing past the first defence.

Step #6: Add the Defender's Counter to the Counter

Add the defender's counter to the attacker's counter to the defence. Again, this is ideally sourced from the book. The logic behind this is the same as for the previous step and, again, you need to be able to explain why you're doing it this way. At the beginner level, or if your goals are purely historical, simply saying "it says to do this in the book" is actually sufficient because this is all about historical authenticity. If you don't understand the *why* of it yet but the book tells you to do it, just do it. But it's a good idea if you have at least a solid working theory of why it would be this way before you start teaching it to some unsuspecting beginner students.

Congratulations, you now have one solid four step drill: attack, defence, counter to the defence, and counter to the counter. That is sufficient for your cornerstone drill. However, you'll have noticed that at every stage there are all sorts of possibilities for variations. You could choose a different attack, or it could be a different defence against the same attack, or it could be a different counter to the same defence against the same attack, and so on. Once you have your cornerstone drill, and you've worked through a few options and come up with something you're really happy with, it will give you the basic structure of the system:

ideally every further drill that you create can be expressed as a variation on this basic drill. This makes the whole syllabus much easier to remember and much easier for the students to absorb as a complete system, rather than as a set of isolated techniques.

For example, if we take the cornerstone drill for my Fiore syllabus for the longsword, first drill, we have:

* *Mandritto fendente* from *posta di donna*
* Parry from *tutta porta di ferro* and strike
* Yield to the parry and pommel strike
* Cover against the pommel strike and do your own pommel strike.

In our second drill, the attack is the same but the defence is from a different guard: *dente di zenghiaro* on the left. The third basic drill is the exchange of thrust, in which the attack is a thrust. Indeed, all of our longsword technical drills can be expressed as variations on First Drill.

Similarly, in our rapier syllabus our cornerstone drill is plate seven, and the second foundational drill is plate sixteen. In that one you stringer on the outside, which is countered by an attack by disengage. You could think of it as "plate seven on the other side."

Tactical Drills

Once you have your cornerstone drill, let's have a look at creating a tactical drill. For a tactical drill, you need two technical drills, or one drill and a variation to it. The tactical drill introduces choice.

Let's stick with plate seven for our example. We can create a tactical drill from it by simply varying whether when "C" disengages, they do so to attack or to feint (to do step #2 or #4). You can play this drill as either "C" training "D" to distinguish between the feint and the attack, or you can have it the other way around so that "C" is being trained by "D" to choose wisely. That is, if there is an opportunity to attack and they think they can get it in, they should take it. If they're not sure they can get it in, they should feint to draw the attack onto their prepared parry riposte.

Syllabus Design

The gap between beginner and expert is vast, and can take years to cross. The function of the syllabus is to provide a ladder for the beginner to climb up to where they want to be. Every step on the ladder should be achievable if the previous steps have been taken.

No syllabus:

Syllabus:

The hallmarks of a well-designed syllabus are:

1. A clear goal. Is the syllabus intended to create a good fencer in one style, an all-round martial artist, a competent researcher, or something else?
2. Every action in the higher levels has been prepared for in the lower levels
3. Students can reliably progress through the levels to reach their goals. If students are getting stuck at a particular point, the syllabus is probably lacking in some material
4. There is scope for more than one route through the material, allowing students to follow their interests at least up to a point.

Build the Foundation

The foundation of your syllabus is a set of between three and seven drills that will form literally the foundation of basic training for your students. The idea is that once they know those three to seven drills, they have a solid handle on the fundamental techniques, tactics and ideas behind the system.

To reiterate, the golden rule of syllabus design is this: you must only teach them a drill for which they already have the necessary components. Every next step in the syllabus must be prepared for by the previous steps. For example, if a new drill introduces a new blow, they have to be taught that blow first – so that when they see the drill, they already know its components.

In a syllabus made up of three levels, everything the students do in level one prepares them for level two, and the new material in level two will prepare them for level three. When you created the cornerstone drill in the previous chapter, you established what you feel is the fundamental technique, the fundamental idea of the system, so you've already done a lot of the preparation work for creating this foundation. We're going to take that same process, those same ideas, and apply them in a slightly broader way.

Firstly, you have to identify the key plays. You've probably already done this as part of the winnowing-out process of choosing your cornerstone drill, but this is just a reminder to identify the key plays. You should look for plays that are repeated, or patterns that are repeated, within the source that you're working with. Your key plays will also solve common problems. For example, if in your system a thrust to the face is very common, your foundational plays must address it. On the other hand, if a cut to the ankle occurs once in a 400 page book, it's probably not going to appear in your foundation. You might include it in the full syllabus but you won't put it into the foundation. So the foundation is, if you like, the 80/20 principle at work – where 20% of actions apply to 80% of the context.

Let's take a concrete example. In my foundational syllabus for the longsword, we have four drills around which everything else is built.

First drill deals with *mandritto fendente* (a forehand descending blow coming to your left shoulder), which is parried from the right.

Second drill has the same attack, but it's parried from the left.

Third drill is the "breaking of the thrust": defending from your right side against a thrust coming from your opponent's left side.

Fourth drill is the "exchange of thrusts": defending from your right side against a thrust coming from your opponent's right side.

What this gives you is an attack with a cut, an attack with a thrust, attacks from both the right and the left, and defences against a cut and a thrust from the right and the left. This is a broad and expandable set of material, with each of these plays sourced directly from Fiore's manuscript. This means they fit together quite nicely as a coherent whole. When the student has that and all the necessary training to be able to do those drills, they have the basic knowledge required to expand outwards into dealing with attacks from below and attacks from above, and so on. A well-built foundation is easily expanded upon.

How Many Drills Should the Foundation Have?

I prefer between three and seven. Less than three is usually not enough to cover the fundamentals, and more than seven are difficult to hold in memory all at once. Ideally, your foundational syllabus – the core drills that you're going to build everything around – can be relatively easily memorised. Most people's working memory is limited to between five and nine individual items, and that's pretty much hardwired. So, seven is on the high side; five, anybody should be able to manage; but three, and you're maybe starting to lose some of the opportunity to make your syllabus a bit broader. The best way to find the exact number is to see where the material takes you. If there seem to be four basic ideas, have four drills.

One of my students on the Recreate Historical Swordsmanship from Historical Sources course is creating a syllabus for the *I.33* sword and buckler manual. It says in the very beginning of the manuscript that there are seven wards or guards, of which three "take the fore". In other words, three are the most important. So my student decided to make three drills the foundation of his syllabus.

Having established what your foundational drills are, you need to figure out what a student needs to know before they can be taught those drills. This may include sword handling exercises, footwork exercises or even fitness training.

The foundation should be enough material that it would normally take about four to six months to cover it all with a beginner who is training about twice per week for an hour and a half each time. Obviously, you might be able to run an experienced swordsman through the whole thing in twenty minutes.

It's a good idea when you're putting together your foundational material to design the basic components of a beginners' course (which is the first section of your foundation) to fill six to ten classes. This will force you to organize and prioritize your material. Your cornerstone drill will be there, and its prerequisites too, but see what other parts of your foundation will fit in. That process of trimming your four to six months' worth of material down to a six to ten classes section will give you a way of prioritizing the material, and a useful way of thinking about it. The function of the beginners' course is to prepare the students to learn the entire foundation.

Create the Syllabus

Creating a syllabus is a monumental task. As with any such challenge, the best approach is to break it down into manageable chunks. You already have your cornerstone drill and your foundation. The next step is to expand the foundation using two approaches, which we might label "Theory" and "Practice."

Theory

First, you need to work out a complete interpretation for your primary source. This may take a very long time, and you should go at it section by section. You have already created your table of contents (see "How to Approach Your Chosen Source", p. 131); now pick a section and work through it, writing down each and every play or technique as a separate drill. You need to know who is doing what at every stage of the action and, unless the book specifically states otherwise, *both* combatants should be doing something that might work. Keep going with this until you have worked through every play in every section, and have your working interpretation of every play written down. This will take a long time, but it's fun, fascinating and useful, so there's no rush.

As you go through the book, note which techniques come up repeatedly, and what appear to be solutions to highly specific situations. Both of these categories need to be incorporated in your syllabus, with the most common actions at the most basic level. Depending on how the plays are written out in the book, you may need to add actions to them to create workable drills;

fencing manuals often have "you're in this situation, do this" instructions, but don't ever tell you what you did to get into that situation. You need to figure that out.

Practice

No book is perfectly comprehensive. It is simply impossible to write down every possible variation, because the art is infinitely complex. There are more possible combinations of sword actions than there are atoms in the universe, because every action can be countered. So there is, in theory, no end to the permutations you might come up with. This is not useful. So instead of trying to work out every possible variation, you need a set of multipliers with which you can develop variations on your foundational drills, which will often magically lead you into plays from the book. I go over these multipliers in detail in the chapter "Skill Development" (p.176), so will just recap them briefly here. The multipliers I use are:

Who moves first? You can start the drill with both players standing still in guard (this is the usual set-up for beginners to start with), or you can change who attacks, or the defender can draw the attack by some prior movement or invitation.

Add a step: you can add a counter to the end of any drill, or you can add a preparation or some other action at the beginning.

Degrees of freedom: at any stage in any drill, a set of decisions have been made. Systematically allowing a different choice to be made on the fly by one player introduces an element of unpredictability for the other player.

The rule of Cs: this is not strictly a multiplier, but it gives you the three main attitudes with which every drill should be practised. Co-operate, Coach, and Compete.

These multipliers (or any you develop yourself) should be incorporated into the syllabus itself, as should any specific drills that they create which you find solve a common problem for your students.

Your syllabus now looks something like this:

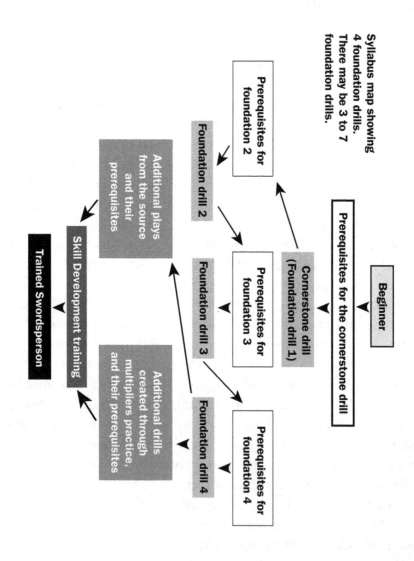

Syllabus map showing 4 foundation drills. There may be 3 to 7 foundation drills.

Now all that remains is to run cohorts of students through it, and see what happens. Are they getting stuck somewhere? Then the rungs of the ladder are too far apart at that point. Are they exhibiting common errors? Then the training needs to be adjusted. For example, we noticed that students coming into the advanced classes were often freezing in fencing. They would do one or two things and then just stop. So we added additional motions to the first step of every basic drill; after that, at no point in the syllabus did the students ever do just one action and stop. Sure enough, the next cohort through didn't have that bad habit.

This process of adjustment will probably go on for years, but it is way easier to adjust a syllabus than create one from scratch. Just remember your goal, and compare the products of the system to the goal it was intended to reach.

ETHICS

I have extensively edited this chapter down from the original version, which was published as *The Swordsman's Quick Guide part 4: Ethics*, to improve the flow of this book. You can download the complete version from my website (for free) by signing up here: https://guywindsor.net/blog/theoryandpractice

Swordsmanship training centres on learning mechanics and tactics: how to strike and when to strike. The latter encompasses more than just finding the opening to throw your sword into; it also has an ethical dimension. This is obvious if you phrase the question properly. "Under what circumstances should I strike?" can be answered according to fencing tactics: "when you have an opening"; "after a successful parry"; "after your feint has deceived your opponent"; and so on. But it also includes "when you are morally justified in doing so".

"What strike should I use?" has similar range, and can be answered in this vein: "in this circumstance, use a descending forehand blow; in that circumstance, thrust through their left eye". But it also has the scope to consider lethal versus non-lethal options: in this case, stab them in the throat; in that case, disarm them and run.

I believe that, to a historical swordsman at any level, the study of ethics is at least as important as the study of mechanics or tactics. One of the larger goals of modern swordsmanship training is the development of character. Through self discipline we become able to behave as we believe we ought, and in ever more difficult circumstances. It is easy to be good when everything is going well. But it is much, much harder when the shit has hit the fan.

One important tool in the study of ethics is the question to which there is no straight answer. Geoffroi de Charny's *Book of Chivalry* contains perhaps the most famous set of questions in historical swordsmanship circles. Charny does not include the answers; they are not the point. The point is to engage with the questions, come up with your own answers, and then live by those answers. For example:

> "When a man at arms has performed in such a way that he is considered to be good in this profession, if he finds himself armed in a place where men at arms are fighting and leaves, fleeing to his dishonor, what is necessary for him to repair and recover his honor? Is it necessary for him to do as much as he has done before or more, or what?"
>
> (Translated by Stephen Muhlberger)

My favourite modern editions are *The Book of Chivalry of Geoffroi de Charny: Text, Context, and Translation* by Richard W. Kaeuper and Elspeth Kennedy; and Stephen Muhlberger's translation, which is published as *Charny's Men at Arms: Questions Concerning the Joust, Tournament and War*, and is available for free online here: http://charnyqs.blogspot.com

There are many other historical examples; every parable and just about every piece of medieval fiction would serve. One of my test readers, Robert Elm, eloquently pointed this out and gave an excellent example, so I'll quote him here:

> "Wolfram Von Eschenbach's *Parzival* is written by a Teutonic Knight, and Parzival's purity is an excellent example of the motivations of a knight who has decided to follow the conscience of his heart as opposed to conscience as dictated by social norms.
>
> Instead of adhering to the social niceties taught to him, had he followed his own conscience and simply asked the Fisher King what ailed him, the blight of the Wasteland would have been lifted. As it happened, even though he was assured he was too late to

gain benefit for the inhabitants of the land, he eventually decided to follow that impulse and return to the side of the King and ask him, just because it was the right thing to do. This act of purity of the heart, doing what he knew in his heart to be right without any promise of reward, lifted the curse and the land rejoiced.

This short tale goes a long way toward describing the ultimate ideal of chivalry from a perspective beyond simple pragmatism. Like the Samurai poets in Japan, the knights of Europe were brought up into a whole culture of war that had to speak to the existential reality of the man behind the warrior's role. Yes, the practicality of war would have to be fulfilled, but why fight for one's life if not for some higher purpose; what is the spiritual side of the equation?

The reason I like *Parzival* so much in this regard is that every ethic must have an ideal that can be demonstrated as an example of the highest good, which becomes a focus for the reasoning behind the ethical considerations that make up a moral code."

To get my students engaged with the ethical dimension of the Art, I occasionally put a question to them and collate their answers. As always with such questions, I am as interested in how they interpret the question as I am in the answers they give. Before we get onto those, here's an easy one: I have two daughters. Should I sell one of them to a brothel?

Easy answer, huh? Noooooooooo!

Sure. Right here, right now, that is not a useful question, because I don't have to think (other than to restrain myself from punching anyone who suggests it in the face). People must not be bought and sold. Fathers must care for their children. Sex trafficking is just plain evil.

But now imagine that I have five children, and I'm a subsistence farmer in the back end of nowhere. This year's crop has failed, and experience suggests that three out of my five surviving kids will be dead in the next year. If I send my eldest daughter to that brothel, she will suffer horribly and might die; but she will probably be fed, and will probably survive. And the money from her sale will feed the other four kids until next year's harvest. What do I do? Sacrifice one to save the others, or watch them all starve? This is where the study of ethics is useful: for helping you make a decision when there is no one good answer; when people will suffer and die no matter which choice you make. It also makes you far less quick to judge the apparently unethical behaviour of others.

My cover designer for *The Swordsman's Quick Guide* series, Eleonora Rebecchi, chose the cover image for the *Ethics* instalment. It is by Albrecht Durer: *Justice, Truth and Reason in the stocks with the Seated Judge and Sleeping Piety*. This was drawn in about 1524, and depicts three women in the stocks: Justice, with her hands tied; Truth, with a lock on her mouth; and Reason, trapped and sleeping.

The fundamental goal of this chapter is to give you tools to unlock Justice, Truth and Reason, and apply them more effectively in your training and daily life.

The Questions

Some of the questions I use are obviously centred on ethics, and some are less so, but they all make the reader think about an aspect of martial arts training that they might not have thought about before. If you read through the list, you'll see it is by no means definitive. It reflects topics I happen to be thinking about, and common areas of dispute; I have not gone into many obvious areas, like the ethics of teaching martial arts at all, ethical behaviour for teachers, or the law. This is intended as a springboard for your own study.

1. When is it okay to stab someone in the face with a sword?
2. Can a duel settle a matter of honour?
3. Can violence be beautiful?
4. To what extent is the practice of swordsmanship the cultivation of virtue?
5. Is the study of ethics necessary for martial artists?

So without further ado, the first question . . .

1) When is it okay to stab someone in the face with a sword?
This question is deliberately vague. Most respondents agree that it means "kill someone with a sword"; some are more specific. It also generates the biggest range of responses.

Personally, I tend to the more homicidal end of the spectrum; I think that if anybody puts your life in danger, or threatens anybody you have a duty of care towards, then they have consented to whatever consequences their actions lead to. The phrase "better judged by twelve than carried by six" is reasonable. But I would also say that it is indisputably more moral to avoid killing when non-lethal options are available. Furthermore: taking a life must, by the laws of conscience, damage you. So avoiding doing so is sensible. But a person who fails to take life for fear of incurring damage is a coward. So failing to take a life can be morally equivalent to running away. Sometimes that's the best thing, but would you leave your child behind?

Most of the responses I've got from this question can be summarised as "in self defence only". But some go into much more detail, and some are closer to my own position above. We also appear to have one or two borderline sociopaths in the wider martial arts community. Who would have guessed?

2) Can a duel settle a matter of honour?
I can see how utterly satisfying it would be to hack off the limbs of someone who has insulted me (or perhaps written a bad review of one of my books . . . you have been warned!), but I have long believed that duelling to settle a matter of honour is just ridiculous. Duelling cultures have always been rife with bullies, who can get away with any bad behaviour thanks to their reputation for being good at duelling. Over the centuries in which duelling was common, many people were coerced into fights they did not want thanks to the prevailing culture. Failure to fight would lead to absolute social ostracism – another form of bullying.

There is a profound romanticism attached to duelling, which induces apparently intelligent people to wish for its reinstatement. Seriously, people, this is madness. That said, I have participated in several grudge matches with blunt swords and protective gear; but in every case, bruises or a cracked rib were the worst likely outcome.

But for me, the duel is the most interesting combat scenario, because all parties present are (at least in theory) equal in rank, training and armament, and have consented to the fight. If I could be sure that nobody was being coerced into the duel, if it was socially neutral, then I wouldn't have any problem with consenting adults engaging in them. Ethically, the institution would be neutral. But whether a person with family obligations of any kind has the right to risk their life like that is a deeper question. I have kids, and yet I drive a car almost every day, and engage in all sorts of other risky behaviour too. Hmm, this one needs some thought . . .

3) Can violence be beautiful?

This one to me is an obvious "yes", because there are so, so many examples of violence in art, in sports, on screen, and so forth. If you doubt it, watch a really good martial arts movie – anything with Jackie Chan or Jet Li, for instance, or any of the new wave of arty Chinese martial arts films that began with *Crouching Tiger, Hidden Dragon*. Some of the sequences depicted are just gorgeous. And I'm okay with some people being badly injured or killed in real life if they've brought it on themselves.

I think violence done well can be as beautiful as any other human art. But to be so, it must be justified and well executed. There are a tonne of videos on YouTube of justified violence done very well; some blameless chap in a store taking out an armed robber, for instance. I see that and I cheer.

4) To what extent is the practice of swordsmanship the cultivation of virtue?

To my mind, that's the entire point. So, my answer would be: 100%. All the way.

But that raises the question of "what is virtue?" Fiore's four virtues of boldness, strength, speed and foresight are clearly not "moral" virtues (except possibly boldness); they are practical ones. But swordsmanship training should also make you more patient and kind, and more likely to do the right thing, whatever that appears to be. If swordsmanship training did not have the capacity to make people into better versions of themselves, I would not have dedicated my life to it.

5) Is the study of ethics necessary for martial artists?

Obviously, I think it is. Without it, we are just thugs or villains.

And Finally . . .

One commenter on my blog summed up the question of ethics with a quote from the *Kalama Sutta: To the Kalamas*. I thought it looked familiar, so dug up the whole quote:

> "Of course you are uncertain, Kalamas. Of course you are in doubt. When there are reasons for doubt, uncertainty is born. So in this case, Kalamas, don't go by reports, by legends, by traditions, by scripture, by logical conjecture, by inference, by analogies, by agreement through pondering views, by probability, or by the thought, 'This contemplative is our teacher.' When you know for yourselves that, 'These qualities are unskillful; these qualities are blameworthy; these qualities are criticized by the wise; these qualities, when adopted and carried out, lead to harm and to suffering' – then you should abandon them."
>
> (Translated from the *Pali* by Thanissaro Bhikkhu, online here: http://www.accesstoinsight.org/tipitaka/an/an03/an03.065.than. html)

To me, the beginning of ethical behaviour is the willingness to engage with questions of ethics. The answers you come up with, and the further questions you choose to ask, are less important than the fact that you are actively engaged with thinking about the ethical dimension of your art and your life. If you are already familiar with the study of ethics, you probably already have a whole range of similar questions in your head. But if not, I ask you: what would your answers be to the ones I have set?

My own answers to ethical questions invariably boil down to this: informed consent. If everyone affected by the issue is fully informed and gives their consent freely, the proposed course of action is ethical. This is actually a very high bar to set. Let's take duelling as an example. History abounds with examples of people coerced into a duel, because the social pressure to take part overruled their own aversion to the practice. On March 21st 1829, the Duke of Wellington, Prime Minister of Britain, fought a pistol duel with the Earl of Winchilsea. The Earl had accused the Duke of "an insidious design for the infringement of our liberties and the introduction of Popery into every department of the State", and the Duke replied with a challenge. This despite years of campaigning against the practise of duelling. But according to the mores of the time, Wellington had no choice. Neither party was keen on the idea: Winchilsea kept his pistol down and did not fire; Wellington fired and missed. Opinions differ on whether he deloped (missed deliberately) or missed by accident. He was known to be a bad shot. In any case, these are two very high-ranking people, neither of whom wanted to duel, yet both of whom did. Their consent was extremely grudging, if it can be said to have existed at all.

Ironically, these days there is no social pressure to duel, and it is not only illegal but you would actually be prosecuted for murder and go down for it if you won and were caught. So I would say that if you could find a willing opponent, there is no ethical problem with fighting to the death. You both know the risks and take them willingly. I'd think you were both idiots, but that's beside the point.

The "informed" half of "informed consent" is also critical. If I don't know my car is about to have all four wheels drop off and I sell it to you, then that's ethical – provided we have both done due diligence. But if I know that the car is a dud and sell it to you anyway, that's clearly unethical. This is why places that sell thrills, such as bungee jumps or rollercoasters, should post their accident records. We are sold on the idea that it's a perfectly safe way to get the experience of extreme risk; actually, people do get killed or maimed at funfairs and the like every now and then.

So let's apply "informed consent" to the problem of the farmer and his five starving children. The first question to ask is whether the daughter being sold is able to understand what is going on. If the issue is explained to her, and she understands that she is being sacrificed to save her siblings, then she is at least informed. If she then agrees that it is the best course of action, she may even consent to it. There are heroes everywhere. None of that absolves the sex traders and their disgusting clients of course, but it may absolve the farmer (not that he is likely to be any less distraught over it). There is no ethical solution (other than a broader social justice that makes these problems extinct).

The fundamental argument against legalising prostitution or drugs is exactly the question of consent. Let's consider prostitution. It is very hard for many people to accept that anyone would ever give their informed consent to be a prostitute, so they assume that those people cannot be choosing freely. This is simply disrespectful of the other person's sovereignty. There are people out there who choose all sorts of things I will never understand (such as to not practise swordsmanship; to eat fried eggs; to have a spike put through their penis – the list goes on), but in each of those cases consent is easily established. Perhaps because so many people have been forced into prostitution it is harder to imagine anyone choosing it, but there is no question that some people do. And there is nothing unethical about it.

It is profoundly unethical not to respect their informed consent.

Let me finish with the best advice I think I ever got. I was sixteen, and angsting about something. My friend Carol said "you must make your own rules, and then live by them".

It stuck in my head, and I have been trying to do it ever since. Making your own rules is hard; it requires deep thought, experience, and willingness to change. Living by them is harder. It requires discipline, and the willingness to put what you believe is right ahead of any other consideration. I have often made bad rules, and often failed to live by the better ones. But through engaging with questions like these, my rules get better; and because I understand those rules, living by them is easier.

PRACTICE

The separation between theory and practice is artificial. As you will have noticed in the previous section, the theory of fencing makes no sense without the practice, and the theory of creating drills and syllabi makes no sense without the practice either. Indeed, the whole purpose of the theory is to improve the practice. In this section I will cover a very broad range of practice, from choosing equipment, to starting a club, to teaching a class, to nutrition and physical training. Not all of that is strictly HMA, because it's neither historical, martial, nor artistic. But I have included it because it's what HMA practitioners ought to know.

SAFETY

At some stage in the recreation of a martial art you have to start hitting people and getting hit. So it would make sense to take a look at safety in training.

> Climb if you will, but remember that courage and strength are nothing without prudence, and that a momentary negligence may destroy the happiness of a lifetime. Do nothing in haste; look well to each step; and from the beginning think what may be the end.

Edward Whymper's admonition, from *Scrambles Amongst the Alps*, elegantly encapsulates the correct attitude to all potentially lethal activities. Substitute "practice swordsmanship" for "climb" and there is the correct mindset for any swordsman, beginner or expert. Take it to heart before you start training with a partner.

When training with weapons, you hold your partner's life in your hands. This is a sacred trust and must not be abused.

Disclaimer: I accept no responsibility of any kind for injuries you sustain while you are not under my direct personal supervision. Earlier in this book you have been taught how to create safe training drills, and I am certain that there is a very low likelihood of injury if you follow the instructions. But if I am not there in person to create and sustain a safe training environment, I cannot be held responsible for any accidents that may occur.

Principles

The basic principles of safe training are:

1. Respect: for the Art, your training partners, the weapons, and yourself
2. Caution: assume everything is dangerous unless you have reason to believe otherwise
3. Know your limits. Just because it's safe for somebody else does not necessarily mean it's safe for you. Never train or fence when you are tired, angry, or in any state of mind or body that makes accidents and injuries more likely.

Most groups that keep going for more than a year have a pretty good set of safety guidelines in place. If you are training with an established group, or are about to create a new group, make sure you know what the guidelines are, and follow them.

As we established in the Seven Principles of Mastery, you cannot afford time off training for stupid injuries. Refer back to page 29 to refresh your memory if needed.

Rules of Engagement

Once you have agreed to fence with someone, it is important to agree on rules of engagement. This is partly to ensure safety, and partly to create an environment in which you can learn. The two most simple rules are these: confine your moves to the safety limits of your protective gear, and also to confine your moves to the technical range of the least trained combatant. For example, do not allow face-thrusts when wearing open helms, or throws when one of you is not trained to fall safely. The rules can be adapted further to develop specific aspects of technique: for instance, you might not allow any close quarters work at all, or even restrict allowable hits to one small target. The idea is to come to a clear common sense agreement before facing off. You are only ready for no-holds-barred, totally "authentic" fight simulation when you can enter such a fight with your judgment unimpaired.

Following the rules of engagement will not make you soft, nor will it dull your edge if it comes to the real thing; rather, it will develop self control.

These rules apply to all fencing:

1. Agree on a mutually acceptable level of safety
2. Wear at least the minimum amount of safety gear commensurate with rule #1. Confine allowable techniques to those within the limits of your equipment
3. Confine allowable techniques to the technical ability of the least trained combatant
4. Appoint either an experienced student or one of the combatants to preside over the bout
5. Agree on allowable targets
6. Agree on what constitutes a "hit"
7. Agree on priority or scoring convention in the event of simultaneous hits. Usually it is better to reward what would have been a fatal blow over one that would produce a minor wound, but simultaneous hits should be avoided whenever possible
8. Agree on the duration of the bout, either in terms of hits – such as first to five – or in real time
9. Acknowledge all hits against yourself. This can be done by raising the left arm, or by stopping the bout with a salute, or by calling "Halt!" and telling your opponent where and how you think she hit you
10. Maintain self-command at all times. If you are angry, frustrated, or at any risk of losing control, stop.

Safe Training

In my experience most injuries are self-inflicted. It is far more common for students to hurt themselves by doing something they shouldn't than to hurt their training partners. Here are a few simple guidelines for joint safety, which should be followed during all training. I am using the lunge as an example of a stressful action, but these principles apply to any physical action.

1. The knee must always bend in the line of the foot. Knees are hinges, with usually a little under 180° range of movement. They do not respond well to torque (power in rotation). So whenever you bend your knees, in any style and for any reason, ensure that the line of your foot, the line of movement of your knee, and the line of movement of your weight are parallel. This prevents twisting and thus injuries. This one simple rule, carefully followed, eliminates all knee problems other than those arising from impact or genetic disadvantage.

2. Whenever performing any strenuous task (such as lunging or lifting heavy objects), tighten your pelvic floor muscles (imagine you need to go to the bathroom, but are stuck in a queue). This supports the base of your spine and helps with hip alignment.

3. Joints have two forms of support: active and passive. Passive support refers mainly to the ligaments, which bind the joint capsule together. This is basically set, and can't be trained. When training your joint strength with exercises or stretching, avoid any action that strains the joint capsule. Any action that causes pain in the joint itself should be modified or avoided, because it may damage the soft tissues (ligaments, tendons and cartilage). These tissues have a very poor blood supply and hence heal very slowly.

Active support refers to the muscles around the joint, and these can be strengthened by carefully straining the joint with small weights and rotations. To strengthen a joint you must stress these muscles without endangering the ligaments. Any competent physiotherapist can show you a range of exercises for building up the active support around your knees, wrists and elbows, where we need it most.

4. Rest is part of training. Your body needs time to recover, and is stimulated by the stress of exercise to grow stronger. However,

the body is efficient and will withdraw support from any muscle group that is not used, even if for only a few weeks. So regular training is absolutely crucial.

If you can't lunge without warming up, don't lunge except in carefully controlled drills. Warming up is essential before pushing the boundaries of what your body can do.

These safety guidelines have been drawn from my books, namely *The Duellist's Companion*, *The Swordsman's Companion*, and *The Swordsman's Quick Guide part 1: The Seven Principles of Mastery*.

EQUIPMENT

Whatever art you choose to practise, you're probably going to need some kit. We can loosely divide equipment into two kinds: the weapons, and the protective equipment. Let's start with the weapons. You're going to need a decent quality reproduction of the weapon or weapons for which the system is designed. You can tell what weapons the system is designed for by looking at the pictures (if there are any) and, if you're lucky, there will be some information in the text itself. It's important to note that most historical swordsmanship writers did not concern themselves in any way with any kind of weapon that wasn't current to them. For example, Capoferro and all the other Italian rapier masters don't talk about rapiers at all. They just talk about "the sword" (*spada*) and it's exactly the same word in Marozzo's *Arte dell'Armi* from 80 years earlier, and in *Il Fior di Battaglia* from 200 years earlier (though in places Fiore does qualify it as the *spada a due mani*, the sword in two hands).

You've already chosen your source, so now you need to come up with a reasoned argument for why the sword is as you think it is. What's your evidence? Once you know the approximate dimensions and form of the sword, you will need to find modern training replicas.

The Sword
Training swords come in three main types: authentic sharp reproductions, which are used for cutting practice and some pair work with advanced students; blunt swords, which try to reproduce the handling characteristics of the sharps; and fencing

swords, which are designed to make fencing safer. These all have their pros and cons, and you should use the sword that's right for your style and the kind of practice you will be doing.

It's perfectly all right to use a wooden waster or something similar to start with, but do not imagine that there is any such thing as a safe training sword. Even modern sport fencing blades engineered for fencing sometimes break and puncture people, and anything heavy enough to reproduce the handling of a medieval or renaissance sidearm is going to be able to do damage.

For specific details on choosing a sword, please see *Choosing a Sword*, which is the next chapter.

Looking after your weapon is largely a matter of keeping it dry, clean, and free of stress risers (a stress riser is a weak point, usually a deep nick, which encourages the blade to fold at that point). Occasional rubdowns with a moisture repellent oil and steel wool or a scouring pad, followed by a coat of microcrystalline wax, should keep the blade and hilt clean (follow manufacturer's recommendations if you have a gilt, blued, or otherwise ornamented weapon). Do not be afraid to file down any large nicks, and file off any burrs: this is important from a safety perspective, because the blade is most likely to break at a nick, and burrs can be very sharp. The edges of a blunt weapon should always be kept smooth enough that you can run your bare hand hard up the edge and not get scratches or splinters. Even the toughest and most cherished sword will not survive repeated abuse: the best guarantor of longevity for your sword (and yourself) is correct technique.

You then need to find at least two or three suppliers who will make you the kind of sword you need as a blunt training weapon. You may find that your particular source requires, for example, an extra-long rapier or a particular kind of hand protection, so you need to find a supplier or ideally several suppliers that will provide you with that kind of weapon. To start with you need two blunt replica swords: one for you and one for your friend who doesn't know he's starting historical swordsmanship because you haven't told him yet. It's always a good idea to have two because then you can always put one into somebody's hand and get them to swing it at you so you can practice.

Equipment

Without doubt the single most important bit of safety equipment is good common sense. Fence according to the limits of your equipment, exercise control, and respect the weapon at all times, and you will never have a serious injury. Minor bumps and bruises come with the territory.

There were some masters who believed that the safest course was to fence with sharp weapons and no protection. This is how it was often done in the past until the invention of fencing masks (though there are tournament records and declarations as early as the fourteenth century that record the use of blunt practice weapons; King Rene d'Anjou's treatise of 1470 is perhaps the best source). Such masters are right in theory, in that freeplay with sharps is the best way for students to learn absolute respect for the weapon, and the importance of absolute control. There are a few contemporary masters with whom I will fence like this, and there is nothing like it for generating a perfect fencing approach. But try explaining that to the insurance companies; or, in the event of a slip, to the police or coroner. It was often said in the eighteenth century that you could tell a fencing master from his eye-patch and missing teeth. Never forget that even a blunt blade can break bones. When free fencing, or when practising drills at speed, it is essential that you wear appropriate safety gear. You do this not for your own sake, though self-preservation does come into it, but for the benefit of your training partner. Your protection allows them to hit you safely.

Choosing protection is a very controversial subject. Too little, and you can end up badly hurt (even in practice). Too much, and you can't fence properly. Firstly, it is important to establish what style of fencing you will be doing. If you are practising armoured combat, then buy the best fitting, best made armour that you can from an armourer who knows how you intend to use it and has seen what you want to do. This is the hardest style of fencing to appropriately regulate, because accurate technique requires you to go for the least armoured spots (throat, eyes, armpits or joints), but safety requirements obviously prohibit that.

As a general guideline, I recommend the following for fencing with most weapons.

An FIE (Fédération Internationale d'Escrime) standard fencing mask. This allows you to thrust at the face (a very common target) and generally attack the head. This does have three major caveats. Firstly, it leaves the back of the head open, and you must be very careful not to strike at this target. An added apron of thick leather affords some protection. Secondly, it does not protect the head and neck from the wrenching force of over-vigorous blows. It is vital that you and your opponent learn control before engaging in freeplay; if your syllabus is properly structured, that will happen naturally. Thirdly, it is designed to protect the face from high-speed, light and flexible weapons – not slower, heavier and more rigid ones. So continually check it for wear, and make absolutely sure that your weapons are properly bated.

A steel or leather gorget, or stiff collar, to protect the throat. Points can slip under the bib of a mask and crush the larynx.

A rigid plastic chest guard for women.

A point-resistant fencing jacket rated at least 500 Newtons.

Sturdy, preferably padded and/or armoured gauntlets, which should extend at least four inches past the jacket cuff to prevent points sliding up your sleeve. I have twice had fingers broken through unpadded mail gloves, and now use a pair of fingered gauntlets from Jiri Krondak, which cost about 150€.

A padded gambeson, or a plastron. If you are making one yourself, bear in mind that it should be thick enough to take the worst out of the impact of the blows, and prevent penetration from a thrust. All openings should be covered. The collar should be high enough that thrusts coming under the bib of the mask or under the gorget do not make contact with your throat. A plastron must wrap around the ribs, and properly cover the collar bones and shoulders. I usually wear a fencing jacket and plastron.

A box for men (called a "cup" in the US). You only forget this once.

Rigid plastic protectors for the knees.

Elbow pads for the elbows. Pads of the sort worn by in-line skaters (worn under the clothes for that period look, if you prefer) will save a lot of pain and some injury.

Suitable footwear. On the matter of footwear, few practitioners agree. In the longsword treatises, there are no heavy boots and certainly no built-up heels. For a completely historical style, it is necessary to wear completely accurate period clothing at least occasionally, because it can affect the way you move. Training barefoot or in smooth leather soled shoes is the most accurate, and often very slippery; though there is some evidence to suggest that knights, at least, wore shoes with whipcord attached to the soles for better grip. I have fenced – on wooden floors, concrete, stone, tarmac, grass and gravel; in sports halls, salles, castles, forests and on hillsides; and in all weathers from heatwave to snowstorm – wearing everything from thigh boots to hiking boots to trainers to period shoes to barefoot. My conclusion is that it does not matter what you wear on your feet provided that you understand grounding, body-mechanics and footwork. Excessively grippy soles can lead to joint injury because you may stop too suddenly, or get stuck when you should be turning (particularly in falls at close quarters). The dangers of wearing too slippery soles are obvious. In the salle I usually wear wrestling boots or trainers, and recommend a thin, flat sole.

That's a lot of gear. To start with all you'll really need is a fencing mask. This is because you're going to be going very, very slowly as you're working stuff out, and the point of wearing a fencing mask is so that whoever is swinging a sword at your head or face can actually make gentle contact so you know they're operating in the correct measure. That's it. You don't need the full Mad Max gear. You also don't need full plate armour unless your source is dealing with armoured combat.

With the equipment it's a really bad idea to get it cheap because the cheap stuff usually winds up being more expensive in the long run: it breaks or fails, and then you have to upgrade or replace it. If you need something cheap just to practice with in the short term, buy a wooden waster or a broomstick or something like that while you save up money for a decent quality steel replica. At this stage we probably don't need to consider sharp swords.

Make a complete equipment list of the weapons that you're going to need. Add a fencing mask to that list. Price the whole lot up and start saving your pennies.

I should point out that if you intend to enter tournaments, you must check their gear requirements and follow them. Also, in the last decade or so a huge range of protective gear has been developed for historical fencing of various kinds. I personally don't like most of it, but your experience may differ. I won't offer specific brand or model recommendations because (a) they change over time and (b) I haven't tested most of the new equipment because I'm perfectly happy with the old gear.

CHOOSING A SWORD

I have bad news for you. Buying a sword will not necessarily help your swordsmanship one iota. It will not turn you into Aragorn, D'Artagnan, or Conan. It will do one thing only in that direction: it will lower the barriers to training. Having a sword in your living room makes it that much more likely that you will do some sword practice. That's all. It is very common to mistake *having the same kit as the experts* as *becoming an expert*. Sure, there is usually some overlap, but I have lost count of the number of things I've bought that would help me be a better writer (pens, notebooks, software, etc.), and you know what? None of it has helped nearly as much as (a) writing a lot, (b) reading a lot, and (c) having people kindly tell me what's wrong with what I've written. I've been very lucky in that the sales of my other books justified getting a decent laptop (this is a MacBook Air, and it's lovely. Linux users please shut up; and those of you on PCs, well, I hope you're happy), in that it can run my preferred writing software (Scrivener) and easily cope with really big photo files. But Shakespeare didn't have one, and I don't think it was the way he sourced his quills from extra-fat geese (I just made that up) which made him the greatest writer in history.

I have had literally hundreds of students coming through one or other branches of my school, and I have noticed no correlation at all between how quickly somebody buys a sword and how good they get at using it. Indeed, it often seems to me that some people attend a beginners' course simply to give themselves permission to buy a sword; what they really wanted was not so much *to be a swordsman* as it was *to be a sword owner*.

And that's fine. Let me make things easier for you: you have my permission to go buy any sword you want, so long as you don't hurt anyone with it. Indeed, collecting swords is a skill and a pastime in its own right, and we owe a lot of what we know today about swords to the dedicated collectors of the past (I'm thinking right now of Mr Stibbert, Mr Wallace and Mr Oakeshott in particular).

So go ahead, buy a sword. You don't need my blessing, and this book is intended for people training in historical swordsmanship, not collectors.

For many students, buying their first sword represents a serious commitment to practice. That commitment should be honoured, as indeed I am trying to do with this book. It's a big step, and for most people, a relatively expensive one.

I will take it as my starting point that you are looking for a blunt steel practice weapon. There is a whole other book in why it should be steel, and another in how to choose a sharp steel sword. The basic tenets of this chapter will serve for choosing sharps, and by the time you need one, you will be experienced enough not to need a book of advice on the subject.

So, the questions to ask when choosing a sword for any given practice are:

- Is it of the right type (rapier, longsword, foil, etc.)?
- Is it of the right construction (intended for use rather than display, for example)?
- Does it handle as you feel it should?
- Do you *want* to pick it up and play with it?

I will analyse the first question in detail later on, giving you the approximate dimensions, weights and so on of the most common sword types practised with today. It's the meat of this chapter, but by no means the most important bit; that would be the last of my four questions. Let's start with that.

143

Do you love me?

Imagine that every sword you pick up, or look at on the internet, was asking you that question. Only ever buy the ones that make you answer a loud and immediate "yes!" If you love it, it will sing for you. If you love it, it will call out to you every time a speck of dust falls on it, saying "why don't you ever play with me any more?" If you love it, you will pick it up every day and let it play. And so it will repay the money you spent on it a thousand times.

Think of it like this. Imagine your sword is properly made, and you use it appropriately. It should last at least a decade. That's 3,650 days. Imagine you use it for two hours per day (I can dream, can't I?). That's 7,300 hours.

Now let's imagine you spent 500 dollars on it (a bit above the median price for a usable sword). That's less than seven cents per hour! And every extra hour you use it will lower that cost.

Now imagine you got a cheaper sword that you did not love. And in those ten years, you used it for only two hours per week (which is still more than most people do). That's 728 hours. If your sword cost only 200 dollars, that works out at over 27 cents per hour. Nearly four times as much per hour as the sword that cost more than twice as much!

Okay, I'm massaging the maths to make a point. Of course you have a budget, and of course there is no direct correlation between hours spent training and the cost of the sword. Many of the most expensive options on a sword have no effect on handling, durability or any other measure of performance (do you *really* want a gold inlay on the pommel?). And my most expensive sword is one of my least used. But in my experience, when faced with both an oh-my-god-this-is-gorgeous sword and a this-will-do-the-job sword, it has never been cost effective to settle for the cheaper option.

In general, those that know what they are doing tend to agree on what makes a good sword and what does not. But give any six swordsmen the choice between any six swords of the same quality, and they tend not to all agree that one is the best. Pick the one you love.

Can you handle me?

The handling characteristics of a sword are like the handling on a car. For some uses, you want a Porsche 911; for others, a truck. And there are a million variations in between. I tend to like a sword that has a bit of weight in the blade to power my cuts, because I tend to let gravity do most of the work of getting it to move. But my go-to rapier is very light in the hand.

For beginners – and I assume you are relatively new to this, or you probably wouldn't need this chapter: when in doubt, go light. As the excellent sword cutler (somebody who puts hilts on swords, but doesn't make blades) Dennis Graves once wrote (I have sadly forgotten where, but I'm sure it was him) "you wouldn't practice tennis with a frying pan, would you?" It is very common for beginners to confuse a heavy sword with a durable one; they often are, but one of the reasons that heavy swords last so long is that you can't use them for very much time before you have to put them down!

Am I fit for purpose?

It is important that you decide exactly what you want this weapon for. Is it for fighting, solo practice, pair practice, adornment, or all four? Will it be used for armoured or unarmoured fighting, duelling, or battle re-enactment? In any case, it must be sturdy enough for its most strenuous likely use. Light, fast weapons intended for unarmoured duelling should not go on the re-enactment battlefield, and too many people come away from a practice session heartbroken when their shiny wall-hanger has been smashed to bits. There is also the consideration of exact historical accuracy. Always check with your supplier or the manufacturer that the weapon is intended for the use you want it for.

Important points to consider include:

145

Blade flex. Blades can vary from completely rigid to floppy. In general, for more intense training with partners, a good flex is ideal. Put the point on the floor or on a wall target, and lean on the sword with moderate force. The blade should bend in a smooth curve, starting from about the middle of the blade. If it bends nearer to the hilt, the blade will feel unstable on contact. You can see the ideal curve on a rapier blade in this image from *The Duellist's Companion.* Sharp swords, of course, tend to be much more rigid for penetrating the target, but good blade flex is important for training and fencing with contact.

(Photo by Ilkka Hartikainen, from *The Duellist's Companion.*)

Rubber Blunts. I highly recommend rubber blunts on all training swords. It allows you to work harder on targets and with a partner, and greatly reduces the risk of penetrating wounds. Stage combat weapons and historical re-enactment weapons usually don't have them because they look wrong. If possible, the point should also have a rebate or a nail head, which is then covered with the rubber.

(Image showing a nail-headed rapier blade courtesy of arms-n-armor.com) Adding a blunt does change the handling a little, so you should use the smallest one you can fit onto the blade. I do not recommend fencing without a rubber tip on the end – it makes a great difference to the likelihood of injury.)

Sharp hilts: if you are going to be fencing with this weapon, you should avoid having a hilt or pommel that is too sharp and pointy. Think of striking with every part of the sword; every sticky-out bit of metal should be safe enough for at least minor contact.

Handle size: the handle is your interface with the weapon, and it should fit in your hand. Most weapon makers these days make them much too thick. For reference, your ring finger should be able to touch the muscle of your thumb, as you see here:

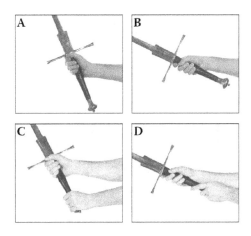

A grip one hand point back; **B** grip one hand point forward;
C grip two hands, point back; **D** grip two hands, point forwards.

(Images by Jari Juslin, from *The Medieval Longsword.*)

Donald McBane, in his 1728 book *The Expert Sword-Man's Companion*, wrote that the little finger should be able to touch the palm when holding a smallsword.

Handling

When you pick up a sword, it should feel like the sword *wants* to go where you want to put it. If you favour a light-pointed super-fast Ferrari, or something with a bit more momentum and presence like a Range Rover, the sword should feel like the use you want to put it to is the use it was born for. The actual physics of what makes a sword feel that way – including resonance nodes, centres of rotation, mass distribution, blade profile, and all the rest – are vastly complicated, and no sword maker I know uses formulae and calculations to produce the desired result. They just know from experience that a slightly shorter grip, or a bit of extra thickness here or there, will make the sword do what it's supposed to. Blade physics are very complicated, and not in my area of expertise. If you are interested in the topic, I suggest checking out these sources:

George Turner: http://www.thearma.org/spotlight/GTA/motions_and_impacts.htm#.WczrhkyZOV4

Vincent le Chevalier's tool "The Weapons Dynamics Computer," developed with help from legendary sword smith Peter Johnsson, is also interesting: https://subcaelo.net/ensis/dynamics-computer/

A Note on Specifications and Units

I am about to annoy the engineers and mathematicians among you. I will give all specs in inches, centimetres (cm), pounds (lb), and grams (g) or kilograms (kg). There are 2.54 cm in one inch, and 2.2 lb in 1000 g. But I will round all numbers up or down as convenient, and without regard for consistency. This is because the soul of a sword is not in its data. A long, heavy sword might be a lovely peach to handle, and a short, light one might be a dog. Unlike in the sporting arena, where the weapons must be practically identical, in historical swordsmanship the specifications are not exact, because (a) the historical record shows a huge amount of variety within any given sword type, and (b) a centimetre here or there, or a few ounces here or there, might make all the difference to the handling of a specific sword, but the effect is not predictable. So the specs are just guidelines.

What About the Hilts?

You might notice as you read through this that I barely mention hilt design. Should your longsword have a plain crossguard or side rings? Should your rapier be a three-ring with shells or a two-poster? It's because these things make very little difference from a practical standpoint, unless it's specified in the manual you are studying. On balance, I'd tend not to use a cup-hilt rapier to do an early seventeenth-century Italian rapier style, nor would it feel right to use a gloriously gothic-hilted longsword to study Fiore. But these things do not really matter in the way that, for example, the length of the blade does. I'll give general guidelines, of course, but that's it.

The test is: does it look right? If the crossguard looks too long, it probably is. If the handle looks too thick, it probably is. And so on. Crossguards should be *in proportion*, which of course changes with every other detail of the weapon.

Types of Sword

Arming Sword

(Image courtesy of arms-n-armor.com)

This kind of sword was popular in Europe in one form or another for centuries. It was usually used with some kind of shield or buckler. In today's historical swordsmanship community it's most often used for practising the system of sword and buckler shown in *Royal Armouries Manuscript I.33*, so I am making the assumption that you are likely to need it for that system. Different practitioners use quite widely different blade lengths for the style, from a long 31" sword to a short 27". The advantage of a shorter sword is that it is stronger in binding actions; your opponent has a shorter lever to use against you. Longer swords obviously reach farther.

Specs summary:
    Hilt type: a simple crossguard only.
    Total length: 33–38" / 84–97 cm.
    Blade length: 27–31" / 68–79 cm.
    Weight: 2–2.5 lb / 900–1,150 g.
    Point of balance: 2–4" / 5–10 cm down the blade.

Falchion, Messer or Storta

There is a huge range of weapons that fit into the category of short cutting sword. I could add to the title cutlass, hanger, hunting sword, machete, and so on.

My falchion, by JT Pälikkö

This is a gorgeous beast, loosely based on the Conyers falchion in Durham Cathedral. Perhaps the most famous storta is the one in the Wallace Collection, once owned by Cosimo de' Medici. It's rather pretty, as this copy by Arms and Armor shows:

(Image courtesy of arms-n-armor.com)

At present, we only have sources for one historical style, which is the German messer. Strictly speaking, messers tend to have straight blades and are defined by their hilt construction: scales riveted to the tang (the part of the blade that extends through the handle). For the purposes of messer training, I'd recommend the following stats:

(Image courtesy of arms-n-armor.com)

Hilt type: a simple crossguard, possibly with a "nail" or side ring.
Total length: 34–38" / 86–97 cm.
Blade length: 26–30" / 66–76 cm.
Weight: about 2 lbs / 1 kg.
Point of balance: 3–4.5" / 8–12 cm from the crossguard.

Longsword (for Fiore)

(Image courtesy of arms-n-armor.com)

Your first sword should be blunt for training with partners and against durable targets. The blade should be of heat-treated spring steel, and the sword should measure between 110 and 130 centimetres (about 43 to 51 inches) from pommel to point. The weight should be absolutely no more than 1.8 kg (just under 4 pounds) for even the longest sword in that range. For most people, a length of 120 cm (47") and a weight of 1.6 kg (3 1/2 pounds) is about right, with the balance point about 5 cm (2 inches) from the crossguard. The handle ought to be at least three of your hand's breadths long. Any shorter and it's not optimum for this style (we know this because Fiore at times has us grab our opponent's sword handle between his hands, so there must be space for three hands there). Much longer, though, and it starts to behave like a two-hander (and looks nothing like Fiore's illustrations).

My preferred suppliers for training longswords are Pavel Moc (www.swords.cz) in Europe, and Arms and Armor (arms-n-armor.com) in America. My students in Asia and Australia tend to go for the European suppliers, which has more to do with shipping costs than anything else I think.

Specs summary:
    Hilt type: a simple crossguard, possibly with side rings.
    Total length: 43–51" / 110–130 cm.
    Blade length: 34–42" / 87–105 cm.
    Weight: 3.5–4 lb / 1.6–1.8 kg.
    Point of balance: 2.5–4" / 6–10 cm from the cross.

Longsword (for Liechtenauer)

The problem (and the glorious opportunity) with Liechtenauer is that his art is represented in dozens of manuals spread out over about 200 years. Unsurprisingly, this means that we see lots of different blade lengths, and especially a tendency towards longer handles. As a general rule, I think that Liechtenauer's system makes most sense with a somewhat longer sword; a total length of about 120–140 cm and a handle length (not including pommel) of a minimum of 24 cm should be okay. I am not a Liechtenauer specialist, so do check with your instructor if you have one. A lot of practitioners use a "Feder" type sword, which is a kind of practice weapon based on an early seventeenth-century original. I've included it below as a special case.

Specs summary:
    Hilt type: a simple crossguard, possibly with side rings.
    Total length: 47–55" / 120–140 cm.
    Blade length: 37–45" / 96–114 cm.
    Weight: 3.7–4.4 lb / 1.7–2.0 kg.
    Point of balance: 2.5–4" / 6–10 cm from the cross.
    Feder specs taken from Peter Regenyei's website:
    Hilt type: a simple crossguard, possibly with side rings.
    Total length: 52" / 132 cm.
    Blade length: 39" / 100 cm.
    Weight: 3 lb / 1.4 kg.
    Point of balance: 3" / 8 cm from the crossguard.

Sidesword

(Image courtesy of arms-n-armor.com)

This is the term that modern practitioners (and only them! – Most museum staff call these "early rapiers") give to the kind of "cut and thrust" sword which became popular in the early sixteenth century, and developed into the longer, thinner rapier by the end of the sixteenth century. It is most commonly used by practitioners of the Bolognese style, and of Meyer's *rappier* (which is not what we would normally call a "rapier," though it may be the origin of the term). The sidesword is arguably the first single-handed sword that was commonly used without a shield or buckler, though of course it was also used with bucklers, daggers and other secondary weapons.

This sword type marks the beginning of the tendency towards more complex hilts. For a full description of how sword hilts developed over time, from a simple cross all the way up to the cup hilt, please see my book *The Duellist's Companion*, pages 9–18.

Specs summary:

Hilt type: a more complex hilt; at least finger-rings, and a side ring.

Total length: 39–44" / 99–112 cm.

Blade length: 34–37" / 86–94 cm.

Weight: 2.2–3.5 lb / 1–1.6 kg.

Point of balance: 2.5–4" / 6–10 cm from the cross.

Two-Handed Sword

(Image courtesy of arms-n-armor.com)

This kind of sword, far too long to be worn at the waist, was used especially in Italy, Germany and Portugal. The sixteenth- and seventeenth-century fencing sources call it a *spadone*, *zweihander* and *montante* respectively. There are style differences, of course, but generally speaking these swords are about 5 feet (150 cm) long with very wide crossguards, and often a secondary crossguard built into the blade. You can get the general idea from these plates from Marozzo's 1536 *Opera Nova*.

Hilt type: a simple crossguard, sometimes with side rings.
Total length: 58–65" / 147–165 cm.
Blade length: 42–50" / 107–127 cm.
Weight: 4–5.5 lb / 1.8–2.5 kg.
Point of balance: 4–8" / 10–20 cm from the cross.

Rapier

(Image courtesy of arms-n-armor.com)

Of all the historical sword styles, "rapier" is perhaps the one that shows the greatest degree of variation. Capoferro and other "rapier" masters refer to the weapon they are writing about as simply "spada", a sword. The Oxford English Dictionary has it as: "a light, slender sword used for thrusting".

The term "rapier" is very imprecise, covering a range of hilt styles, blade lengths, and so on. It has been variously used to describe everything from a Bronze Age thrusting sword (in archaeological texts) to a sports sabre with a funny grip (in a modern SCA equipment catalogue). The word is probably not Italian at all; according to the OED it comes from a German, Dutch or possibly French root. Meyer for example refers to the "rappier." The term as it was used in English sources in the period in question (the late sixteenth and early seventeenth century) describes a complex-hilted sword with a long slim blade, used mainly for thrusting.

A glance at the historical record shows swords we would call rapiers in an abundance of different weights, lengths, hilt configurations, points of balance, and so on. As I see it, the hilt type that you choose matters much less than that the blade length, mass, and point of balance be within the following parameters. In my opinion, Capoferro's system works best with a sword that weighs between 1 kg and 1.6 kg (2.0–3.5 lb); and has the point of balance between 6 and 15 cm (2.5–6 inches) in front of the crossguard, a complex hilt that allows you to put your forefinger over the crossguard safely, and a blade length from crossguard to point of at least 97 cm (38", for short people) up to a maximum of about 114 cm (45").

Capoferro himself tells us in "Chapter III: The Division of Fencing That is Posed in the Knowledge of the Sword," section 36:

"Therefore the sword has to be twice as long as the arm, and as much as my extraordinary pace, which length corresponds equally to that which is from my armpit down to the sole of my foot." (Translation by William Wilson and Jherek Swanger.)

I have never met anyone for whom those three measurements were the same, and in my book *The Duellist's Companion* I worked them out like so:

"My arm is 52 cm, shoulder to wrist; my lunge about 120 cm from heel to heel, and it is about 140 cm from my foot to my armpit when standing. When standing on guard, it is about 115 cm from foot to armpit. When in the lunge, it is about 104 cm from foot to armpit. Also, it is not clear whether he refers to the length of the blade, or of the whole sword.

If we resort to the unreliable practice of measuring the illustrations, in the picture of the lunge, the sword blade is 73 mm, the arm from wrist to armpit 37 mm, and the line G (front heel to front armpit) 55 mm. The distance between the feet is 67 mm. So, the measurement most consistent with the text would appear to be the length of the arm, from wrist to armpit, as it approximately correlates to half the length of the blade. Given this as a guide, my blade ought to be 104 cm or about 41" long from the guard to the point."

Specs summary:
Hilt type: a full complex hilt; either swept, Pappenheim, or cup.
Total length: 45–53" / 114–135 cm.
Blade length: 38–45" / 96–114 cm.
Weight: 2.8–3.5 lb / 1.25–1.6 kg.
Point of balance: 2.5–6" / 6–15 cm from the cross.

Smallsword

(Image courtesy of arms-n-armor.com)

Ah, the glorious smallsword; my first love as a swordsman, and never was there a nastier, tricksier, more vicious death-dealer than this.

The smallsword refers to the successor of the rapier, popular from about 1650 to the end of the eighteenth century (and surviving to this day in some civilian ceremonial forms, such as the Finnish PhD regalia). The smallsword was shorter than the rapier, with a blade length of about 30" to 34" (approximately 76 cm to 86 cm), and was lighter, weighing in between 500 and 1000 g (approx. 1–2 lb). It would often have a triangular section blade, and usually a relatively simple shell guard, with or without arms. One interesting variation on the smallsword, the colichemarde, had a broad forte, suddenly narrowing at about the middle of the blade.

Domenico Angelo, in his 1787 *The School of Fencing*, makes the following recommendations:

1. Have a triangular section blade for single combat, and a flat, heavier one for battle
2. The sword should be proportional to your height and strength
3. It should not exceed 38" "from pummel to point."
4. "It is an error to think that the long sword hath the advantage."

Specs summary:

Hilt type: a simple shell guard, vestigial quillons, and usually a knucklebow.

Total length: 35–39" / 89–99 cm.

Blade length: 30–34" / 76–86 cm.
Weight: 1–2 lb / 500–1,000 g.
Point of balance: 2–4" / 5–10 cm down the blade.

Backsword, Broadsword or Sabre

(Image courtesy of arms-n-armor.com)

As Capt. John Godfrey wrote in his 1747 *Treatise Upon the Useful Science of Defence: Connecting the Small and Back-sword, and Shewing the Affinity Between Them*: "The Small-Sword is the Call of Honour, the Back-Sword the Call of Duty". Variations on the theme of a solid military cutting sword have been around since before the pyramids, but this distinct style is characterised by a broad blade (hence "broadsword") often with a blunt back edge (hence "backsword"), and a quite enclosed hilt offering excellent protection to the hand.

It is not strictly true to say that if the blade is curved it must be a sabre (there are straight-bladed sabres, and curve-bladed swords that are not sabres, such as falchions and katanas), but it works as a rule of thumb. These are not hard and fast distinctions. The specs here work for all three sword types. Note though that systems which use a heavily curved blade tend to make use of the curve not only for devastating cuts, but also for sneaky blade angulations. So if your system calls for a curved blade, make sure you get one.

Specs summary:
  Hilt type: fully enclosed.
  Total length: 36–42" / 90–107 cm.
  Blade length: 31–36" / 79–92 cm.
  Weight: 2–3 lb / 1–1.5 kg.
  Point of balance: 2–4" / 5–10 cm down the blade.

Sabre (duelling)

(Image courtesy of www.therionarms.com)

Light sabres for light cavalry (not Jedi) were usually of a similar style to the heavy version, just shorter and lighter. The slim, very lightweight fencing sabre did not become common until towards the end of the nineteenth century. At the time of writing, this kind of sword is usually called a duelling sabre, and is available in several styles as described by the nineteenth-century authors that defined them (Radaelli, Hutton, etc.). As these tend to be all about the same size, I'll list just one spec.

Specs summary:
   Hilt type: shell with integral knuckle bow.
   Total length: 37".
   Blade length: 31".
   Weight: 1.5 lb / 700 g.
   Point of balance: 4–5" / 10–13 cm down the blade.

Historical Examples

We are very fortunate in that thousands and thousands of swords have survived into the modern age, largely thanks to museums and collectors. So we have abundant examples of the real thing to copy and draw from. All good HMA sword suppliers take these existing examples into account, and many do accurate reproductions. A few words of warning though: just because it still exists doesn't necessarily mean it's good. Or representative. You can find some really awful historical swords, and you should be careful about buying a copy of an original if it falls outside

160

the specs range I have noted above. Then as now, people had varied taste and varied ideas about what made a good sword. Think of the massive range in quality and style in the tools we use today – smartphones, cars, and so on. It was like that back then. The legal record is also interesting: some countries issued edicts limiting the length of swords, such as Elizabeth I's famous proclamation from 1580 limiting the length of sword blades to 36 inches. This led to swords with blades that could retract four or five inches into their handles, so conforming to the law until the moment you were about to fight!

Our written sources are sometimes useful in this regard. What could be better than a recommendation from the master himself? Unfortunately it is relatively unusual to get detailed information from actual fencing treatises regarding the size or weight of the sword. I think that this is largely due to the fact that most of the intended readership didn't need any help in that regard, and that no worthwhile system is very sensitive to small changes in the weapon.

One notable exception is Ridolfo Capoferro, who at least tells us the length of the weapon, as noted above. Another is Domenico Angelo, also noted above. We also have some specifications from Philippo Vadi regarding the proportions of the sword, which are found in his chapter 2 "Measures of the Two-Handed Sword". This is a rather more complicated matter than it first appears; I went into it in some detail in my book *Veni Vadi Vici* (pages 39–41) and have reproduced that section as a free download from the resources page for this book on my website, here: https://guywindsor.net/blog/welcome-hma-fans/

Choosing a Supplier

As a general rule, go with suppliers who advertise their swords for the use you intend. It is a good idea to go with suppliers that have a track record of reliability. It is strangely common for makers to produce excellent swords for a while, get overloaded with orders, and then collapse (which can lead to you losing your deposit, or waiting a year or more longer than agreed for your order). Running a business is a totally different skillset to that of swordsmithing, and ideally your supplier has both. Or he lives in your town and you can go bribe him with beer, or threaten him with dire retribution (watch out though, he has both hammers and swords! The beer approach is better).

Ordering Online

In a perfect world, you'd find the sword you want on a stall or in a shop, swing it around, fall in love and buy it. But most probably, you will be ordering one online.

The things to look for in a sword supplier or smith are:

• The swords should be advertised for use. Look for HEMA or something like that in their website blurb
• The swords appear to be of the right style and size. A good maker will always provide detailed stats – at least length and weight
• Ideally, one or more of your friends has bought one of their swords and been happy with it.

The online suppliers I use most for swords are:

Pavel Moc: www.swords.cz
Darkwood Armory: www.darkwoodarmory.com
Arms and Armor: www.arms-n-armor.com
Albion: http://www.albion-swords.com

Ordering a Custom Made Sword

For many of us, ordering a sword is our first experience of dealing with an artisan and ordering something custom made. Like with your doctor, your tailor, and your spouse, you should never lie to or deliberately mislead your smith. Be honest and you will get exactly what you want; and be fair. People who have never made stuff by hand for a living tend to have no clue whatsoever what it entails. If that's you, and you are ordering something custom made, here's my advice:

Find a maker whose work you love.

Tell them exactly what you want the thing you are ordering to *do* (such as impress your friends; cut through a car door; be perfectly historically accurate down to the molecular arrangement of the iron and carbon; or whatever).

Tell them your budget. Trust their artistry. Do not, not, *not* overload them with obsessively detailed specifications. They are not a 3-D printer.

Agree to the time frame, and then wait patiently.

If they say they want the job and you can meet their price, great. If not, go back to step one. Do NOT haggle. You can ask if there are any unnecessary embellishments that they can leave out (that solid silver pommel, for instance) to bring the sword within your budget, but do not ask them to drop their prices by one penny. I made my living as a cabinet maker and antique furniture restorer for five years after graduating from university. I know what it is like to have someone, who probably earns ten times what you do, bitch about how much you are charging them to make something. I flat guarantee that no sword maker on the planet who is working on his own or in a small shop is in it for the money. Because there isn't any.

Sword Specifications Table (metric)

	Arming Sword	Messer/ Falchion	Longsword (Fiore)	Longsword (Liechtenauer)	Longsword (Feder)*	Sidesword	Two Handed sword	Rapier	Smallsword	Backsword/ Sabre	Duelling Sabre
Hilt type	Simple crossguard	Simple cross, plus nail or sidering	Simple crossguard	Simple crossguard, perhaps with siderings	Simple crossguard	Often finger rings, siderings, knucklebow	Simple cross, perhaps siderings	Complex: swept, Pappenheim, or cup.	Shell guard, knucklebow	Fully enclosed	Shell, with integral knucklebow
Total Length	84-97cm	86-97cm	110-130cm	120-140cm	132cm	99-112cm	147-165cm	114-135cm	76-86cm	90-107cm	82cm
Blade Length	68-97cm	66-76cm	87-105cm	96-114cm	100cm	86-94cm	107-127cm	96-114cm	76-86cm	79-92cm	68cm
Weight	900-1150g	1000g	1.6-1.8kg	1.7-2.0kg	1.4kg	1-1.6kg	1.8-2.5kg	1.25-1.6kg	500-1000g	1-1.5kg	700g
Point of Balance	5-10cm down blade.	8-12cm down blade	6-10cm down blade	6-10cm down blade	8cm down blade.	6-10cm down the blade	10-20cm down the blade	6-15cm down the blade	5-10cm down the blade	5-10cm down the blade	10-13cm down the blade

Sword Specifications Table (Imperial)

	Arming Sword	Messer/ Falchion	Longsword (Fiore)	Longsword (Liechtenauer)	Longsword (Feder)*	Sidesword	Two Handed sword	Rapier	Smallsword	Backsword/ Sabre	Duelling Sabre
Hilt type	Simple crossguard	Simple cross, plus nail or sidering	Simple crossguard	Simple crossguard, perhaps with siderings	Simple crossguard	Often finger rings, siderings, knucklebow	Simple cross, perhaps siderings	Complex: swept, Pappenheim, or cup.	Shell guard, knucklebow	Fully enclosed	Shell, with integral knucklebow
Total Length	84-97cm	86-97cm	110-130cm	120-140cm	132cm	99-112cm	147-165cm	114-135cm	76-86cm	90-107cm	82cm
Blade Length	68-97cm	66-76cm	87-105cm	96-114cm	100cm	86-94cm	107-127cm	96-114cm	76-86cm	79-92cm	68cm
Weight	900-1150g	1000g	1.6-1.8kg	1.7-2.0kg	1.4kg	1-1.6kg	1.8-2.5kg	1.25-1.6kg	500-1000g	1-1.5kg	700g
Point of Balance	5-10cm down blade.	8-12cm down blade	6-10cm down blade	6-10cm down blade	8cm down blade.	6-10cm down the blade	10-20cm down the blade	6-15cm down the blade	5-10cm down the blade	5-10cm down the blade	10-13cm down the blade

*these specs taken from swordsmith Peter Regenyi's website, and so represent one common model of feder.

164

For more details on sword types and designs, the go-to books are:

Oakeshott, *Records of the Medieval Sword*. This is the "bible" of medieval sword designs.

A. V. Norman, *The Rapier and Smallsword 1460–1820*. This magisterial work does for the rapier and smallsword what Oakeshott did for the medieval sword.

HANDLING THE SWORD

The purpose of the grip is to form a seamless interface between you and the weapon, allowing you to manipulate the sword as necessary. The sword is a tool, a labour-saving device. Most of the time we will want to be hitting things with the edge or the point, so our grip must allow us to deliver force through those parts of the blade. Pick a target: a bit of wood screwed to the wall will do, anything that doesn't mind a few dents. Then pick up your sword with one hand and poke the target gently. Don't think about it, just do it. Now press down on the floor with the edge near the tip, hard enough that it's difficult to stop the blade bending sideways. Imagine that you are trying to crush a tomato. Still one-handed, write your name in the air with the point, as beautifully as you can and as large as you like. Chances are, you are now holding the sword correctly.

For swords that use a two-handed grip, what do we do with the other hand? Usually, grip the pommel to support our efforts with the edge. Try all of the above exercises using your other hand to help your dominant hand.

Now that we have the sword in hand, we need to notice that one edge faces away from us, and is easy to hit things with: that's the true edge (*filo dritto* in Italian, or "long edge" for German-style fencers). The other faces towards us: that's the false edge (*filo falso* in Italian, or "short edge" for the Germans).

Just to make sure we're on the same page, here are some pictures of my hand with a longsword.

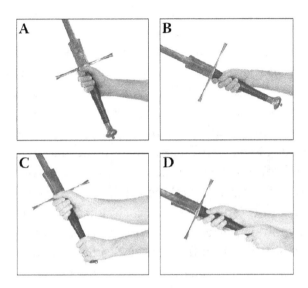

A grip: one hand, point back; B grip: one hand, point forward;
C grip: two hands, point back; D grip: two hands, point forwards.
(Images by Jari Juslin, from *The Medieval Longsword.*)

Notice that the sword is either held back against the web of the thumb – with the blade close to 90° to the forearm – or point forwards almost in line with the forearm, and the hilt resting in the heel of the hand. The shift between these two positions is a key part of most blows and parries. When the sword is held back, the grip is "chambered" (like a bullet in a gun, ready to strike); when the sword is extended, it is "released". In most circumstances, when the sword is held close to the body, away from the opponent, the grip should be chambered; and when the sword strikes or parries, it should be released.

Most thrust-oriented weapons should be held with the grip already extended, so the blade is more or less in line with the forearm. Your forefinger will often hook over the crossguard. Some sources (such as Thibault) specify a particular way to hold the sword; in those cases you should of course follow their instructions!

Teaching the proper grip is tricky, because adjustments that are invisible to the naked eye can have major consequences in using the weapon. As a general rule, align the part of the grip that corresponds to the false edge with the lifeline of your palm, and shake hands with the sword. Keep your grip as relaxed as possible to allow the sword freedom of movement. The weight of the sword rests on the middle phalange (section) of the middle finger, and the back of the handle presses into the middle of the heel of the hand. You should be able to hold the sword with just those points of contact: try taking off your forefinger, ring finger, little finger and thumb. The sword should not move.

There is no one perfect grip. With practice, you will come to hold the sword slightly differently depending on what you want to do with it. Just as a learner driver grips the steering wheel, knuckles white from the tension, but an experienced driver just feels through their hands what the car is doing and responds effortlessly; so with swords.

Striking Practice

Whatever swordsmanship style you practice, it is very important that you make time to practise striking. This is precisely analogous to boxing training; we use the equivalent of shadow boxing, the speed ball, the heavy bag, and focus mitts.

You need to learn to be able to strike accurately and hard – without damage to yourself – first against stationary targets, and then against moving targets. In friendly sparring and pair drills, it is of course also vital that you can hit gently without damage to anyone. The main tools we use to practise these skills are the tyre, the pell, the wall target, and the buckler game.

Hitting the Tyre

An ordinary car tyre, held by a helpful partner, is an ideal striking target because it absorbs some, but not all, of the impact. You can hit it with absolutely full force without endangering the person holding it (unless you miss), and while it gives some shock back into the sword and your hands, much of the force is taken by the elastic give of the tyre. Every target hits back – every action has an equal and opposite reaction. If your technique is correct, you can direct the returning energy down into the ground. If not, the tyre will bounce your sword up and off. I recommend adding a strip of duct tape as a more precise aiming point. When you hit the tyre, the energy going into it should be absorbed by the tyre (and your partner). You should feel almost nothing. Start gently, standing still, and work your way up, adding speed and power slowly. Then try adding footwork, such as striking with a pass.

Your body knows that to hit hard, it should step first and strike with the rotation of the hips. This will give you maximum power, but get you killed in a sword fight because it will expose you as you step into measure. In fencing you will always lead with the sword, not the foot. It is critically important to remember that the tyre is not waiting with a sword to kill you, and therefore will let you get away with wildly incorrect timing – you can step into measure and then strike. You and your partner should watch for this.

The Pell

The pell is a post, often with a crossbeam, fixed upright for you to cut and thrust at. The oldest reference we have for this kind of training is Vegetius's *De Re Militari*, written (probably) in the late fourth century. Try the following exercises:

- Pick one blow, and see how hard and fast you can strike at the pell without touching it
- Repeat with multiple strikes (use your imagination)
- Strike fast, but stroke the pell gently on a marked spot (about as hard as you would like to be hit in freeplay). See how hard and fast that really is
- Repeat with multiple strokes
- The 99 strikes exercise: make 100 cuts at the pell without

touching it. Every time you touch it, the counter resets to zero. So if you touch on strike 99, you go back to the beginning . . .

• Choose a specific strike and approach the pell from far away, moving smoothly and without stopping with blows from guard to guard: see if you can arrive in measure with your sword in the right place to launch the pre-arranged strike. This is harder than it sounds.

The same caveat applies as with the tyre – be careful to time your strikes to land a fraction before your passing foot touches the ground.

The Wall Target

(I have adapted this from my rapier training manual, *The Duellist's Companion*.)

The wall target is a padded striking surface for thrusting at. We know that these have been in use since at least the late sixteenth century, when a primarily thrust-oriented style of fencing became common. I use it with every weapon though, because the pell in my salle is set in a bucket of cement, and so topples over easily if you thrust at it too hard. The wall target is fixed to the cladding around a steel girder, so I can hit it as hard as my joints will allow!

I make my own. It is a piece of plywood covered with camping mat foam and a layer of leather. Additional leather patches to reinforce the target points are a good idea. Wall targets can range in size from a few inches squared to 30" by 30". They should be large enough that you are never likely to miss the target altogether; holes in the wall are hard to explain. The main school target has three main striking points, approximately at face, heart and groin height (for an opponent standing on guard), with two additional points placed like eyes. There is enough space around the target for all footwork actions, for both left and right handers.

For any thrust-oriented weapon this is perhaps the most important solo practice you can do: in addition to accuracy, it teaches you distance, power and control. Make sure before you start that your blade is designed to take the repeated bending, and if you are using a triangular section blade, make sure that the point of the triangle is in the inside of the curve. Symmetrically cross-sectioned blades (such as the common lozenge shape) can bend in both directions. Regular practice on the wall makes up about 80 per cent of my own rapier, smallsword and foil training. It is very important that the blade bends when the point touches the wall, but there is no "give" anywhere else. Ensure that the blade stays in line with your forearm, and your wrist locks to support the pressure.

Wrist position when hitting target. (Photo by Ilkka Hartikainen from The Duellist's Companion).

A common mistake is to allow the wrist to "break."

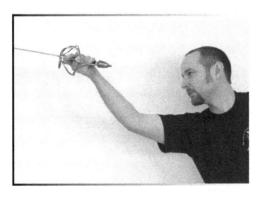

Wrong wrist position on target. (Photo by Ilkka Hartikainen from The Duellist's Companion)

Or the hilt to lift.

(Photo by Ilkka Hartikainen from The Duellist's Companion)

The purpose of the lunge is to drive the sword through the target. With a practice blade and a wall target, the energy is absorbed by the blade; with a sharp blade and a penetrable target, that energy is used to puncture the target.

The sword/swordsman combination should be perfectly aligned so that no energy "leaks." The lunge is the perfect long attack with all your weight and energy focussed in one direction, on one point.

Point control exercise #1
5. Establish your guard position, and extend your sword.
6. Approach the target and place your point on the marked spot.
7. Withdraw your arm to the normal guard resting position.
8. Extend in *quarta* and place your point on the spot (or as close as possible). You should be close enough that your blade bends convincingly.
9. Repeat ad nauseam.

Point control exercise #2
Multiple targets: once you are reasonably successful at the above exercise, it is a good idea to practice striking at different marks,

at varying heights, and from all guards. Try numbering the points and have a friend call out numbers randomly; you must strike that number as fast as possible.

Point control exercise #3

Finally, when your point will go reliably within an inch of where you want it when striking in the straight line, practice the exercise using all the footwork actions you know (the *scansi*, the passes, the *sbasso*, etc.). I sometimes execute many steps and passes changing distances constantly, and striking using whatever action is best suited to the distance at which I happen to find myself.

Point control is the hallmark of a good swordsman. Practice it whenever possible. I often turn the CD player on and off, and change tracks, with my point. I also turn the lights on and off with my sword (though an engineer friend thinks that's crazy dangerous, so perhaps you'd better not try it).

When walking with an umbrella, pick spots on the pavement (litter, chewing gum marks, etc.) and tap them with the point as you go past. No one will notice, and you can get some useful training done while walking to the pub. For extra difficulty, you could fix a tennis ball or squash ball to a piece of string, hang it up, and try to hit it. After the first successful hit it gets much harder, because it's moving.

There is a delightful variation on the wall target that you might want to set up: it comes from a rather controversial book by Baltazar Ficher published in 1796. It is controversial because he stole the entire text from Olivier's 1771 book *Fencing Familiarised*, but he added original engravings, and the book includes a complete translation into Russian. This machine has a wooden heart that drops when you let go of the string, and you have to pin the heart to the wall before it hits the bottom. I would have a friend holding the string so you don't know when it's about to fall! It is pictured overleaf.

L'ALONGEMENT DU COEUR

This is one way to learn timing, but our next exercise is (I think) even better.

The Buckler Game

For this exercise we use a simple wooden buckler as a thrusting target. Your partner holds it in one hand (and wears a mask just in case), and offers it up for you to thrust at. Their job is then to make you move about, offering the target at various heights and distances, and for decreasing lengths of time, making it difficult for you to get the thrust in. This should be calibrated so that you can hit it about three to four times out of five attempts. Less than that, they should slow down; more than that, they should make things harder. This is just like using focus mitts with a boxing coach.

Circuit Training

There are usually not enough wall targets for everyone in class to use at the same time, nor are there enough pells and other things (except bucklers – we have lots of bucklers!). So we set up a circuit with our two wall targets, a hanging target, a mirror, and the pell, which keeps five people busy, and equip the people left over with one buckler per pair or, if using a cutting weapon, add in a tyre or two as well. The mirror is used for slow, careful, perfect form practice. Everybody spends two minutes in each station, with a one minute warning so they can switch hands if they like (I do recommend it). One sadist has the stopwatch (usually me, though I usually take part in the circuits as well). We do one round, which puts everyone through the entire circuit, and takes between ten and twenty minutes depending on how many people are in class. That is usually enough!

SKILL DEVELOPMENT

It is relatively easy to teach set drills to a student or class. He does this, you do that. And it is relatively easy to set up a freeplay (sparring, fencing) environment that is reasonably safe. I have seen many groups and schools that have nice set drills, and which freeplay quite a bit, but there is no real relationship between the two kinds of training. The things done in freeplay bear scant resemblance to the actions in the drills. The point of this chapter is to show you how to build a bridge between set drills and freeplay. This is especially important for historical swordsmanship because the manuals tend to show short, simple sequences (an attack and a defence, usually), which are easy to turn into drills but very hard to pull off in friendly freeplay.

Freeplay, sparring, fencing – whatever you want to call it – is a key component of most martial arts. How you should prepare for it depends on what your freeplay is supposed to accomplish, and where freeplay-like activities fit into your system. Schools that emphasise winning tournaments tend to introduce it very early, using heavily modified weapon simulators and lots of protection (my earliest formal weapons training was sport fencing; I seem to remember that we did freeplay at the end of the first class); schools that emphasise other things, such as historical accuracy or self defence, tend to modify the weapons less and use less protection, and so naturally introduce freeplay much later.

We can divide the challenges you face in getting from beginner to expert freeplayer into personal and practical challenges.

Personal Challenges

The main personal challenges facing a martial artist getting themselves ready to freeplay are:

- Fear of injury
- Fear of embarrassment
- Fear of loss of control.

None of which are about technique! I'll get to technical issues in a moment, but let's deal with these first.

Fear of Injury

Beginners should run into little to no risk of injury; if you do, there is something wrong with the school and you should probably find a better one. So this is an irrational fear, and should be handled by gradually building up the complexity of your training (I will show you how to do that in a moment) until you find yourself doing a "set drill" that is effectively freeplay.

Fear of injuring your partner is also very common (in my experience, it's actually more common than fear of getting injured yourself). There are several approaches for this. First, you must learn to respect your partner's integrity and sovereignty. It is up to them whether they take the risk of fencing with you. If they are keen and your behaviour is appropriate, it's not entirely your fault if you do hurt them. Those risks ought to be pretty small, but nobody trains hard for many years without ever accidentally hurting a partner at least a little bit. Remember how you feel about your bruises; they are part and parcel of training, and you accept the risks. Your partners have every right to take the same risks.

If you have valid doubts about your ability to physically control your weapon under the stress of freeplay, then I recommend the pell and the "99 strikes" exercise.

If you still have valid doubts about your ability to remain in control of yourself when in freeplay, don't do it. In my salle, nobody is ever required to do freeplay. Had a frustrating day and think you might take it out on someone? Don't fence. Too tired to think straight? Don't fence. I have a scar on my scalp from the time I persuaded a friend to fence me, against his better judgment. He said he was too tired. He was right. I got three stitches. I have bled so you don't have to.

Fear of Embarrassment

You will probably suck at fencing the first hundred times you do it. I did. So did everyone else I know. In any well-run group or school, you will get respect for putting yourself out there, training hard and trying hard – far more than you will for any actual skill or fencing success. People who laugh at beginners are arseholes. Ignore them, and then surpass them. They do not deserve your attention, far less your embarrassment.

Fear of Loss of Control

This is tied up with fear of injuring your partners through loss of self control, and fear of getting injured yourself. At the end of the day though, set drills can become a crutch that replace training. If you are uncomfortable and struggling at the edge of what you can do, you are probably learning and growing. Comfort is for the pub after training, not the salle. Get over it!

Practical Challenges

Let's say you were fencing or building up to fencing, and got hit when you were not supposed to. Here's why:

- The actions were familiar, but too hard or fast
- You came across an unfamiliar action
- You have no idea what just happened.

The answer in every case is to repeat what happened, but slowly. This is a key skill, perhaps the key skill, in skill development; at least one partner must know what just happened. If you can't repeat it, you can't train it, correct it, recognise it next time, or defeat it. We call this "fencing memory," and we have a simple drill for training this skill. You will need it for every stage of building the bridge.

Developing Fencing Memory

This drill works best with three fencers: an attacker, a defender and an observer. Switch roles after each phrase to develop your ability to remember phrases you have both done and seen.

- Designate an attacker and a defender
- Allow free choice of attack and defence, but no continuations (attacker can't counter)
- Attacker attacks as they like, defender tries to defend. Notice who gets hit
- First one, then the other, and then the observer describes in clear fencing language, in detail, exactly what occurred.

For example (using Fiore longsword jargon – sorry you non-longsword readers!): "Mary was in *coda longa*, I was in *posta di donna*. Mary attacked with a thrust to my face. I tried to exchange the thrust, but my sword caught on the back of my mask and I missed my parry. Mary's thrust landed in my face." Then Mary describes what she thought happened "well, I started in *tutta porta di ferro*, and attacked with a *mandritto fendente* . . ." (You'll be amazed how rarely you'll agree with each other to start with.) Lastly, the observer states what they think happened. If the observer doesn't have a reliable fencing memory (and even if they do!), use a video camera too.

When one attack and one defence can be reliably described and repeated, add the attacker's counter. When that is easily recalled, the defender can counter that, and so on. Once you have built it up so that you can accurately reproduce a phrase of at least six actions (three from each side), your memory is ready for useful freeplay. When you are reconstructing what happened, it's usually best to start with the blow that landed and work out the fencing sequence backwards from there.

Building the Bridge

Every martial art I have ever come across uses set drills of some kind, even if only at the beginning (and in some cases, set drills were the whole art). So if you are reading this, you are bound to know some. Whatever actions you are practising when you do a drill are usually specific to some kind of attack or action by your opponent. He punches you in the face with his left hand, for example, so you deflect with your left forearm and punch him in the ribs. Or as you try to stab him with your dagger, he covers your attack with his right hand, so you trap his wrist and throw him.

To start with, I imagine you have been taught to do this action slowly and co-operatively. And you have probably seen more experienced people do something like it in freeplay. But it's likely that if you tried to do it in freeplay on day one, it would fail. That's not the technique's fault (if it is, change systems!); it's because either:

- you did it in the wrong context, or
- you did it wrong.

We call the first problem "tactical" and the second "technical". Tactical problems are all about knowing the right thing to do, and technical problems are all about doing the right thing well enough for it to work. Most of the more complex training set-ups can go wrong at either point, so it's good to have a clear idea of what kind of problem you are working on, and you should be able to identify the type of problem before you rush off to fix it.

Every drill should have a clearly defined tactical context, and a clearly defined technical solution. They usually look something like this:

- Attacker and defender are ready to go
- Attacker attacks with action A
- Defender defends with action B
- Attacker continues with action C
- Defender counters C with action D.

. . . and so on. Let's call this drill ABCD. Action A is the tactical context for defence B. So let's begin with the kind of drill that establishes where your technical gaps are.

Work the Combinations

Set up the drill ABCD. Then, from the same starting point (whatever that is in your system), the attacker varies his attack: actions F, J, N, and so on. Be that "thrust from the left", "beat attack and lunge in *quarte*", "go for the hip throw", or whatever. In each case, the defender should make the proper defence.

The next stage is for the attacker to use whichever attack they have chosen to set up their counter: A draws B, so they can do C.

Then of course, the attacker does A–C so the defender can practice D.

In most systems, attack A has more than one defence. So once you have worked through all the main attacks, go back to one of them and work through all the main defences against it. (My longsword students know this as the Four Corners Drill.)

Then do the same for all the attacks.

Then do the same for the attacker's counter to each of the defences generated by each of their attacks.

Then do the same for the defender's counter to each of those . . .

This generates a combinatorial explosion. Very quickly, you could end up with a ridiculously complicated set of useless drills. So your goal is to survey the system quickly, establish where you are weakest, and set about chunking the actions together. You should not have to remember more than three or four basic defence ideas (e.g. block, counterattack, avoid) or three or four basic attacking ideas (e.g. strike, go around, feint). As you can see, I only know three of each. But each one can be usefully expanded upon for hours.

Please note, we are still in the basic form of the drill.

This is where many schools get stuck. They can get this far easily enough, and it generates all sorts of cool new sequences for students to remember, but it doesn't really help them develop workable skills. So let's move on. I have a set of "multipliers" that add complexity in a systematic and approachable way.

1. Who Moves First?

In any set drill, you can:

- Start the drill with both players standing still in guard (this is the usual set-up for beginners to start with)
- Change who attacks
- Draw the attack by some prior movement or invitation.

In my salles the students spend a lot of time doing basic drills, but starting from way out of measure. The trick is to arrive at the right time and in the right place to do the initial actions of a particular drill, without exposing yourself. This is very hard at the beginning.

But we are still stuck in an artificially short sequence of a maximum of four steps.

2. Add a Step

Another simple means to make a drill more useful is to allow the "loser" to counter the last step if he can. So for instance: you set up the drill and, as the attacker counters, the defender may – if he sees it coming and can think of something useful to do – counter the attacker's action. There is in theory no end to this drill, because every action can be countered. Add one step at a time, and stop when it becomes difficult to remember how you got to where you are. This uses a set drill to set up a kind of slow freeplay.

3. Degrees of Freedom

This is the beginning of the bridge between set basic drills and advanced fencing skill. At any stage in any drill, a set of decisions have been made. Systematically allowing a different choice to be made on the fly by one player introduces an element of unpredictability for the other player. For example, we might allow the attacker to choose his counter to the defence at random. This can be either to develop the attacker's decision-making skills (so the defender is helping him), or to develop the defender's ability to adapt (so the attacker is helping him). When there is a choice like that to be made, we say there is a degree of freedom – the attacker in this case has one degree of freedom – one point in the drill where he gets to make a choice. The other has to respond appropriately in real time. By adding degrees of freedom one at a time, we can get all the way from ABCD to freeplay. Common places to add a degree of freedom are:

- The defender doesn't have to wait for the attack, but can pre-emptively attack (thus switching roles)
- The attacker can vary the type of attack
- The defender can vary the type of defence (the most common change is from parry-riposte (two motions – one to defend, and one to strike) to counterattack (defence and strike in one motion))
- The attacker can vary their reaction to the defence (e.g. feint, or parry the riposte, or enter on the parry, etc.).

4. The "Rule of Cs"

The "Rule of Cs" is then applied to all of the above, in which every drill is first worked through with the players **co-operating, coaching,** or **competing**.

1. **Co-operating:** creating correct choreography.
2. **Coaching:** Once the choreography is smooth, increase the difficulty by increasing intensity or introducing a degree of freedom (e.g. is the attack a cut or thrust?), with one player adjusting the difficulty for the other to learn at their most efficient rate. If it works all the time, ramp it up; if it fails more than twice in ten reps, ease off a bit.
3. **Compete:** Finally, the players each try within reason to make the drill work for them. In First Drill for instance, the degree of freedom that has just been coached might be that the attacker is either continuing with a pommel strike or angulating around the parry. When coaching, he tries to make sure the defender can usually counter him; when competing, he just tries to make his action work. This can be dangerous if it gets out of hand, so be careful, and wear full protection just in case. In practice, the more experienced fencer should get most of the hits, without departing from the drill. This is fine, and gives a good indication of whether your training regime is working. There is a significant risk of this getting out of hand; be mindful as you play the drill competitively that you must stick to the constraints of the drill that you have both agreed upon. Otherwise you lose track of the rationale behind what you are doing, and mistakes creep in that are difficult to spot and trace back to their source.

To recap then, we have the following means of expanding on set drills:

- Specific variation multipliers, such as going through every type of blow and defending against them
- Who moves first?
- Extending the drill
- Adding degrees of freedom, so either partner gets one or more decision points
- The Rule of Cs.

5. Pressure Drills

You may have noticed that the core of my approach is to isolate variables – technical complexity or degrees of freedom, for instance. Pressure drills are exercises whose specific function is to get you used to performing under, you guessed it, pressure.

The most basic set-up has you with two partners – all of you in full freeplay gear, whatever that is for your school or system. Each partner will give you the same attack, alternating, ten times each. You will defend against each attack as best you can. In theory, you do the same technique perfectly twenty times. Your partners' job is to keep you moving, keep you under pressure. They do not wait for you to sort yourself out after each action; as soon as your defence is done, the next attack comes in.

That's why you have two partners. As fatigue sets in, you will tend to make mistakes and get sloppy. Ideally, you will find it really, really hard to defend yourself.

The next level has the attackers using different attacks; one from the left with a cut and the other with a thrust, say; and you have to do two different defences correctly.

Then the attackers can attack as they please, their only job being to keep you working under pressure.

Of course, in whichever set-up, immediately after you're in the middle, you take one of the attacking roles and then the other. So on the fourth round, you're back in the middle again. Good luck. You'll know you've really done this when you've felt like puking into your mask.

It's an age-old secret of martial training that acute fatigue is a good mimic of combat stress. When your heart rate is up at 180 and your legs and arms feel like they are falling off, and you can still get your actions right, then you have truly learned something.

What we need now is a drill that allows either person to attack or defend with any action, and for the play to continue until an action is successfully concluded. We call it freeplay!

6. Setting up Freeplay

Let's start easy. If getting beginners to freeplay quickly is your goal, all you have to do is have:

- Safer weapons (e.g. nylon longswords or sport-fencing foils, or similar) and adequate protection
- Rules, such as a list of what is allowed and what is not (e.g. no throws, kicks, chokes, or whatever)
- Supervision. Make sure that everybody is wearing the right protection and follows the rules.

As your students develop their skills, your school might graduate them to more realistic weapons or less protection, or allow a wider variety of techniques. Some students will be put off if the freeplay appears too unstructured, so be ready to introduce beginners gently, such as by letting a senior student, who can be relied upon to go easy on them initially, be their first opponent.

The trap that most beginners fall into, as I did myself, is the realisation early on that practising technique while fencing, rather than relying on your wits and instinct, can often mean losing a match you could win. These lost bouts can be an embarrassment, and can certainly lead you to doubt the validity of so-called "good technique". This is why I believe it is a bad idea for relatively untrained students to freeplay in uncontrolled conditions or too often. Not all instructors will agree with me here, because their emphasis on teaching swordplay as the art of self defence leads them to treat all bouts as practice for the real thing: if losing equals dying, the student must be trained to win at all costs, and from the outset. I disagree with this approach because it is predicated on two mistaken surmises: that freeplay is fight simulation, and that the will to win is the main component in winning.

If we go back a couple of hundred years to the fencing schools of the eighteenth century, we find a totally different attitude towards freeplay. These masters were teaching the art of survival in a culture where everyone went armed, and every gentleman was expected to be ready to defend his honour with his life. Yet in those salles it was the height of bad manners to brutalise or wound an opponent. During freeplay, one might even be expected to delay a riposte to allow your opponent to return to guard. This was in part a safety consideration in an age when fencing masks were uncommon. But it was also because the instructors at these schools clearly believed that the purpose of freeplay was to practise good technique, not to score touches. There has never been a good excuse for unsafe play. The first schools of fencing to emphasise winning in the salle, that I know of, were mid-twentieth-century sport-fencing schools. An interesting coincidence: only fencers who were never likely to fight to the death were trained to fight only to win in practice.

Once you have agreed to fence with someone, it is important to agree on rules of engagement. This is partly to ensure safety, and partly to create an environment in which you can learn. Please review the Safety chapter. To recap, though, the two most simple rules are these: confine your moves to the safety limits of your protective gear, and confine your moves to the technical range of the least trained combatant.

JUDGEMENT

Training happens in the brain and, in my experience, the biggest barrier to training exists between a student's ears. One of the most common problems I have seen (and experienced myself) is the tendency to stop and make judgements when things aren't going well. For example, I'm practising my still-imperfect *mandritto fendente*, as part of the *Farfalla di Ferro*. I make a noticeable mistake, so I stop, berate myself ("you bloody fool, couldn't swing a sword through a wet paper bag, come on, what kind of idiot are you?") and then get back to practising.

Or for another example: I'm fighting someone for real. I get hit but am not dead. So I stop fighting back, and start criticizing myself for getting hit. Meanwhile my assailant keeps hitting me.

Do you see the problem? Do you ever do this? I have seen this problem so severely ingrained in a student that he actually stopped in the middle of the class and hit himself three times in the head for making the mistake. He did this about five times per session, three sessions per week, until I trained it out of him. This corrective technique has never once in the history of mankind ever been shown to work.

So what does?

At its core, the mistake is allowing your attention to be taken off what you are doing, and onto what you were doing. This is followed by an emotional reaction to the mistake or imperfection, which locks your attention on what you have done. This is the very opposite of mindful presence. But because it is disguised as paying attention to what you are doing, because you are indeed paying close attention to what you have done, it can feel like something you should do. And if you are not alone at the time, it can feel like you need to indicate to everyone else that you have noticed the mistake. The social pressure to do this is actually quite severe. But think on this: it's not they that need to fix the mistake, so bringing it to their attention does nobody any favours. If they are not well trained, they haven't spotted the mistake anyway; if they are, they will be less impressed by your reaction than they would have been by your dispassionate correction of it next time the opportunity arises.

The trick is to notice the mistake dispassionately, and calmly correct it next time round. It should not break your flow; not so much as a flicker of a frown should cross your brow. There should be no emotional reaction clouding your ability to actually enact the correction. Noticing something and reacting to it are two completely different things.

This is a skill, and can therefore be trained. Here's how:

Set up an exercise in which you know you'll make a natural error. Do a form a bit faster than usual, or do a pair drill at a level of complexity that challenges you.

Knowing that a mistake is coming, decide that when it does you will notice it but not react.

Pay attention to your emotional state. When the error arises, spot your reaction. Just notice it, and don't interfere.

Keep running this exercise, the point of which is to practice noticing mistakes without judging them. If this is a common problem for you, every training drill you do should be done as a way of generating natural errors for you to practice noticing without judging.

Beating yourself up about mistakes simply reinforces the mistake. Noticing them dispassionately allows you to correct them much more quickly and easily. It took my head-bashing student several months to change the habit; because his case was so severe, I had him replace the head-bashing with push-ups to change his reaction before getting rid of it altogether. This worked quite well, and no doubt saved him many brain cells.

HOW TO START A HMA CLUB

One of the most common questions I get asked is this: "there are no HMA clubs near me. What should I do?" My answer is always the same: "start one." So the next question is "how do I do that?"

The most difficult part of starting a HMA club is deciding to do so. Once the decision has been made, the rest is not so hard.

I've been involved in starting many groups. There was the Dawn Duellists' Society (DDS) in 1994, the British Federation for Historical Swordplay in 1999, The School of European Swordsmanship in 2001, and literally dozens of satellite clubs since then. So I have some ideas on the subject, as you might imagine.

Let's begin with some general principles (this is extracted from an article of mine that was published in *Teaching and Interpreting Historical Swordsmanship* in 2005):

"Starting a group is not as hard as it may seem, it just requires determination, and some basic social skills. The obstacles vary so widely in different countries and cultures that it is very hard to advise on the specifics, but I use a set of basic principles to run my school, which are applicable to any group (summarised in these terms by Mike Stillwell).

- **Group purpose**: every group must have a purpose, clearly stated. "The study and practice of historical swordsmanship" covers most, but you may wish to narrow the focus.
- **Group needs**: every group has specific needs, which must be

190

met for the group to flourish. Typically they include financial health, sufficient membership, and the specific means to achieve the purpose, such as weapons, treatises and a place to practice.

• **Individual needs**: every group is comprised of individuals, who will leave if their needs are not met. Such needs include sharing in the common purpose, assistance for beginners, and the various social needs that we all share. Most practitioners prefer a group where they feel welcome and needed to one where they are looked on with suspicion until they have "proved" themselves. Even the most inexperienced beginner should be recognised as a vital part of the group: without such beginners, the Art, and the group, have no future.

A group will succeed if all the above needs are met, and kept in balance. Once the needs of any one individual (including the illustrious founder) take precedence, the group is doomed. Likewise, any group decision, whether made by the individual in charge, by a committee, or by the whole group, should be arrived at based on how well it serves the three needs. Individuals whose needs are met by the group will stay, and enable the group needs to be met, which enables the group purpose to be met. Of course, many individuals will fall by the wayside when they discover that their needs are not met by a group with that purpose; this is normal, so expect attrition. Also there are some individuals who feel a need to take over any group they join; this is not a problem provided that the group purpose and needs are served by their ascendancy. Just beware of political infighting, and establish the aims of the group clearly enough to prevent slippage."

Now we have established the principles, let's get into the specifics. You want to start a HMA club: what's the first step?

1) Find a friend who'll have a go at swords. One friend is good; two is better. What, you've got three interested friends? Then this will be easy . . .

2) Be honest with yourself and your co-founders about your interests, and agree on exactly what, at this stage, the club is going to do. Establish in clear and exact terms the **group purpose**. For example "we are going to train for HMA tournaments in longsword and take part in as many as we can." Or "we are going to recreate Meyer's swordsmanship from his book." Or "we are Jedi and will train accordingly." Look for the sources and help you might need. For groups wanting to "recreate Fiore's art of arms," you could use my books, syllabus and so on; but if you want to study Liechtenauer, those won't be much help. Many of my branches started out as "we will train from this book by this Windsor fellow" and grew from there. Choose a book, a syllabus, a historical source, or even a YouTube channel – whatever suits your **purpose** – and say "we'll do this and only this." It is much better to add things later, once the group is established, than to start out trying to please everyone. To begin with, focus on one thing, and make it absolutely clear what that thing is.

The key question at this stage is "does being part of this club actually meet my **individual needs**?" If you wanted a club so you could learn to teach eighteenth-century smallsword, and nobody in this club wants to do smallsword (e.g. they're all obsessed with polearms), then start a different club and be clearer about your goals. It is perfectly okay, normal even, for the founders to start the club to scratch their own itch. Start the club you'd want to join.

3) Meet regularly – once a week at a minimum – at the same time and in the same place. Depending on the weather and local laws, you could meet in a park, or (as the DDS did for years) train in a courtyard outside a pub in the centre of Edinburgh. You don't need money for this; there are lots of free spaces in most places, if you just look. When you start out, you will be ignorant and unskilled. *That is okay!!* Everybody starts at zero. But you have SO much more help available than I did in 1992, and I turned out all right. So you will probably do even better.

4) Advertise in any free medium (Twitter, Facebook, etc.) for like-minded people in your neighbourhood. If you're training in a public space, be ready for curious people of all ages and types to come up and talk to you. Be very clear about what you are trying to do, so Viking re-enactors won't come along and be disappointed by your sword and buckler club, or vice versa. Being specific means that people can see in advance whether the club is likely to meet their **individual needs**.

5) When you have 6–10 people coming regularly, it's time to establish a formal club. Start collecting fees. This is essential. Price it at the cost of a night out per month, minimum. For example, in the UK, perhaps 25 quid; in Finland, maybe 35 euros, per person per month. (I don't recommend charging per session – it's a convenience for the uncommitted, and not good for the club.) One of the biggest mistakes beginner clubs make is to not gather fees, and they do this mostly because they don't feel they are providing a service that is worth paying for. But you are not selling a service (unless you are setting up a professional school, which I am not covering here); you're gathering the resources the club needs to meet its goals. Members who don't want to pay are not going to help meet the **group needs**.

What is the money for? To help accomplish the **group purpose**. You can use it for whatever helps pursue the **purpose**, such as to pay for a teacher, buy club equipment, send your most active class leaders to events they can't afford to go to on their own, or pay for a better venue. The list is endless. My point is that clubs that have money can pursue their purpose much more easily than those that don't. I advise having members use a "set it and forget it" direct debit or PayPal regular payment; it's much more effective than manually collecting dues.

6) At this stage you will need to register a non-profit organisation. This is usually quite easy to do, if you don't mind filling in

forms. Use whatever umbrella organisations are available. University students can start a university society to get access to university facilities. Your local sports fencing club might let you set up a sub group within their umbrella (as, for instance, my branch in Oulu, Finland, did). If there is a suitable umbrella available, consider joining it. Be careful that doing so does not interfere with your **group purpose**, though. If joining an umbrella organisation means giving up your core purpose, or unacceptable changes to equipment or rules, don't do it.

Be careful that you understand the rules around what a non-profit organisation can and cannot do. I can't advise you on the law in your country, but in general, you *can* hire a teacher (but the employee cannot usually be part of the governing board). You *cannot* use the funds to pay for your personal sword collection. You will also probably have to file annual accounts and a list of members. This is not too much work if there are many hands helping: maybe one person handles the paperwork; another handles finding new members; and a few others run regular classes. At this stage the thing to watch out for is that the **individual needs** of the people doing all the work are being met. Some kind of compensation for their efforts is appropriate (such as not having to pay dues, or subsidised attendance at an event, or a guarantee of never having to clean the training space, or something). The last thing you want is for the essential administration to not get done because the poor bugger doing it has been snowed under by mounds of paper and can't get to class, and so quits. Look after your officers – they deserve it.

It's really not so hard. It *is* a lot of work, but that's true of almost everything worthwhile.

How a club treats beginners is a defining feature of its culture. In my schools, beginners are considered the future of the Art and welcomed accordingly. In general, clubs either run beginners' courses or expect beginners to just show up to a class. I ran my school without formal beginners' courses for the first year and a half, and it doubled in size when we ran the first beginners' course. Most beginners just don't feel comfortable showing up unless they know that they are expected, and expected to be inexperienced. I run my beginners courses with two rules and four principles.

The Rules:

1. Every student must finish every class healthier than they started it.

This is accomplished by:

2. Every student must behave like a reasonable adult (whether they are adult, or reasonable, outside the Salle or not).

The Principles

1. Funnels not filters

Beginners' courses should be funnels, not filters. They should entice people in and seduce them to the Art, not hold up artificial barriers to entry (such as the push-ups-till-you-puke approach). A beginners' course is either a filter or a funnel. A club that is trying to produce competition champions will usually try to filter out students that will never do well in competition. They do this by making the beginners' course a selection procedure, requiring a certain level of grit or fitness to get through. That's perfectly legitimate behaviour; special forces units do the same. But if your club is run as an open learning environment, interested in progress rather than attaining a specific goal, a funnel makes more sense. Your purpose then is to equip students to take part safely in regular classes.

2. Movement

Get them moving: movement is the foundation of swordsmanship. Good movements create good guards, good blows, and so on. This starts with the warm-up and continues throughout the class.

3. <u>Start with what they can do</u>

Start with what they can do, and then adjust that towards what you want them to do. Every action must be taught from the familiar: walking across the salle becomes passing steps; swinging the sword from shoulder to shoulder becomes striking; and so on. If your art has passing steps, start with having them walk. If your art has lunges, start with having them reach out their arm for something. If it's a bit too far away, they'll shift their front foot naturally. Then take this natural action and modify it in the desired direction.

4. <u>The rule of beginners</u>

Show it to them correctly a thousand times, and they will eventually get it. Show it to them wrong once, and they'll copy it accurately first time.

HOW TO TEACH A BASIC CLASS

Teaching a basic class can be quite daunting for an inexperienced instructor. The purpose of this chapter is to give you a set of guidelines for organising and teaching a basic class. You may need to refer back to the sections on drill design and syllabus design, and forwards to the physical training section, to fill in gaps in your basic knowledge before attempting to teach. If you are planning a formal beginners' class, you should read through the reports on running two beginners' courses in my school to get an idea of how they are structured. You can find them here: https://guywindsor.net/blog/theoryandpractice

I have been teaching basic classes of one sort or another for well over twenty years, and it's my nature to refine anything I do regularly into a system. If I wasn't teaching swordsmanship, I'd be teaching something else; giving instruction is my best learning environment. If ever I'm having difficulty with any skill – be it woodwork, writing or getting my sword to go where it should – I conjure up an imaginary student and, in my mind, teach them how to do it. Instant improvement, every time.

My training focus between 2009 and 2015 was on my teaching skills. This was really kicked off by my attendance at a British Academy of Fencing (BAF) coaching course in April 2010. We trained from 9 a.m. to 9 p.m. for five days straight, and I was deeply uncomfortable and out of my depth almost the entire time. It was not very enjoyable, as such, but seriously good for me. It opened my eyes to a pedagogy of teaching, and crystallised for me a clear and simple set of goals for teaching. The Art of Arms is a way of organising the practices and principles of combat so that they may be studied and taught. The BAF has done for the art of teaching fencing what Fiore did for the art of arms. It is irrelevant that the techniques and theory of sport fencing are radically different from those of my core systems. What matters is that there is a clear body of technical and tactical knowledge, a perfectly defined environment in which it is supposed to be applied, and a systematic way to get students from one to the other. That system is priceless. Of course, what follows is not that system, it's my adaptation of their pedagogical approach to the goals of my Art and my school. You may find similarly useful pedagogical approaches in dance classes, classical fencing or, indeed, in any environment that teaches skills to be used under pressure.

Let us quickly define what I mean by "basic class". There are, generally speaking, three kinds of class: beginners', basic, and advanced. Of these, the basic class is by far the easiest to do well. Beginners are hard to teach well because they have absolutely no frame of reference; you have to build that for them. They have to be taught everything, from how to safely take a sword off the rack, to how to do a push-up. In a basic class, everyone has at least the beginnings of a common frame of reference. They know at least the choreography of some drills, and have understood the group's safety protocols. At the advanced level it is very challenging, because you have to be able to teach people who are already quite skilled.

At the basic level, you have a simple hierarchy of goals:

- Safety
- Teach one thing
- Inspire them
- Get out of the way.

1. Safety
Your job as the instructor is really simple. At the basic level, your job is to provide a safe environment in which training will

occur. That's it. You don't need to be able to teach the *punta falsa* from first principles, nor customise the class to the interests of its members: just open the doors, give folk stuff to do, and make sure no one gets hurt. In short: *create and maintain a safe training environment*. Get everyone to the end of class without injury. The prime directive is this: "everyone finishes class healthier than they started it". Swordsmanship is naturally dangerous, so this overrules all other goals. An airline pilot thinks the same way. It's vastly more important that everyone survives the flight than that they get to the destination airport at the scheduled time. You do this by making sure that all students present are aware of the dangers, and have a set of safe practices to follow.

2. Teach One Thing

So long as it doesn't conflict with the prime directive, your next goal is to teach them one thing. That could be a technique or drill they didn't know before, or how to apply a drill they already know. One thing per class. Not more! The most common mistake a junior instructor makes is to try to pack it all in. That one thing might be "control of measure" for instance, in which case you use only drills they already know to apply that skill; or the one thing might be teaching the steps of a new drill, in which case you go easy on the measure. You might sometimes get two or even three things into a basic class, but fewer is usually better.

When teaching, always, *always* start with something they can already do, and then modify it towards what you want them to do. For example, assuming an able-bodied class (but the rule holds even more strongly for disabled students), if you want them to learn a particular passing step, start with simple walking. Everyone can do that. Great. Then do the step again, but modify it towards the specific kind of stepping your style demands. An upright body, for instance: do the step again, with an imaginary bowl of single malt whisky on your head. Don't spill a drop! In this way, everything you teach them is a modification of something they can already do. This makes it much less confusing and gives them a stable base to work from. When I teach beginners to cut with a longsword, the process goes like this:

1. Swing the sword from shoulder to shoulder, standing still. Stay relaxed
2. Swing the sword from shoulder to shoulder, aiming at head height (most students do the previous step aiming at the floor, like golfers)
3. Swing the sword and follow it with a step each time. Make sure the correct foot is stepping
4. Swing the sword with the step, and adjust the line to the one Fiore shows (jaw to knee)
5. Swing the sword along the line with the step, and align the edge with the blow
6. Swing the sword along the line with the step and with the edge aligned, pausing at the moment of maximum extension.
7. Swing the sword along the line with the step and with the edge aligned, gently tapping your partner on their mask.

Everybody can do step one. And very soon, usually in under twenty minutes, everyone can do step seven safely and with acceptable technical accuracy.

You might ask, what is the "one thing" I'm trying to teach you right now? Fundamentally, I want this chapter to give you the confidence to stand up in front of a class and do your best. That's it. Please do let me know if it's worked!

3. Inspire Them
So long as it doesn't interfere with the "one thing" or the prime directive, your next goal is to inspire the students with the sense that they can do this. They can become the swordsmen they want to be. It is usually not helpful to dazzle them with your skill; it is much more useful to surprise them with how much *they* can do, with a little help. A little flash and dash goes a long

way, but as a general rule, only show them the things you want them to actually do. It should be just outside their current competence, but they should be able to touch it. One thing I cannot stand is attending a seminar in which the instructor puts on a show, however glittering. It should never be about what the teacher can do; only about what the students can do.

The most inspiring message you can give them is "you can do this." Swords are cool. Swords are aspirational. Your students probably aspire to be excellent swordsmen. Show them the path that will take them there.

4. Get Out of Their Way

And lastly, so long as it conflicts with none of the above, your job is to create an environment in which learning happens naturally, and then get out of their way; do not interfere, and let them practise. This, for most instructors, is the hardest step. You can see the errors they are making, and you want to dive in and fix them. So, the question is, when should you? I use a rule of three: see the mistake once, ignore it. See it twice, watch to see if it happens again. On the third time, make the one most basic correction. To identify that one correction, you need a hierarchy of correction.

Every time anybody does a drill or technique, no matter the level (and I include the best swordsmen you have ever seen or heard of in this), there is always something to improve. As an instructor your job is to identify one thing they should change, and bring it gently to their attention. Usually, especially in a basic class, there are lots and lots of visible errors. So the question is: which one first?

1. Start with gross choreography. If the drill needs to be done with the left foot forwards or the feed is a cut to the head, but the student is starting right foot forwards or thrusting to the belly, fix that; but with no technical correction (such as *how* they should do it).
2. If there are no gross choreographical errors, identify the

201

technical error that is interfering the most. Measure is the most common. Failing to organise the body properly behind the action (aka grounding or structure) is also very common.

3. If the measure and the timing are okay, now finally go to the internal specifics, such as their groundpath or the slight unnecessary tension in their shoulder.

Making Corrections

The goal of any correction given while the student is practising is always to improve the student's immediate performance of the drill in question. This is not the time for lengthy explanations, nor teaching them something new. This is so very context dependent that I think it's impossible to give you a comprehensive list of how and what to do, so here are some simple guidelines that will help in 99% of situations.

- Correct one thing at a time. At any given moment, the student should be focussed on only one thing. Let everything else slide while they get that one thing under control.
- Correct the biggest, most obvious mistake. Leave the rest.
- Do not make negative corrections. See what I did there? Do NOT think of a pink elephant. There it is again! Telling your student what you want them to do is okay. But use only positive statements. "Do not keep your left leg straight" is not very helpful. "Bend your left knee" is better. But best of all is to set up an exercise in which the student naturally bends their leg the way you want them to and without thinking about it, because it helps them accomplish a goal they understand. For the knees, I usually use grounding and mechanics exercises to give the student the experience of doing the exercise with the leg bent; and with it both working and feeling better, they will naturally keep doing it that way.
- Show them a couple of times how you want it done. Let them try. Show them again if needed.
- Keep verbal technical correction to an absolute minimum. It's

better to tap the offending leg to remind them than to say "bend your knee," because the language centres in the brain are not involved with making physical movements other than speech.

- Praise effort, acknowledge success.

How to Structure a Basic Class

It is very useful to establish a basic structure for your classes. It allows you to progress naturally from the simple to the complex, and it establishes a set pattern within which you can add variation without losing your way. It's good for the teacher because it creates a framework with which to construct your class plan, and it's good for the students because it makes one aspect of every class predictable, which reduces confusion.

The structure of a typical basic class in my school looks like this:

- Opening salute
- Warm up.
- Footwork/mechanics specific to the system
- In *Armizare* (Fiore) classes, we usually have a long section on dagger or wrestling related to the sword material we'll be doing
- Solo sword practice
- Pair sword practice, working from simple towards complex
- End salute.

Within each section there should be a typical structure: for example, the warm-up usually goes something like:

- Open joints
- Heat body
- Activate stabilisers.
- Establish range of motion specific to the style
- Establish smooth movement.

The content of each section is determined by the theme of the class (see "How to Write a Class Plan" below for more on theme). For beginners, it may be just teaching them some specific footwork actions, but more often it's about preparing the students to do the sword material better. Likewise for the solo sword practice, I focus on the mechanics that the students will need for the pair drills, unless mechanics are the theme. It's a good idea to structure each section with a progression from basic towards more advanced or complex actions, so as the class progresses from section to section, the material is going from simple to complex to simple again, in the form of a wave.

I could go into terrible depth on this, but because the purpose of this chapter is to help less experienced instructors gain confidence and experience in teaching basic classes, I'll restrain myself and start writing "How to Teach an Advanced Class", and possibly "How to Structure Long-Term Training".

There is no way to predict exactly who will show up to a given class, or what their interests will be, so in general I don't plan my classes at all in advance; we do it in the first few minutes of the class itself. But I've been doing this a long time, so I don't need time to think about how to put the pieces together. For less experienced instructors I highly recommend that you plan your classes beforehand, at least in broad strokes. It's also a good idea to then let everyone know what the subject will be, so they know what to expect.

How to Write a Class Plan

Start by deciding your theme: what exactly do you want the students to know or be able to do by the end of the class? If possible, ask the students what they would like to cover, giving yourself time to plan the class before it starts. Examples would be "controlling measure", "survey the content of level 2 in our curriculum", "using counterattacks", or "sword handling". Then block out the allotted time in ten minute chunks. So a ninety minute class has nine chunks. The warm-up is usually the first one or two chunks (two if you are teaching the exercises from scratch, or one if you are just running through them for students who have done them before). A good class has a clear connection between each of its parts: a story that the students can follow, with every drill related to the one before it and after it, and the theme running as a clear guideline throughout.

It is really helpful to distinguish between breadth and depth. A class will usually focus on broadening the student's knowledge base or adding depth to their skills. You must begin with breadth; beginners do not know very much to start with, so teach them something new. But once they know a few things, start helping them get better at the things they already know, rather than continuing to add new material. The trick is that adding breadth is easy, especially for an inexperienced teacher. "Here is this cool new technique" is an easy win. But it is essential that you are also able to add depth: "So you know this technique. Okay, now let's apply it in more and more difficult circumstances". I cover how to do this in detail in the chapter "Skill Development", p. 176.

Here is a sample rapier class plan for a class starting at 6 p.m. You can find each of the drills I mention on video on our syllabus wiki. I've assembled a list of them on the welcome page for this book: https://guywindsor.net/blog/theoryandpractice

Time	Content: Teaching the Attack by Cavazione to students who don't know it well.
Before class	Planning. Establish theme: attack by cavazione. Select and order exercises and drills.
18.00	Salute. Everybody must know that class has started.
18.01-18.10	Warm up. Theme requires lots of lunges, so emphasise the necessary flexibility and stability for them.

18.10-18.20	Footwork exercises, related to the theme, so emphasis on the lunge. We use the "Rapier Footwork form" as our starting point, usually.
18.20-18.30	Mechanics exercises, related to the theme. "Hunt the debole."
18.30-18.40	Teach the basic action as a technical drill.
18.40-18.50	Plate 7, emphasis on step two, the attack by cavazione. The counter shown on plate 7 (step 3 of the drill) is done by the coach in the drill, to improve the attack, not defeat it.
18.50-19.00	Plate 16, same emphasis.
19.00-19.15	Plate 15: contracavazione: using an attack by cavazione as a defence against itself.
19.15-19.30	Review the basics again. Allow free choice of which exercises to repeat.
19.30	End salute. Every class must have a clear end-point.

For students who already know the material, it's time to focus on training them to use it. A class on the same topic for a more advanced group might look like this:

Time	Training the Attack by Cavazione for students who already know it well.
Before class	Planning. Establish theme: attack by cavazione. Select and order exercises and drills.
18.00	Salute. Everybody must know that class has started.
18.01-18.10	Warm up. Theme requires lots of lunges, so emphasise the necessary flexibility and stability for them.
18.10-18.20	Footwork exercises, related to the theme, so emphasis on the lunge. We use the "Rapier Footwork form" as our starting point, usually.

18.20-18.30	Mechanics exercises, related to the theme. "Hunt the debole."
18.30-18.40	Review the basic action briefly, then straight into Plate 7, emphasis on step two, the attack by cavazione. The counter shown on plate 7 (step 3 of the drill) is done by the coach in the drill, to improve the attack, not defeat it.
18.40-18.50	Plate 7, emphasis on step two, the attack by cavazione. The counter shown on plate 7 (step 3 of the drill) is done by the coach in the drill, to improve the attack, not defeat it.
18.50-19.00	Plate 16, same emphasis.
19.00-19.15	Tactical drill: draw the attack by cavazione onto your prepared defence (eg Plate 7, 16, or allow free choice of plates the students know).
19.15-19.30	Review the material briefly. Allow free choice of which exercises to repeat.
19.30	End salute.

As you can see, the material gets more and more tactical, and with a significant degree of freedom allowed so that students can progress at their own pace.

Demonstrate, Explain, Demonstrate, Practice

Within each of these ten-minute blocks (apart from the warm up) you will usually need to show the students what to do, and then let them practise. Every keen young instructor I have ever seen shares a common failing: we all talk too much. What should be a one minute demonstration becomes a fifteen minute lecture. When teaching teachers, I use a stopwatch to time the relationship between demonstration and practice. In an exam, more than one minute of demonstration for every three of practice is an automatic fail. The students aren't there to listen to you; they are there to practise swordsmanship. If what you want them to do takes more than two minutes maximum to explain and show, it is too complicated for the class you have in front of you. If they need to learn something academic, by all means begin or end the class with a lecture, with the students seated, taking notes, and so on. But when they are standing in class, sword in hand, they need to be kept moving.

How Should You Demonstrate?

Demonstration is a critical skill for an instructor. You have to show them the drill exactly the way you want them to do it, with just enough verbal explanation that they know why they are doing it. So, show them the action, slowly and accurately. Then briefly, briefly, *briefly* explain it. Then show it to them again, one to four times, switching direction so they can see it from both sides. I quite often get asked to show the action again; I'll demonstrate it as often as I'm asked to. But I don't ask for questions. Students who need to ask a question to get the drill will do so whether I ask them to or not, so long as I have established a class environment in which they feel comfortable with me; and as I go round the class, they can ask their question without disrupting everyone else's practice. If you need to sell them on the action, do it hard and fast once with an experienced assistant, as the first demonstration. Do not screw this up! If needs be, while they are working on the previous drill, grab your assistant and go over what you'll want them to do. Never, ever, show students the drill done wrong; it's a common error in less experienced instructors to anticipate the likely errors, and advertise them to the students. I stopped doing it when I found a young student, whose English skills didn't quite catch which of the two possible versions he'd seen was the one I wanted him to do, faithfully copying the wrong one. Certainly not his fault!

Demonstration Guidelines:
- Show them exactly what you want them to do.
- Keep the roles the same: if you start out as the defender, stay that way until the end of the demonstration.

- Highlight the bit you want them to focus on, such as the footwork.
- Show it at the speed you want it done, or a bit slower. They will naturally speed up on their own.
- Focus on getting them to do it, not doing it yourself.
- If necessary, prepare the demonstration with your partner beforehand.

So, the time in each block will go something like this: 1–2 minutes of demonstration; 5–6 minutes of practice; possibly 1 minute of class correction; and 3 minutes of practice. When in doubt, talk less. Only stop the class if you need to. So how do you know when you need to?

Class Progression

The class plan almost never survives intact. A question here, a problem there, and very soon you have taken fourteen minutes for a ten minute block. You may have spotted that my example above might be twelve minutes long (two minute demonstration, six minute practice, one minute demonstration, and three minute practice). This is okay so long as you don't try to compress the rest of the material into the time left. Take your time and drop as much of your material as necessary. I have seen hundreds of class plans in my time, and I have never seen one with insufficient material for the time allowed.

How do you know when to move on, or when you've gone too far and need the class to take a step back? In short, if everyone is busy training, leave them to it. If the flow starts to clog up, the class is either unready for the current assignment, so bring them back a step; or ready to move on, so add the next action or move on to the next drill.

The flow of the class is greatly affected by the level of difficulty. Too easy, and everyone gets bored and stops. Too hard, and they get confused or frustrated, and stop. There is a sweet spot where everyone is challenged but not overwhelmed, and you know they are there when everyone is busily engaged with the content you've set them. This is of course an application of the principle of flow, which I wrote about in the chapter on The Seven Principles of Mastery.

You should stop the class for one of the following reasons only:

- Safety. Things are looking dangerous, so stop
- Obvious error: more than half the class is making the same mistake. Stop and correct the group, rather than make individual corrections
- Training flow is clogged: see above. Either move onto something harder, or step back to something simpler
- Time: classes *must* finish on time. It is disrespectful to your class to keep them past the allotted time.

What is the difference between setting the class a new, unfamiliar exercise, and setting them something that most of them know? In short, for new material, demonstrate step by step, and have them do each step before adding the next. Demonstrate for two minutes, and have them train for four. For familiar stuff, demonstrate for one minute or less, and have them practise for five.

If your class is struggling with the material, take a step back. If they are having trouble with mechanics, the best solution is to give them an exercise that requires them to make the correction in a natural way. For example, if your style requires an upright stance but the students are tending to lean forward, have them do footwork exercises with something balanced on their heads to keep them upright. Then ask them to focus on the feeling of being upright as they do it. Then have them recreate that feeling during the previous exercise that they were struggling with. If the problem is choreographical, take them back a step or two in the drill. In every case, bring them back to a place where they can do the actions reasonably well, and then build the difficulty back up.

I am working on the assumption, which may be flawed, that if you have been teaching for a short while (or are about to start), you have a basic training in your style and a comprehensive arsenal of drills and games to draw on for teaching it. If the class has a problem and you don't have the tools to fix it, the best solution is probably to change the topic of the class to something else. Or you can cheat: present the class with the problem, and ask them to come up with ways of fixing it. Don't do this with beginners (unless the problem is very simple). I use this a lot, and it works very well for getting the students involved in the development of new drills and approaches.

Different Kinds of Practice

The excellent Rory Miller talks about four different kinds of training in martial arts: teaching, training, operant conditioning, and play.

- Teaching, by which he means verbal explanation, is good for theory and background, but useless for teaching fast, hard physical responses to actions
- Training, by which he means repetition of known actions, in a low stress environment. This is better than nothing but is a very slow and insecure way to generate useful stress responses
- Operant conditioning is hard to do well, but is by far the most effective training tool for actual violence
- Play. It is very effective training to set up games that reward the desired actions.

How should teaching, training, operant conditioning and play be distributed in class? In a lecture on the history of combat, it's 99% teaching and 1% play, and that's it. In a basic martial arts class though, it should be 5% teaching, 65% training and 30% play, or thereabouts. Too much play and you lose the structure; not enough, and it becomes very ineffective. One of my most common exhortations in class is "got it? Now play with it." At the more advanced levels of training, it should be pretty much all operant conditioning and stress management. Most of this book has been about teaching and training, so I'll expand a little on operant conditioning.

Operant conditioning is the shortcut to ingraining reactions. It works by short-circuiting the OODA loop. The OODA loop occurs when you Observe something happening, Orient to it (which means you recognise it as something that is actually occurring and requires a response), Decide on your response, and finally Act on your decision. Surprise attacks generally work because you either never see them coming (no Observation), or don't recognise the threat until it's too late (you're still Orienting to it), or your Decision is too slow. It's worth noting that the more options you have, the slower you are at choosing between them (this concept is formalised as Hick's Law, which states Reaction Time = Movement Time + Processing Speed · log2 (n), where n is the number of options).

Operant condition is the process of making you jump from Observe to Act, with no Orient or Decide phase. It's done by creating the stimulus for you to observe, and then rewarding you for acting immediately on it or punishing you for not acting immediately. It's the secret sauce of all good fencing coaches and martial arts teachers (of any style), because it's how you get students to learn really fast. In a fencing context, the teacher gives the stimulus, and the student either strikes without being struck (success!), or gets hit (fail!). It's instant, real-time punishment or reward. It's amazingly effective but very hard to do, because the teacher has to be able to identify the correct response and allow it to hit them, or strike the student in the moment – and get it right every time. Because at this level, individual repetitions matter. If the student is rewarded for doing the wrong thing, even once, then that response can become ingrained.

The key to making it work is consistency first, and then intensity. If the student has time to think, you're probably not doing operant conditioning. It's also worth noting that the key thing you're training is making the desired action instantly – not necessarily doing the desired action particularly well. It's generally best to get the basic actions trained to a reasonable technical level before moving on to operant conditioning.

Teaching from a List of Requests

When I show up to teach a seminar to a group, even one I don't know at all, I always start by gathering them together and asking them what they want. Why am I there? What do they need me for? This usually generates a very varied list of interests, from a specific action ("how do I do the third play of the first master of the dagger?") to a more general problem ("how do I stop people hitting my hands when I'm fencing?"). A well-organised group will often gather the questions in advance, and email them to me. Here is an example:

"Here are some wishes for the seminar from the intermediates and class leaders:

How to train with someone who is much stronger than you? How to prove that their technique is wrong if they succeed in it only because of their strength?
How to get the most out of training with a beginner? How to benefit from this situation?
Safe ways of training and ergonomics at work. Maybe focus on shoulders? (Four people in in our club have shoulder injuries at the moment.)
Second drill *stretto* (there were some confusions about the way it should be done correctly).
Punta falsa.
Could we learn some Vadi techniques?
PS: There will be beginners attending this seminar. They know some techniques with dagger, but haven't learned all parts of the first and second drills yet."

As you can see, there is not much obvious connection between teaching the *stretto* form of second drill and teaching students to train with others that are much stronger or much less experienced than they are. I spotted a teaching opportunity. I began the seminar by discussing this list with the students present, and I explained to them the order in which we were going to do everything and why.

The first step was to identify the most general item. In this case it was ergonomics: correct form and structure are required for everything you ever do, both inside and outside the salle. So we spent quite a long time working on perfect push ups and perfect squats, and the structural foundation of Fiore's movement dynamics.

Then, using ergonomics as our base, we moved on to the skill of how to use a beginner partner to develop your own skills. This is a very common request and, given that since I came to Finland in 2001 the vast majority of the people I have crossed swords with have been my students, I have an awful lot of experience in making less experienced training partners nonetheless useful. There are basically three ways to do it: either you take advantage of their unpredictability to create genuinely random drills to train your responsiveness; or you demonstrate perfect form within the bounds of a set drill, because they will copy your every mistake; or you aim to win by the narrowest possible margin in a competitive drill. We used the standing-step drill as a good example of this last idea, and I demonstrated with someone clearly smaller and weaker than myself who had been training for about a month. By allowing her to push me to the very limit of my balance, I was able to use the minimal resistance she was able to give to practise at the edge of my skill.

The Standing-Step Drill
Stand opposite your partner, both of you in a wide stance, as if standing on parallel lines. Touch your wrists together. When you are both ready, the goal is to make your partner move a foot without moving one of your own. You must yield, avoid their pressure and destabilize them, usually by pushing them in the centre of their chest. You can allow joint locks and even strikes if appropriate.

At the next level, you are each allowed one step: you can move one foot once, in attack or defence, but on the second foot movement, you lose.

This should be played with a minimum of strain. Aim for fluid movement, like Neo avoiding bullets in the Matrix, not solid resistance. You can see it on video here: http://www.swordschool.com/wiki/index.php/Standing_Step_drill

This introduced the idea of customizing your actions to the specific training partner that you have, and in this case how, without being dramatically more skilful, you can train a beginner out of using their superior strength. There is nothing wrong with strength: strength is good, skill is better, and strength applied skilfully is best of all. The trick, of course, is to make it so that their action fails if they stiffen up, but their action succeeds if they execute it in a relaxed way. They will only learn to let go of their strength if they don't need it. We used the third and fourth plays of the first master of the dagger as our example plays for this exercise, because most students already knew them well. I then had them all look for actions that made them tense up. This was in order to better understand the problem of relying on strength and, within the context of those actions, focus on using only the minimum necessary force.

So with ergonomics underpinning all, and focussed experience in working usefully with the beginner and working usefully with a much stronger partner, we can then address the system-specific technical requests.

We started with the cutting drill, emphasizing shoulder stabilization from the perfect push-ups, and I spotted and corrected some branch-wide errors. From there we went into first drill and used that as the basis for working on the *punta falsa*. At this stage those that had difficulty with the basic drill were separated out, and they worked on that. We needed to make sure that the mechanics of the *punta falsa* were clearly understood, which our ergonomics study had prepared us for. Then the two groups were put back together. The seniors were required to make sure that the circumstances were correct, when they attacked and the blades met, for the defender's set response; and when they defended they had to respond correctly to the exact conditions of the blade relationship that actually occurred. This made them work on parts one and two of the training with beginners' theory above.

From there we went into second drill and built the *stretto* form of it step-by-step from the basic form. Again, those that didn't know the basic form were taught that, and those that did know it learned the more difficult *stretto* version. This was classic, straightforward teaching of basic drills from the set syllabus. The trick was to connect them explicitly to the foundational skills we worked on before: namely, ergonomics, using beginners, and dealing with stronger partners. Of course the *stretto* forms of the drills explicitly deal with resistant partners, and so fit nicely with the theme.

By finishing up with the *stretto* form of second drill, the *zogho stretto* situation had been introduced, and so it was easy to segue into spending the last hour working on Vadi's solutions to the *zogho stretto*, and why they differ from Fiore's.

To summarize, this is the process of teaching from a list of requests:

- identify the most generally applicable concept and start with that;

- take each request in order of specificity, from most generally applicable to most specific;
- organize the parts into a logical sequence, paying particular attention to the connections between the items on your list; and
- make the organization of the material part of the lesson, so that the students can see how their requests are being dealt with.

To do this on the fly with no advance warning and taking up less than five minutes of class time requires a deep knowledge of your material, and a lot of experience as a teacher. But the principle of organising a coherent class is always the same: there should be a narrative thread that runs from start to finish, and every drill should build on the one before it. The class should always finish with a review, and with time for the students to reorder the material, play with it and make it their own.

How Do You Get Your Own Training Done?

Given that very few people who lead classes get paid for their time, it is unfair to expect you to sacrifice all your training time to running classes. So we should look at when and how you can incorporate your own practice into the class. One such technique is to join the group, have everyone train in two straight lines and, when it's time to change partners, you hold the corner and everyone else shifts one place to their right. The person you just trained with goes across to your right (or waits out one turn if there's an odd number in class including you). This is okay, but rather limited.

You can also treat every demonstration as training: pay close attention to your assistant, and pull them up on any errors. Never assume that they are doing it right.

However, if you have a mixed-level class (and most classes are, in my experience), there are great opportunities to train without anyone feeling left out. The pattern of a mixed level class should go:

Everyone together, with seniors helping juniors.

Juniors and seniors split into groups – juniors practice what they just learned, and seniors do something at their level.

Back together, but this time seniors get to play a little, taking advantage of the junior's predictability or beginner's unpredictability.

Repeat from step one.

Every time you get to step two, given that the juniors have all had some personal attention, you can join in the more advanced group without guilt. Just make sure the class is safe, and keep an eye on the time. You can of course delegate one of the more experienced students to supervise the juniors and keep time while you're training.

The basic goal is that everyone in class gets something they can do and something they can almost do, and that the students at various levels learn to value each other.

Using Beginners

Beginners are the future of any martial art, and the best learning environment is when you are the least knowledgeable person in the room; anyone you train with can teach you something. It is more difficult to keep learning when you are surrounded by relative beginners. When I moved to Finland in 2001, I was – by a mile – the most experienced practitioner of European swordsmanship in the country. Literally everyone I crossed longswords with knew less about the subject than I did. This could have easily led to stagnation, but I managed to keep learning through the following ways.

I cross-trained 3–4 times per week in other martial arts, one-on-one with senior instructors – basically trading classes. The potential for contaminating my interpretation was huge, but the upside was I developed a lot as a martial artist.

I travelled a lot to international events, paying for it by teaching classes there. I treated these trips mostly as recruitment: when I saw an instructor I thought my students and I could learn from, I hired them over to teach seminars. We averaged about three such seminars per year.

I learned how to train usefully with beginners.

The last step is the critical one here. I will summarise the approach below for students about to work with beginners, then describe the class step-by-step as a potential class plan for instructors facing this perennial problem.

Recall the rule of beginners: show it to them right a thousand times, and they will eventually copy it correctly. Show it to them wrong once, and they will copy it perfectly first time. (I mean no disrespect. This is just true, and I've never seen a beginner for whom it wasn't.) So having beginners around demands that your every action is as perfect as you can make it. No pressure then.

Use the drill for your own purposes. One of the things beginners have to learn eventually is the terminology of the art. So on the beginners course we do things like call out the names of the steps (*accrescere, discrescere, passare, tornare,* etc.) and they have to do the named step. For more experienced students in the same class this could be unimaginably tedious, but should not be: they are expected to work at their own level. So while they are all doing the same thing, some are working on remembering the terms; some are working on perfecting their mechanics; and some are working through possible applications, from power generation, to avoidance, to specific plays.

In pair drills, the beginner will naturally get parts of it wrong. Excellent. A genuine randomiser! The attack may be too strong, too far away, too close, in the wrong line – anything. And of course your job is to effortlessly and spontaneously adapt the drill to the specific conditions of the attack you get, not the one you expect. This demands 100% focus on what is happening. And when it is your turn to do what they just attempted, you have to demonstrate it perfectly according to the drill, of course.

Your training alternates between 100% perfect tactical choices in real time, and 100% perfect mechanics in your own time. Sounds like 100% perfect training, no? You should also note the following:

- The strike is never "wrong": you get hit because you failed to defend. But the attack can always be improved
- Your correction of the attack will be much more convincing if it comes after the attack has failed than after it succeeded (that is, after you just got hit)
- Coach by modelling, not explaining. Beginners are not stupid: they are just unskilled. They need opportunities to practise, not a lecture
- This kind of training demands 100% focus on the specifics of the attack that you get, not the one you expect.

When training with beginners, you have an opportunity to go deep, making a few actions better. But you have less chance to go wide, using a broader range of actions (because this will bewilder the already overwhelmed beginner). When paired with more experienced students, you could take the chance to go wide if it doesn't conflict with the overall class goals.

So relish the influx of new perfection-demanding random generators, and relish the fact that in a decade or two, they may well be vastly better at this than you are now; but they will always remember and be grateful for the help you gave them when they were starting out. You may be helping to train the next Bruce Lee, Aldo Nadi, or even Fiore dei Liberi.

What Happens if There's an Accident?

Swordsmanship training is inherently dangerous. Accidents will happen. Your job is to make sure that they happen as seldom as possible. There is a fundamental difference between being responsible and being culpable. While students are under your care, you are responsible for their safety. Provided you stick to the syllabus and safety guidelines of your school or club and behave responsibly, you are not *culpable* even if you are the one *responsible*.

Before class even starts, there should be at least the following things in place: a first aid kit (check it now!), someone present who is trained in first aid (ideally everyone who ever leads a class is so trained), and a working phone in case of an emergency.

What should you do if? :

You see a student sitting out? Ask them what's wrong, and help them if needed. They may just be tired, or may have been hit badly but did not want to make a fuss. Always check.

There is an accident? Stay calm. Depending on the severity: either apply first aid, apply first aid and organise a lift to the nearest Accident and Emergency room, or apply first aid and call an ambulance.

On a related note, I would say that it is immoral to teach any martial art that requires actions to be repeated which will generate injury over time even if done correctly. It's just not okay to have your students do things that will reliably create (for example) joint problems in the long term. Assuming that your style is fundamentally mechanically healthy, it becomes your responsibility to make sure that the mechanics you teach are sufficiently correct that they will not injure the student. This is very hard to do, and is probably beyond the skillset of the average reader of this book, which is aimed at the less experienced instructors. So what's the solution? Keeping everything slow and gentle is the easiest way to reduce the likelihood of self-inflicted mechanical injury before your own skills are sufficient to teach actions correctly at a deep level. The lower the forces involved, the less likely an injury is to occur, and the less severe it will be. In the long term though, you should be carefully studying the ergonomics of your style. Refer back to the sections on grounding, page 58 and ahead to the "Physical Training" section, starting on page 265, for guidelines on this.

A system is inherently unsustainable if it is not clearly optimised to reduce injury. I'd actually include almost all major sports in this category. That athletes have to retire in their thirties due to injury is a pretty clear indication that the training is not sustainable. What you are looking for at every stage is an emphasis on long-term health over short-term achievements.

COMMON PROBLEMS
Disruptive Questions
You have a student asking too many derailing questions. Tell them to ask them after class. If they persist in talking too much, ask them privately not to. One student had this problem, so I bet him 50 push-ups he couldn't get to the end of class without talking. He won. I did the push-ups. He said "I get it," and the problem was solved.

Your Students Know More Than You Do
Of course it often happens that a class session may have students who have more experience than the person in charge, so how do you teach those people who are already ahead of you? This is quite daunting for the inexperienced, but just remember your prime directive and try some of these key phrases:

- "Add a degree of freedom to that"
- "Coach for the first two passes then do the drill competitively"
- "How's your grounding?"

An Unresponsive Class
This can be hell. And it is especially difficult with a class of people you don't know. It is very easy to let yourself spiral out of control trying to get a reaction out of them. I suggest the following instead: get them playing a game as a group. Try the "glove game," for example, which works in any style. The rules are:

1. Everybody has to keep moving
2. Throw two gloves into the class
3. Students can pick up gloves from the floor, and have to hit

other students on the back with them. If you are hit on the back, you're out

4. Anyone holding a glove can also be knocked out of the game by being tapped on the back with a hand
5. If you're holding a glove and are knocked out, you throw the glove away
6. If it's safe with your students, allow disarms.

You can also get them to plan the class they want: gather them round in a circle and ask them what they want to learn or practise today, then run the class accordingly. Above all, don't take it personally. You're not an entertainer. If they don't want to be there, they can leave.

"Hopeless" Students

There are some people who find even the most basic actions or sequences incredibly difficult to learn. If you have someone like that in your class, here are some points to remember:

They can walk and talk. These are both fantastically complicated skills. So they probably *can* learn swordsmanship. You just have to help them figure out how.

Reduce complexity as far as possible. For example, give them sword exercises they can do standing still.

If possible, assign a different senior student to help this person every time the class moves on.

Keep rotating the class pairings, so that nobody gets stuck with them, and they don't feel like they are holding someone back.

Praise their effort. Tell them that progress will come.

Suggest taking a short video of them now, which nobody will look at yet, and another video of them doing the same exercises in three or six months' time. Watch the two clips side by side, together with the student, to give you both a clear sense of their progress. They will probably be amazed by the difference.

Aggressive or Unsafe Students

They do exist, and it can be hard to get through to them that their behaviour is unacceptable. Let me remind you though of the prime directive. Your first and highest responsibility is to the wellbeing of your students. So you must be able to ask a person to sit out an exercise, or even leave the class. I have had many senior students with the physical competence to teach great classes, but whose promotion to teaching has been delayed while we worked on their ability to take command when necessary. Age can also be a factor; very young students (under 20) learning to run classes can find it especially hard to command older students. It is well worth modelling this situation (as you would model accidents in a first aid class), and actually practise asking a person to leave. You will have the backing of your other students, because nobody wants to train with an unsafe person. If you have any doubts on this score, appoint a back-up person, someone you trust, whose job in class is to back you up if you need to confront a student.

"Confront" is a bad word. If this situation arises, do everything you can to let the person in question save face. Take them quietly aside and gently remonstrate; if that doesn't work, take them aside again and ask them to leave. Have your backup person standing next to you when you do it, but ideally nobody else in class should even be aware that someone has been expelled. Of course, if their actions have been obvious and public, you need to face them down. But again, leave them their pride, and let them leave in peace.

Dojo Busting

Back in the bad old days of martial arts, "dojo busting" was quite common. People would go round challenging martial arts teachers to fight. If the teacher lost, all their students would leave them and join the school of the dojo buster. When I opened my school, I was concerned that it might happen to me, and I'd either kill someone or lose my school. It never did happen, and

I've not heard of it happening in real life in the last twenty years. But I asked a senior Finnish martial arts teacher about it, and his answer was simple: if someone comes dojo busting, just ask them to leave. If they don't, call the police. Good advice.

Defining Success

It only remains to define success. In order of importance, your basic class was successful if:

- There were no injuries
- Everyone was busy
- They ended class better than they started it
- The theme goal was met.

Perhaps the most common problem that inexperienced instructors face it is that they are not sure whether they have the right to teach anything. I don't see it like that, and never have. Instead, I ask this question: "is this group of people better off with me, or without me? With my classes, or without?" Most of what we teach, most of the time, is at least somewhat wrong. This is entirely normal, and is true at every level in just about every field worth studying. What matters is whether you and your group *get better*. Whether they improve faster with your help than without it. So don't ask yourself the question "could Guy teach this class better?" Or "could Jake Norwood teach this class better?" Because unless Jake or I are standing right there ready to teach, it's irrelevant.

The question is only "does this class benefit from my being here and am I doing my best to serve them?" Your first few classes will be a horrible mess compared to your thousandth. But they will probably also be pretty bloody good compared to what would happen without you. We have a system in place in my school to help less experienced teachers learn. Simply, after any class, the teacher's peers get together and, starting with the least experienced, praise two aspects of the teacher's class (e.g.

you kept them moving very well; your demonstration of drill X was very clear) and point out one thing that could have been better (e.g. your explanation of X went on too long). It's at least as important to say what went well as it is to say what could have been better.

Teaching is a skill. You learn it by doing. So get to work!

Further Reading

Two of the best books I've read on the subject of teaching physical arts are *The Inner Game of Tennis*, by Timothy Gallwey, and *Fencing and the Master*, by László Szabó. I have also been heavily influenced in the way I teach by reading *Thinking, Fast and Slow*, by Daniel Kahneman, and *The Art of Learning*, by Josh Waitzkin. I would also highly recommend the British Academy of Fencing's coaches' courses. I know that most of my readers aren't interested in modern sport fencing, and neither am I; but it's the best coach training I've ever come across.

HOW TO TEACH AN
INDIVIDUAL LESSON

Individual lessons, where you help one student at a time, are usually more about coaching (getting already known actions to work) rather than teaching new material. In an individual lesson, the coach should create an environment in which the desired behaviour results in the student striking, and undesired behaviour results in the student being struck.

You don't have to be technically superior to your students to run a good class, but you do need a high level of skill to give a good lesson to an individual. Coaching requires the highest levels of technical skill because you have to be in sufficient control of the situation that you allow yourself to be hit when the student has done what you want, but whenever their action is undesired, it must fail and you must strike. This way the student learns very, very quickly, because the environment they are in makes learning and improving absolutely natural.

As with all high level skills, it's best to build up to it in stages. I've broken it down into four steps for you. You can do some of this work within a class context, but be careful not to spend too much time with one student if there is a class running. It's much better to schedule the individual lessons separately.

1) Verbal Correction of a Solo Drill.
The "student" does one iteration of a solo drill, and the "coach" watches it and makes one verbal correction. The student then

repeats the drill, applying the correction. See if there is an improvement. When coaching with your voice, use single words to draw the student's attention to specific details (e.g. "parry" or "foot"). Where possible, avoid "good" or "bad" type judgement statements; reserve those for praise at the end of the lesson. Praise is useful, necessary even, but must always be sincere. Even if the student totally screwed up the lesson, find something to praise. And always focus on their efforts, not their accomplishments.

2) Prescribe a Drill to Improve a Solo Drill.

The same set-up as above, but this time the coach has to prescribe a specific exercise to be done – either solo or with the coach – to improve the solo drill. Then the solo drill should be done again to see whether the coach's prescription worked. Ideally, the prescription is followed there and then, but you can also use this exercise to set homework for the student.

3) Improve One Step of a Specific Pair Drill.

Take a basic drill and improve the student's execution of one step of it. Set it up so that if the action is improving, the student succeeds; if not, they fail. Adjust the difficulty level such that the student usually succeeds, but only by working at their upper limit.

For example, take a drill beginning with a simple attack from wide measure. The trick is to get it better and better, and faster and faster, by having the student beat the coach's parry. The parry should be done such that it creates a closing window that the attack should just sneak through.

What we have covered so far in this chapter is the bare bones of how to coach, but you can apply this kind of approach to any class situation in which you are a student. You don't have to be giving individual lessons all the time to learn how to do it. Any time you are paired off with a student of lower skill, make it your aim to raise your partner's skill level without actually giving them a formal lesson. Just subtly modify what you do so that they naturally improve. (This is high level stuff!)

4) Plan a Short Technical Individual Lesson Lasting 6–7 Minutes.

This is plenty of time to create a clear improvement. The process is similar to what you have already done. In the individual lesson you should:

- Identify or illustrate the problem (get the student to show you it, not describe it)
- Identify the cause of the problem (usually not what the student thinks it is!)
- Prescribe a specific drill or exercise
- Assess the results. If good, go to the next level; if not good, go back to identify the cause of the problem
- Increase the pressure under which the student performs the corrected action.

This begs the question of diagnosis: how do you know what problem to solve, or find the cause of any difficulty? This is one area where experience counts more than anything else, but you gain that experience by trying to improve students as systematically as possible and noting what works with which problems. In general, I ask this question and then use the following checklist: is the problem technical or tactical?

If technical:
- Is the measure correct? If not, the problem is in the feet. Fix the footwork
- Is the timing correct? If not, teach them the proper rhythm of the action
- Is the structure correct? Are they grounding properly, and are they aligning their strength to their partner's weakness?

If the problem is tactical:

• Give a tactical lesson: improving the student's choice of action, rather than the action itself. Adding a degree of freedom is of course the usual tool: in circumstance a), do this; in b), do that. You, the coach, then set up the circumstances such that you control when a) or b) occur.

Common Problems:

The main challenges most students face when starting to give individual lessons are:

• reaction times, and
• teaching a student who is stronger than you.

Neither of these are easy to overcome, so expect it to take a lot of work.

Reaction times are a tough nut to crack. Basically, if you can't see the student's error in time, you can't give the lesson. So you must either slow the lesson down to give you more time, or learn to read the error earlier in the student's action. Work on your foresight! (See page 283 for this.)

It is technically challenging to teach a student who is stronger than you are, because you have to make their strength insufficient. This is not too difficult when you are sword against sword, but is much more difficult when grappling. In essence, you need to give the student a reason to use correct technique (i.e. insufficient accuracy leads to being hit). There is no shortcut to this; you just have to have a sufficiently deep technical skill to make it work.

How to Get Your Coaching Practice In:

You can practise these coaching skills in a normal class where you are not the teacher. In any pair arrangement, one of the following will be true:

Your skill > your partner's: subtly tweak what you do to bring out their best.

Your skill < your partner's: ask for a (non verbal!) lesson on the drill in question. Or simply study how they do it.

Your skill = your partner's: play with the drill.

In all cases, be careful not to disrupt the lesson.

I would recommend getting significant experience with teaching basic classes, and by coaching solo drills and simple drills (steps 1–3 above), before trying to teach an in-depth individual lesson. In my experience, it's the highest expression of the art. Good luck!

TOURNAMENTS

Sport longsword is not a new phenomenon. Meyer, 1570. This image courtesy of Adelheid Zimmerman of Draupnir Press.

I love the HMA tournament scene. This will come as a surprise to many people, because I am not really involved with it in any direct way. In fact, I have seen people referring to me as "anti-tournament." (I wrote about this in *Swordfighting*, pages 82–83.) Nothing could be further from the truth. Just because I am not personally interested in entering or organising tournaments, it does not mean that I don't understand their value.

My own tournament life extended from 1987, when I entered my first foil tournament, through to 2002, when I entered (and won) a rapier tournament in Italy. The sport-fencing scene is especially tournament dominated. It is fair to say that tournaments are the only meaningful measure of success in that sport (and most others). I was never a great sport fencer, but I won a local competition or two, and ended up in the last eight in sabre at the Scottish Universities tournament in 1993. Tournaments were great if you did well; but it was equally possible that you would travel for hours, wait around for hours, get a few bouts in, wait for more hours while your more successful teammates got to fence, and then travel for hours back home again. The ratio of time spent to fights fought always bugged me. You got far more bouts in far less time in less formal environments.

At high school I was involved in organising our annual tournament, and so I have a pretty good idea what a huge amount of work it is to set up and run a tournament. That's why I've never organised an open tournament in Finland; it's way too much work for something I'm only peripherally interested in. But I do encourage my students worldwide to enter tournaments if they are interested, and it's always nice to see a current or past student doing well in that environment.

As with every training environment, tournaments have their limitations.

1. They serve no useful research purpose, unless you are studying historical tournament rule sets and applying them. "It works/doesn't work in tournaments" is just not a relevant statement when considering martial arts that have been developed for other purposes

2. They privilege the gifted. In any sport, there is an optimum body type. As the tournament scene develops and the stakes get higher, we will start to see the different rule sets privileging certain body types. Read *The Sports Gene* by David Epstein for detailed information on this phenomenon

3. They are good for highlighting areas of weakness, but do not provide an ideal environment for fixing those weaknesses.

From a training perspective, it's more useful to be able to stop testing and start fixing immediately

4. They reward outcome over process. The people who "succeed" are by definition winning specific bouts. It doesn't take into account how much they have improved or how hard they have worked. With a long enough head start, somebody could (in theory at least) win many tournaments without improving at all!

But the tournament scene has many benefits, too.

1. It provides a sense of community for a very widely distributed group of like-minded people. Other events do this too, but the advantage of the tournament scene is that anyone can show up and take part, with any background, and every competitor is (at least in theory) equal and welcome. Your club or style don't determine your value

2. It provides external validation for fencers who need it. This can hurt as much as it helps, because poor performance on the day can be hugely discouraging. In the long run, internal validation is much better, but most fencers go through a stage of needing to test themselves, and tournaments provide one straightforward way to do that

3. It creates an easy-to-explain model of what we do for the casually curious. One of the most common questions I get asked is "do you have tournaments?" If I don't want to explain exactly what I really do, then I can just say "yes, there's a big international circuit now, though it's not really my focus." It saves me so much time. Tournaments also attracts media attention, because everyone understands them.

4. It creates a much, much bigger market of fencers with particular equipment needs: the current availability of (for example) longsword free-fencing kit is directly due to the tournament circuit that has developed. This is huge: those of us doing HMA in the early 1990s will remember that our

equipment was a hodgepodge of sport fencing kit and some dodgy re-enactment or SCA gear. Without sport fencing, there would have been no masks. How much would that have slowed our progress?

5. It provides training opportunities for working under pressure, and developing attributes such as timing, measure, speed and tactical sense

6. It demonstrates the effect of rule sets. One of the hardest things to explain to beginners is how much rule sets affect behaviour. Tournaments have clearly defined and published rule sets, and that determines more than any other factor what kind of actions work

7. Tournaments shine a spotlight on diversity. Who, exactly, is really welcome?

8. Most people like the idea of tournaments to give them something to train towards. So the sport-HMA scene is always going to attract lots and lots of people. Excellent. For me and many others in the early '90s, sport fencing (and the SCA for many of my friends) provided our first entry into the sword world, but in the end proved frustrating. It was not real enough. So we left to create HMA from scratch. The tournament scene provides a similar easy-entry route into the sword world. I look at the sport-HMA scene as a massive pool of potential future historically-minded HMA students and teachers.

Training for Tournaments

Let's briefly dispense with the question of how to win tournaments, and then look at how to get the most out of them, win or lose. Fair warning: to many readers, the method for winning tournaments looks like "legal cheating." I'm including it here for the sake of completeness, not because I particularly like it.

All world-class tournament competitors in low-contact combat sports use this method to succeed in tournaments. Whether you want to treat your tournament career like this is a whole other question, but, at the top level, everybody is doing this because it's the only method that works.

1. Analyse the Rules

Analyse the rule sets, equipment, and every other aspect of the tournament environment. Your job is to score more points than your opponent in that environment *and that's it*. You are not there to look good, be popular, or gain respect. You are there to win, and win only, according to the rules that are set.

Here's an example of this in action: in 1999 Tim Ferriss, with a couple of months of preparation, won the Chinese kickboxing US national championship. He did this only because he found a loophole in the rules that allowed him to win by dehydrating himself before weigh-in down to 165 lb, rehydrate back up to over 180 lb between weigh-in and the tournament, and, avoiding kicking and punching altogether, pick up his much lighter opponents and throw them out of the ring. Did he beautifully represent the spirit of the Art? No. (In the article I link to, he writes about "how to win at kickboxing the wrong way"!) Did he win? Yes.

Here's another example: Johan Harmenberg, who pretty much single-handedly destroyed sport fencing (in my eyes at least). He did this by ignoring conventions and analysing the rules to figure out a new and more effective way to score and not get scored on with the electronic scoring apparatus. He got from nowhere to World Champion and Olympic Champion in a few years. I highly recommend his book *Epee 2.0*, which recounts the details of how he did it. Did he beautifully represent the spirit of the Art? No. Did he win? Yes.

2. Create An Area of Excellence

Pick one, or at maximum two actions that lead to you striking, and train the hell out of them. Start with the action itself, and then work back to create the situation in which you can pull it off. Harmenberg's action was the parry sixte-riposte. Ferriss' was throwing people out of the ring (he has a background in judo and college wrestling). In every match, your only job is to lead your opponent into your area of excellence, where you can beat them. You need one world-class action in your repertoire – but only one, and it should suit your physical and mental strengths. Don't waste time getting good at things you are not going to get world-class at. Will you beautifully represent the spirit of the Art? No. Will you win? Maybe.

3. Analyse Your Likely Opponents

Who are the few individuals you are most likely to be beaten by? Go over every second of their tournament footage and analyse exactly what they are doing to win. What is their area of excellence? Your job now is to train ways to keep them out of their area of excellence, and lead them into yours. Your coach's job is to model their behaviour to give you the opportunity to train against their specific game. For lower ranked opponents, you have to rely on your general skill at leading people into your area of excellence; you can't train specifically against more than a few opponents, there just isn't enough time.

Will you beautifully represent the spirit of the Art? No. Will you win? Probably.

The problem of course is that all world-class competitors are doing the same thing: they're analysing you (once you become successful enough to become a threat and so warrant attention). This is why every now and then a complete outsider comes out of nowhere and wins: he or she has prepared to fight the best; but the best have never seen his or her one area of excellence before.

This process is simple. But it is not easy. And, personally, I am much more interested in the spirit of the Art. Which is why I don't normally train students for tournaments, but will if I'm asked to. I have the necessary skill set, but it's not a terribly interesting field for me.

I would also note here that I do not think that everyone should train like this for tournaments; there are plenty of ways to have fun and learn useful things from tournaments without going all-out to win them. This might seem like cheating, but the beauty of tournaments is that they have a very clear rule set. So long as you do not break the rules, you are by definition not cheating.

Further Reading

The best books on this subject that I'm aware of are Josh Waitzkin's *The Art of Learning*, which details how he went from chess champion to world champion in push-hands (the moment when he realised that the one opponent he had trained to beat was now in a different weight class was priceless. As was the moment when he realised that the ring was now a tad smaller), and the aforementioned Johan Harmenberg's *Epee 2.0*.

Preparing for Tournaments

Other than the "how to win" stuff above, you will benefit from the following preparations:

1. Get fit. Really fit. Tournaments are usually very long days with lots of waiting about, and lots of fencing. And the most important matches tend to come at the end. So anything you can do to improve your core fitness (see the "Physical Training" and "Nutrition" chapters for details on this) is a good thing
2. Make sure your regular training has a strong freeplay component. You should probably be doing some freeplay in every class, either as a diagnostic tool during class or as a blowing off steam exercise at the end of class, or both
3. Fence with as many different people as possible. Go to other clubs if you can, and fence with anyone who will let you.

Get your club to organise regular fencing meets with other clubs, as informal or formal as you like

4. Actively seek out fencers who can beat you. The more you get hit, the more you will learn. Treat fencing less experienced students as a necessary "paying it forward", but emphasise fencing your superiors. If you are fencing with a beginner, see what you can do to handicap yourself. Limit yourself to specific actions, perhaps

5. Create artificial restrictions. We use our *Audatia* decks for this: have the fencers pick a guard card, for example, which determines their start position; or a technique card, which determines the only action they can score with

6. Above all, get out of your comfort zone. Get good at dealing with stressful situations.

How to Use Tournaments in Your Training

Now that we've had a look at how to *win* tournaments, and looked a little at how to train for them, let's have a look at how to *use* tournaments – a topic that is probably much more interesting to most of my readers.

The tournament scene is good for many things, as we saw earlier. In terms of your fencing development, entering tournaments can be a really useful step along the path. This is because it exposes you to fencing styles outside your usual training environment, and it gives you an opportunity to train under a degree of pressure. If you really care about winning, that pressure can be extreme. Suddenly all your careful technical training flies out of the window, and you hang onto the sword for dear life and swing like a fool (I speak from personal experience). This is normal, and if you have followed the steps in the "Skill Development" chapter, you should find yourself able to relax a bit, because it's actually not that much different from normal training. Breathe, relax, and focus on your opponent.

You will get the best results by changing the way you think about the tournament itself. You must believe in your heart of hearts that you are there to give your opponents a tough fight. That's it. Make it as difficult as possible for them. If it's your first tournament and you are up against a veteran fighter, a tough fight might be one where you last three seconds longer than your opponent expected. Or it may be your tenth tournament, and your opponent is a beginner; you can effortlessly dominate them, and they will have a tough fight.

The point is, you can *always* succeed if that's your goal. Winning a specific bout, pool, or match is not 100% under your control. You may slip at the last moment. Your opponent may have trained under a really good coach just to beat you. The judges might be blind, biased, or just plain incompetent. You don't control any of that. But if you can finish every bout and say to yourself honestly "I gave them the toughest fight I could," you can succeed every time. And success is the heart of training.

You can also put tournaments to work for you in terms of technical development. Can you create the circumstances for a specific technical action? Can you go into a bout and count it a success if you manage to create the opening, whether you pull off the technique or not? Let's say the technique you're working on requires your opponent to make a parry from their left and take their point offline. Some opponents will give that to you naturally; others will have to be forced into it. Creating the opening is at least as difficult as getting the technique it exploits to work, and it's a necessary pre-condition. Tournaments are a great place to find non-compliant people you can practise that on.

You will get even more rewarding results (though might not get so high in the rankings) by aiming to give your opponent the best fencing match of their life. What can you do to bring out their most interesting moves onto your most stylish responses? Can you make Fiore, Ringeck, Fabris, Girard or Carranza come alive in the arena? You will rarely succeed because it is a very hard thing to do, but cast success and failure in these terms: were you able to make the quality of the fencing your primary goal, and hold to that throughout the bout?

In each case, the key skill is to make success or failure a matter completely under your control. No external factors are involved. You will still fail a lot, but you can improve very quickly regardless of the quality of the opponents, the rule set or any other external factor.

One of the best fencing matches I ever had was the first time I fenced Christian Tobler. We found a quiet space in a rackets court at the 2006 WMAW event in Dallas, and set to. We were so absorbed in what we were doing that we never even noticed that the spectators area filled up with students as word got round. I think it was a burst of applause that caught our attention. We continued until we were both thoroughly satisfied. I know he hit me quite a bit; I'm pretty sure I hit him too.

When I got home I told my students about it. One of them asked "Who won?"

I was baffled for a moment, then replied: "We did."

ATTRIBUTE TRAINING: HEALTH, STRENGTH, SPEED

There is nothing particularly historical, artistic, or even martial about this section. I should also point out that I am neither a doctor, a physiotherapist, nor a sports coach. But several of my test readers asked for this section to be added to the book, so here it is: the basic principles of physical training, as I understand and apply them. I'll add some suggested reading at the end if you want to dig deeper. I have also added a guide to breathing exercises, because I think they are critically important for long-term training. Just be aware that they are not HMA at all!

I think of health as a three-legged stool. The legs are: activity, nutrition and sleep. Take away any one of those, and eventually the stool will fall. Perhaps the most common mistake I see people making is to only consider activity when they think about training, so I'm going to put sleep and nutrition first!

SLEEP

We live in an absurdly sleep-deprived culture. When someone tells you they pulled an all-nighter, you should not be impressed by their dedication: you should be appalled at their lack of organisation and understanding of basic health principles. It is simply childish to think of staying up late as some kind of cool thing to do. Read Matthew Walker's *Why We Sleep: the New Science of Sleep and Dreams* if you don't believe me.

There are three kinds of sleep: REM (Rapid Eye Movement, dream sleep, in which your brain is very active), light sleep, and deep sleep. Your body and brain cycle through these in a rhythm that takes usually about 90 minutes, with deep sleep usually coming towards the end of that. You will need about four full cycles per night, minimum. How do you know if you're getting enough sleep? If you wake up naturally without your alarm clock, and if you are not tired during the day, then you are sleeping enough. Otherwise, you're not. Almost everyone (according to Walker at least, and he should know) needs about eight hours. If you suffer from any kind of insomnia, go to the doctor. Avoid sleeping pills, obviously, but there are many kinds of sleep problems, and many of them are easily treated. If you snore, get yourself checked for sleep apnea. I had it for a long time, and eventually went to the doctor and had it treated with a minor surgery. I suffered the worst sore throat ever for about three weeks, but within a couple of months the difference in my energy levels was incredible thanks to improved quality of sleep. Friends of mine with apnea caused by being fat (when the muscles of the neck relax in sleep, the weight of the fat in their neck literally crushes their airway, so they choke and wake up) have found that a CPAP machine (continuous positive pressure; literally pushing air into the lungs, keeping the trachea open) has made a gigantic difference. Help is available.

The basic principles of getting enough sleep are:
- Go to bed and get up at the same time every day. Earlier to bed is better: my Grandma used to say that "one before eleven is worth two after seven," and as usual, she was right
- Avoid caffeine (for at least six hours before bedtime). Using a sleep tracker I was able to confirm my suspicion that simply not having tea or coffee after 2 p.m. made an enormous difference – not to the total amount of sleep I was getting, but to the amount of deep sleep
- Avoid alcohol (for at least four hours before bedtime). Again with the sleep tracker, I found that a couple of glasses of wine made no difference to sleep quality, so long as the alcohol was out of my system before going to bed
- Avoid eating a heavy meal (for at least three hours before bedtime). This makes a huge difference, I find. If my body is working on digesting a big meal, my heart rate remains much higher all night than if I go to bed long after the last calorie went in
- Avoid screens for at least an hour before bedtime. If you absolutely must be using a screen, on an iOS device enable Night Shift, or use F.lux or something similar to adjust the wavelengths of light your screen emits
- Avoid social media for at least an hour before bedtime. There is nothing more likely to keep you awake than some foolish thing said on the internet. Remember that social media companies hire really clever people whose only job is to get and keep your attention; and nothing says you're not paying attention like falling asleep
- Keep your bedroom as dark as possible: use black-out curtains, and cover or switch off any sources of light pollution such as

luminous clocks or devices with LED lights on them. This to me is one of the hardest things to get right when travelling. One hotel room I stayed in had an illuminated light switch in the middle of the headboard of the bed. I had to get my old boarding pass out and stick it over the damn thing with chewing gum to get any sleep

- Create a wind-down ritual that persuades your body that it will be going to sleep soon. Keep it gentle. I find reading a good novel is hopeless, because I stay up late to get to the next bit, but reading a fairly dull but useful non-fiction book is great

- Get a decent mattress. It's worth it. You literally cannot put a price on sleep.

I also use naps extensively. If your schedule allows it, cutting your night time sleep by an hour or so is okay if you get a full sleep cycle (so a solid 90 minutes of sleep) in the afternoon. Shorter naps can be helpful, but nothing replaces deep sleep. As this book is also concerned with history, I should mention that throughout most of human history artificial lighting was incredibly expensive. It is only in the last century or so that ordinary people can afford brightly lit rooms after nightfall. Thanks to Roger Ekirch's book *At Day's Close, Night in Times Past*, we know that at least some Europeans used to sleep in two blocks, with an hour or two of wakefulness in between. In the 1990s, Thomas Wehr (a psychologist) found that people who live in darkness for fourteen hours per day spontaneously develop a similar pattern, so it may be very natural. It's worth experimenting with, I think.

For a layman's overview, see the article entitled "The myth of the eight-hour sleep" by Stephanie Hegarty, published by the BBC on February 22nd 2012. http://www.bbc.co.uk/news/magazine-16964783

The key with this – as with every aspect of health habits – is to experiment carefully, and track what makes a difference *for you*.

NUTRITION

Every serious practitioner of any physical discipline is careful about what they eat. I'm not a nutritionist, but I've been living in my body for 43 years now, and paying attention for most of that time. I also read a lot. So here are my key ideas, and there's a reading list at the end of this chapter. Please bear in mind that I am not a doctor. And even if I were, I'm not *your* doctor. If you have any kind of medical issue, don't get your information from swordsmanship instructors. Do some research, and then go talk to your doctor. Clear?

In the Beginning
In the late nineties, the metabolism I inherited from my father started to kick in. When I was 21, my sister gave me a leather belt for my birthday, and I've been wearing it round my waist ever since. It started out wearing a groove into the leather at the fifth hole from the end.

When I got to Finland in 2001, what with the stress of starting the school and lots and lots of training, I ate what I wanted and stayed skinny. On a normal day, I was training for two or three hours and teaching for two or three. I had to eat every three hours or so, or Hungry Guy would appear and make everyone's life miserable. The closest I have come to murder was probably when I hadn't eaten for four hours, went to a Thai restaurant for an emergency feed, and the waiter seemed to dilly dally about getting the food on the table.

I (mis)diagnosed the problem as too-low body weight. I was about 73 kg at that point. I ate like crazy to try to put the weight on, but was too stressed and training too much to gain an ounce. Then I met Michaela in 2005 and chilled out considerably. One of the ways I knew she was The One was that within a few months of meeting her, I'd put on the 4 kg (9 lb) I was looking for. That did help with Hungry Guy, but only up to a point. I still needed to eat every four hours or so. At this point, my weight was up to 77 kg,, and I was wearing my belt at the third notch so I instituted a rule: if my weight got up to 80 kg, I'd cut out sugar and alcohol until it was back below 78 kg. Then I could eat what I want. This very often (maybe five times a week) included an entire 200 g bar of chocolate after dinner, "shared" with Michaela (she'd get maybe one row, so an eighth of it).

What with one thing and another, by April 2014 I was seriously considering adjusting the rule to anything below 80 kg is fine, but over 82 and I'd cut out sugar and alcohol. (Self-indulgent bullshit is a specialty of mine.) I was at 83 kg, and my belt was on the penultimate notch. It still has the deepest groove; it was there for a long time. I had already read Michael Pollan's *The Omnivore's Dilemma* and Gary Taubes' *Good Calories, Bad Calories*, so I should have known better. But sugar, oh, sugar; sweet heaven.

Then, on a flight to Melbourne, I read Tim Ferriss's *The Four Hour Body*. It was the final straw. There was just no way I could justify the level of sugar I was eating, especially given my family history of high blood pressure, my father's serious weight problem, and everything I had ever read on the topic of metabolism, nutrition, health and longevity (not counting the junk science rubbish that occasionally made it onto my reading list. I highly recommend *Bad Science* by Ben Goldacre to help you distinguish the good from the bad).

When I got to Australia, I decided to try the Slow Carb diet. Let me summarise it for you.

1. No fast carbs, no sugar, and no starch. No potatoes, no rice, no bread, no biscuits and no pasta – no white food except cauliflower, in other words
2. Eat the same few meals; perhaps half a dozen different dishes.
3. Don't drink calories. Avoid alcohol and sweet drinks (especially sodas, obviously, but less obviously also fruit juice)
4. Cheat one day per week. On that day, eat and drink whatever you like, as much as you like. But just one day per week.

If you think about it, rule #3 is really just the same as rule #1, rule #2 is a bit boring, and rule #4 should be optional in my opinion. What I ended up doing was basically just rule #1, and I was reasonably strict about it.

On the day I arrived in Australia, jet-lagged to hell and about to teach a four-day intensive seminar, my metabolism was still demanding I eat every 3–4 hours. So obviously, I never went anywhere without back-up chocolate. I arrived on Friday morning and started the Slow Carb diet right away. I taught from Saturday to Tuesday, five or six hours per day. Up until this point there had been no way I could get through a six hour seminar without a sugar hit in the afternoon. I'd crash about 3 p.m., sugar up to get me through to the end, and then need a large and fast dinner.

On the Monday, after teaching for three days straight, I was digging through my bag for something, and found my chocolate stash. In three days of teaching, in the most energy-demanding situation (jet-lag, long days), I had forgotten to eat in the afternoons. I was astonished.

This was because I was not spiking my blood sugar at any point, and so was not crashing. Cutting out starch and sugar proved to be a complete game-changer, because it evened out my energy demands. Please note though that I was not cutting out carbs; only fast carbs. I was still eating about eight tonnes of vegetables every day, and a lot of meat (the food in Australia is superb!).

Slow Carb, Low Carb, and Ketogenic

Let's take a moment to define a few things:

1. Slow Carb vs. Low Carb. They are very different. A classic low carb diet gives you most of your calories from fat and protein. A slow carb diet gives you a lot of carbohydrates, but all with a low glycaemic index, so you avoid the blood-sugar spike. I think any diet that tells you to steer clear of vegetables is fundamentally dangerous.
2. Ketogenic versus Low Carb. A ketogenic diet, as the name suggests, is a diet that keeps your body running on ketones instead of glucose. Ketones are created in your body from fat. It is a very high fat diet and obviously restricts carbs, but it also restricts protein. This is because protein is easily broken down into glucose, and so your body will switch back to a glucose-based energy delivery system rather than stay in a fat-based energy delivery system. Ketogenic diets are mostly used medicinally to treat children that have drug-resistant seizures. I personally would not recommend long-term ketosis, because it is very hard to do in the modern world, and there is no evidence that any human population has ever subsisted long-term on a ketogenic diet (the Inuit may be an exception, but probably not). Ketogenic diets should be further subdivided into calorie restricted (less than 1,000 per day) and unrestricted versions. The best-known proponents of the unrestricted ketosis diet are Dom D'Agostino and Peter Attia (both medical doctors). Their podcasts and websites are well worth a listen/look.

Bye-bye Hungry Guy

What I was doing in Australia was a not-terribly-strict Slow Carb diet; after class, at dinner, I quite often wolfed down a bunch of fast carbs in the form of beer and chips with my steak – that sort of thing. But breakfast and lunch were fast-carb-free. The difference in my energy levels was enough to sell me on the idea. But when I got home less than three weeks later and trod on the scales, I got a shock. I was down from 83 to 74 kg, and had not once, even once, gone hungry. My belt was back at the fifth notch, though I ate like a pig, just not starch or sugar. I was so pleased with the results that I decided to keep it up. I now hover around the 73–74 kg mark, and some days I need to tighten my belt to the sixth notch. Most incredibly, Hungry Guy has disappeared. To test this, in September 2014 I decided to see what would happen if I missed a meal or two. I had lunch on Monday at about 1 p.m.; taught class on Monday night; ate nothing when I got home; had one cup of coffee instead of breakfast on Tuesday; missed lunch; and ate dinner with the kids at 6 p.m. So, about 29 hours of not eating anything. And I was completely fine. Not even that hungry. Certainly no dizziness or feeling of weakness. Nothing associated with low blood sugar problems.

Food is Personal

Food is one of those topics that entire lifestyles can revolve around. It is a critical part of every culture; there are no culturally-neutral cuisines. Foods also tend to have deeply personal associations. My grandma's cherry pie is, I'm sorry to have to break this to you, way better than yours. Roast turkey with all the trimmings, but at Easter instead of Christmas? That would be weird, right? My brother-in-law is Jewish and my sister-in-law is Muslim, so neither are likely to be found scoffing bacon. And so on.

Just because a food is culturally mandated or culturally taboo, it does not necessarily make it healthy or unhealthy. But it does make it very hard to objectively assess whether a specific food belongs in your diet or not. Your belief in the health-giving properties of apple pie may be unfounded in medical fact.

Food is a Drug

The human body is a fantastically complicated machine, and the precise effect of any given thing on it is hard to predict. I think we can all agree that decapitation is unhealthy and breathing air is healthy, but between those two extremes, there is a massive amount of variation. For example, I once ate a lovely healthy salad with chicken at a hotel in Edinburgh, while sitting across from someone who would have been dead in 24 hours had she eaten the same. She was in the last stages of kidney failure, and the protein would have been utterly toxic to her. She died a couple of months later, having extended her life by several years by severely restricting her protein intake. So while it is important to have a good idea of what any given food tends to do to most human bodies, it is vital to know precisely what it does to your specific body. And just like with other drugs, a large part of food's effect is placebo or nocebo. Honestly believing that cyanide is good for you does not make it so; but in the normal range of foods, how you feel about what you eat has an effect on what it will do to you.

Alcohol is a good example of this. There are measurable, non-imaginary chemical effects of alcohol ingestion, but the behavioural changes brought on by intoxication are entirely cultural. It makes you gregarious, badly behaved, or whatever else it does because you are conditioned to think it will by the culture you live in. Kate Fox, social anthropologist and director of the Social Issues Research Centre, has this to say:

> In high doses, alcohol impairs our reaction times, muscle control, co-ordination, short-term memory, perceptual field, cognitive abilities and ability to speak clearly. But it does not cause us selectively to break specific social rules. It does not cause us to say, "Oi, what you lookin' at?" and start punching each other. Nor does it cause us to say, "Hey babe, fancy a shag?" and start groping each other.
>
> The effects of alcohol on behaviour are determined by cultural rules and norms, not by the chemical actions of ethanol.
>
> There is enormous cross-cultural variation in the way people behave when they drink alcohol. There are some societies (such

as the UK, the US, Australia and parts of Scandinavia) that anthropologists call "ambivalent" drinking cultures, where drinking is associated with disinhibition, aggression, promiscuity, violence and anti-social behaviour.

There are other societies (such as Latin and Mediterranean cultures in particular, but in fact the vast majority of cultures), where drinking is not associated with these undesirable behaviours – cultures where alcohol is just a morally neutral, normal, integral part of ordinary, everyday life – about on a par with, say, coffee or tea. These are known as "integrated" drinking cultures.

http://www.bbc.co.uk/news/magazine-15265317

So the effects of alcohol, and indeed many other ingestibles, are in part culturally determined.

The Problem with Doctors

Doctors, like soldiers, tend to be very conservative. If something appears to work, don't change it. Don't experiment. Because when the consequences of a failed experiment is that people die, conservatism and caution are not just advisable; they are a moral imperative. *Non nocere* (do no harm) is the essence of the Hippocratic Oath. But this conservatism can also work in reverse. It took Dr Alice Stewart decades to convince the medical establishment that it is dangerous to x-ray pregnant women; thousands of children were killed by cancers caused by in-utero irradiation *after* she had proved that it was happening. Margaret Heffernan wrote about this heartbreaking disaster in *Willful Blindness: Why We Ignore the Obvious at Our Peril*, pp. 60–67. So, just because a doctor says it's so, does not necessarily mean it is. Doctors are highly trained experts with a professional aversion to change, and they are all, every last one of them, human. It is foolish to think that doctors are infallible health gods.

So, the problem with doctors is often the patient. Doctors are not responsible for your health. You are. Doctors are professionals you hire to fix problems that are outside your competence. The person who services your car probably does not fill it up with fuel every time it runs low – you do. You don't call a plumber to flush the toilet (I hope). The point at which your competence ends and you need to call in an expert varies hugely from person to person, and domain to domain. I don't need a mechanic to check my oil level, but I never touch my car with a tool. I can change a washer in a tap, but I would not install a boiler. I don't need a doctor to diagnose a cold, or to mop my fevered brow (that's my wife's job, poor woman), but if I can't figure out what's wrong, I call in a professional.

A doctor's advice on what you should eat will tend to stick with what usually works okay for most people, and be extremely moderate. It is very unlikely to hurt you, but it may not boost your performance at all.

Be a Soldier or an Athlete

World-class athletes tend to have their diet planned down to the last grain of rice (if their diet allows rice), and meals are scheduled extremely precisely to ensure maximum performance at a single thing (running 100m OR a marathon; boxing OR wrestling) on a specific, known, future date. When the difference between Olympic gold and obscurity are measured in fractions of a percent in difference in performance, this only makes sense.

Soldiers on the other hand cannot tell in advance when they will be under fire; when they will be lumping 25 kg packs over desert hills or sprinting for cover through jungle; nor when they may be resupplied or will be living off the rations in their belt pouches for a week or even longer. So while general good nutrition is essential, and while a good quartermaster will win more battles than a good general, soldiers tend to eat what they can get when they can get it. The key skill there is tolerance for variation.

In my view, martial artists (as opposed to combat sportsmen) should follow a healthy diet, yes, but never get precious about what and when they eat. "I didn't get my organic bacon for breakfast" or "I timed my protein intake wrong" are not valid excuses for losing a fight.

A Good Story is Not Always True

Story 1: "Fat makes you fat."

Makes sense, but there is no evidence for it. Plenty of people on a high fat diet are skinny – if they also avoid sugar. Likewise "energy in, energy out". Yes, the laws of thermodynamics are absolute. But the variables of what your body does with the energy that comes in as food are huge. A friend of mine worked in a lab where they put mice on a low-calorie diet, but also injected the hormone leptin into their brains. The results, in my friend's immortal phrase: "furry tennis balls". Food is a drug. Some foods trigger fat deposition, yet other foods can trigger fat burning. The body is complex. Perhaps the most important book on this topic is *Good Calories, Bad Calories* by Gary Taubes, which demolishes once and for all the notion that it is your fat intake that controls your weight.

Story 2: "We evolved in an environment in which certain foods were available; reproducing that (e.g. the Paleo diet) must be healthier, because it's the diet we evolved to survive on."

Well, yes and no. I tend to agree that eating like a caveman is probably closest to the diet we evolved to survive on, but:

1. We don't know exactly what cavemen ate, nor how often
2. Cavemen did not all eat the same things. Compare for example the known diets of pre-agricultural Native American tribes. Pre-industrial societies invariably ate what they could get
3. We cannot reproduce all aspects of the caveman diet, not least because the ranges of produce are huge and locally specific
4. We cannot know what else they did that may have improved

their lifespan. For instance, for sure they didn't sit on chairs, nor sleep in beds. But they also had a horrifically high rate of infant mortality and death by violence: pre-industrial tribes that survived into the modern era had rates of death by violence of about 25% of males. Today, on the mean streets of New York, that risk is about 1 in 100,000, or 0.001%. (Read Stephen Pinker's *The Better Angels of Our Nature* for details on mortality rates from violence)

5. Paleolithic life expectancy is generally thought to have been pretty damn low. Was all of that environmental, or may some of it have come from their diet? We don't know

6. We do know that early agricultural societies appear to have much higher rates of disease and lower life expectancies than comparable pre-agricultural societies. Diseases such as diabetes, heart disease, arthritis and many cancers do appear to be diseases of modernity. But how much of that is down to diet as opposed to (for example) exercise? Nobody knows for sure

7. Many modern inventions (like antibiotics and surgery) save lives. It is also possible that modern foodstuffs could, in theory, do the same (yes, I doubt it too. But you never know).

So, don't be taken in by a story. Test any dietary changes systematically, give each change time to take effect (at least a couple of weeks, I would think) and be ruthlessly honest with yourself. Take nothing on faith (especially not if it comes from a book by some sword-swinging lunatic).

APPLYING CHANGES
The 80/20 Principle
In all things where you don't want to invest major effort in becoming a world expert, the 80/20 principle (also known as the Pareto principle) applies. It states that 80 percent of outcomes come from 20 percent of causes and, so long as you don't take the numbers too literally, it is largely true. I do not agree with

any diet that requires really specific foods at really specific intervals, unless you are seriously ill and under doctor's orders, or an Olympic hopeful. If you'd like to see self-experimentation taken into 99.999–0.001 extremes (with a lot of good material on a range of health and training subjects), read Tim Ferriss' *Four Hour Body*. The man even had himself fitted with a real-time blood-sugar monitor to test the effect of various foods. Fascinating stuff.

So here are some general guidelines, which will probably lead you to a healthy diet if you follow them (and thus make you healthier, and therefore able to train more, and therefore a better martial artist).

1. Change one thing at a time. The first step, I would suggest, is to avoid refined sugar. Nobody has ever demonstrated that it is at all good for you, so save it for treats. Be ruthlessly honest with yourself and pay attention to what effect each change has on you

2. Eat lots of vegetables. If it is not obviously part of a plant, it doesn't count (unless you process it yourself). Major starch sources don't count either (potatoes, corn, grains, etc.). Fresh and in season is best, frozen or canned are okay too. Michael Pollan is good on this, with books like *The Omnivore's Dilemma* and others

3. Eat high-quality meat only. Avoid processed stuff. This is not only a matter of health, but also of morality. What people do to cows to make them fat is way beyond disgusting. Cows should eat grass outside. (Be a vegetarian if you must, but veganism is, for the overwhelming majority of people, a deeply unhealthy long-term life choice. It's just not practical to get your omega 3s and essential amino acids from a purely plant-based diet. Humans are omnivores, as you can tell from our teeth and our guts, not herbivores. Just don't.)

4. Only consume things that have been produced the same way and product tested for a minimum of 500 years. Coffee, beer,

tea, wine, meat, vegetables, and bread (made properly, none of this absurd twenty minute rising nonsense) are all good. Factory-produced stuff? Might be good, might be bad; you have no way to know. So be conservative. Food should come from a garden via a kitchen, not from a factory. See *The Omnivore's Dilemma* (again), and *Brave Old World* by Tom Hodgkinson

5. Cook. Take an interest in and control over what you eat. It doesn't have to be complicated or take much time, especially if you are preparing food from good quality ingredients. By far the best book I have ever come across for people who might think "I have no idea about cooking, it's intimidating and difficult" is Tim Ferriss' *Four Hour Chef*

6. Give each change time to take effect before you assess its effectiveness.

Indicators of a Good Diet

When making changes to your diet, the key indicator is of course how you feel. But it is well worth keeping track of the following, to see what effect each change is having.

- Weight: Since dropping most sugar and a lot of the starch from my diet, I lost 10 kg in about 3 weeks. I now weigh 75 kg, which is a kilo heavier than when I was super fit and trying really hard to keep weight on at age 30. Weigh yourself at the same time of day, and on the same scales, once a week

- Waist size: Weight gain and loss can come from anywhere, and a lot of it may be simply water. As a general guideline, if your waist is smaller than your hips, you'll fit into your kit better. But I find buying trousers is hell. If they can be pulled up over my thighs, I could fit a couple of hardbacks in the waistband

- Poo consistency: as every parent knows, poo is a great indicator of general health. Parents, especially of babies, can discuss poo at length. Anything that makes pooing harder, or painful, or especially stinky, is probably bad for you. There is no better indication of good diet, really

- Energy levels: These are very subjective, and can be affected by many factors other than diet. But if you find you need to snack to get through the day, you are probably eating suboptimally. I found cutting sugar evened out my crashes very effectively
- Frequency of minor illnesses: again, this is actually quite hard to track. But if a diet leaves you feeling tired or it feels like you are more prone to picking up stray bugs, abandon it. And vice versa, of course.

In short, when it comes to nutrition, you should pay attention to your body, read up on some science-y books so you know what's going on inside you, and use some good common sense. Fresh vegetables? Good for you. Ice-cream? Not a staple food. A martial artist must take care of their body, just as a soldier takes care of their rifle or a swordsman takes care of their sword.

Fasting

This has led me to do some further research on fasting. It comes in all shapes and sizes. The simplest is just don't eat for a while. I would not try that without preparation, if I were you. The health benefits of at least occasional ketosis are well-documented; I think of it as a metabolic spring clean. But you can fast for a couple of days and not get into ketosis because your body breaks down your muscles to produce glucose. So if you don't want to (a) feel too hungry and (b) lose muscle mass, it's a very good idea to get into ketosis before you fast. Here's how.

1. Be very strict about fast carbs for a week or two. This gets you off any sugar-high rollercoaster. When you fast your blood sugar will probably fall a bit, so make sure that it's not a dramatic drop

2. Follow a ketogenic diet for a couple of days. Use pee-sticks to make sure it's working. Not everyone can handle a ketogenic diet, so if it makes you feel ill, stop. Try step #3 instead

3. You can dose yourself with exogenous ketones to speed up the process of switching over. Exogenous ketones or ketogenic foods that I have used successfully (as measured by pee-sticks) include medium chain triglyceride (MCT) oil, branch-chain amino acids (BCAAs), and raspberry ketones. When your pee-sticks tell you that you are in a moderate state of ketosis, such as about 2-3 mmol/L, stop eating. See how 24 hours feels. If you get really hungry or dizzy, your blood pressure drops, or anything like that, then BREAK YOUR FAST. With breakfast, obviously. But unless there are some odd medical issues, 24 hours should be no big deal. Just remember to drink plenty of water. Tea and coffee are also okay.

Just to test this, I skipped breakfast and ate lunch at about 2 p.m. At 11 a.m. I had a ketone level at or close to 0. Lunch was a small salad with a tin of smoked mackerel in oil, two teaspoons of MCT oil, and a splash of olive oil. I also took 2x 125 mg capsules of raspberry ketones (Hi-tech Pharmaceuticals brand) and a 6.33 g dose of BCAAs (USPlabs "ModernBCAA+" brand). At 4 p.m. my pee-sticks told me that I was in ketosis at a level of 4mmol/L. Easy enough!

Further Thoughts on Fasting

1. I got all of my weight loss done without fasting. It's not necessary for that purpose, but there is a ton of evidence to suggest that it is good for you to fast occasionally. It's not clear yet whether the benefits come from being in ketosis (which can be achieved without fasting), from the short-term calorie restriction, or from some other mechanism. But it is abundantly clear that throughout human history, we have had to be able to function for short periods without food,

and indeed many traditional cultures incorporate longer fasts into their yearly calendar (e.g. Christianity's Lent and Islam's Ramadan)

2. There is nothing inherently virtuous in not eating. It's just a training tool, like push-ups and meditation. Do it because it generates specific benefits. Biochemist Dr Rhonda Patrick explains how it works in detail (such as on her podcast and website foundmyfitness.com), but the short answer is that your body only does certain clean-up operations in a fasted state, which is one of the reasons that most healing is done when you sleep – it's the longest non-eating period in most people's schedules

3. Don't overdo it. Fasting gets much easier with practice. These days, I routinely fast for 24 hours with no preparation, about once a week. It does wonders for re-setting my metabolism. After Christmas the other year I was so full I didn't eat for 48 hours. No big deal. I'm planning a 5 day fast for later in the year; it takes planning because eating meals with the children is a big part of family life for me. If you don't have kids, it's probably much easier

4. For me, the point of fasting is to reap the metabolic benefits and to test that my diet allows me to be free of the need to eat for 24 hours or so. I never feel deprived when fasting, so I don't feel any need to "make up for it" with a stupid blow-out. I do stupid blow-outs every now and then just because I like them, and I can get away with the occasional splurge because my habits seem to be good

5. I think that as a martial artist I just jolly well ought to be able to work fine without food for a short time – not eat for a day or two, and still fight. It feels simply unmartial to me to be slavishly dependent on a totally reliable food source for my effectiveness. An army marches on its stomach, yes. But I don't think there has ever been an army in combat that didn't go hungry at least occasionally.

Time Restricted Eating

A version of fasting that you probably do already is not eat for about eight or ten hours at a time: over night! There is a growing body of evidence to suggest that it is very good for you to restrict your eating to a limited window during the day, of eight to twelve hours. This gives you a longer period between the last thing you consume (other than water) at night, and the first thing (other than water) that you consume in the morning.

This is called time-restricted eating, and gives your body plenty of time to perform the metabolic clean-up operations that it can only do when you are in a somewhat fasted state. It also gives your gut a rest. When you ingest food, your gut becomes inflamed, which is normal and necessary. But if your gut never rests, it remains inflamed all the time, which leads to a higher level of systemic inflammation.

This is not the place to dive into the science of it: check out the work of Prof. Satchidananda Panda (of the Salk Institute). But it's a relatively easy protocol to implement, and I've been practising it for a while now, with very pleasing results. According to Panda (and others) it helps with almost everything.

Some Further Thoughts on Nutrition.

If you are trying to control your weight, try changing one thing a time. The first big thing I would do is avoid sugar, and then add vegetables. A decent serving of green vegetables at every meal will do wonders all by itself to make up for any dietary deficiencies and will fill you up a bit, which will reduce the amount of other stuff you eat. Also, the fibre in the vegetables will slow down sugar absorption, at least up to a point.

The next thing to try is to cut out fast carbs. Cheat once a week if you must, but make sure you are always eating lots and lots of vegetables, and some decent high-quality fat. So fry your vegetables in organic butter. If this is too hard, do it for just one meal a day – ideally breakfast.

Then implement a gentle time-restriction, such as being careful to stop eating anything late at night, or if that's impossible, have breakfast much later, but leave a solid twelve hours between last thing in (other than water) at night and first thing in in the morning. The reason to do this *after* coming off the fast carbs is simply that if your body is lurching from one sugar high to the next, it's very hard to avoid eating for a long enough period.

The scales are a very blunt instrument. You might drop a bunch of weight and actually be getting fatter, if you are losing muscle mass instead of the lard. I would take waist measurement over weight as an indicator of progress. I would also take all measurements once per week, at the same time of day, and on the same day – and not more often. This is much more reliable and less depressing than watching your weight fluctuate from morning to night (as it invariably does).

Systems are better than goals. If you are trying to get your weight down to a certain point, you are a failure every day that you are not at your target weight. This is not good. Better to try a different system (such as replacing your starch intake with extra vegetables) and just see what happens. Systems are sustainable. Goals are less so: when you reach them, then what?

And let me reiterate: I'm not your doctor. I believe in trying things out sensibly and building healthy habits. This approach works for me; we have a lot of DNA in common, so it's probably at least worth trying for you. I wouldn't put it more strongly than that.

PHYSICAL TRAINING

Martial arts usually require a good level of fitness, especially when you are learning them, because you will tend to use strength and fitness to compensate for imprecise technique. Once you are more advanced, the martial art itself may not keep you fit because you are too efficient, so incorporating conditioning into your training is a good idea. A large part of my job is getting modern office workers fit enough to be able to take part in medieval martial arts.

I have created two free online courses that you may find useful: Knee Maintenance and Arm Maintenance, available here: swordschool.teachable.com. They will teach you how to look after your joints.

Every movement you make requires these three elements, in this order:

1. Flexibility: can your joints make the necessary movement correctly?
2. Strength: can you make the correct movement with enough strength?
3. Speed: can you make the correct movement under the necessary load fast enough?

In addition, we should consider:

4. Stamina: can you make the correct movement under the necessary load at the required speed as many times as it takes to win the fight?

Perhaps the most important way to prevent injury is to be really careful about getting these elements in order. Regarding training for these things, the rule of thumb is this:

- Range of motion is about the muscles and the joints. Will the muscles and the structures of the joints allow the movement?
- Strength is about the muscles and the nervous system. Can you recruit enough large motor units?
- Power is about the fascia and the muscles. Can you store and release energy quickly?
- Stamina is about efficiency in motion and the metabolism. Can you do the action as efficiently as possible, and generate enough energy to keep it going?

In this section I will cover flexibility first, and then strength and speed. Given that a huge component of apparent speed is foresight (seeing what's about to happen and so reacting earlier), I'll cover that too; and because my core art, Fiore dei Liberi's *Armizare*, is based on four virtues (strength, speed, foresight and boldness), I felt I should complete the set and include training for boldness. Boldness is about overcoming fear, for which meditation and breathing exercises are very helpful – as is creating specific training scenarios to practise boldness in.

Before we get started, though, you should be aware that from a health perspective, sitting for long periods for any reason will kill you. It is almost as bad as smoking. We know this thanks to the work of scientific studies like this one: http://annals.org/ aim/article/2091327/sedentary-time-its-association-risk-disease-incidence-mortality-hospitalization-adults

That study concluded: "Prolonged sedentary time was independently associated with deleterious health outcomes regardless of physical activity." In other words, exercising for an hour per day does not undo the damage done by sitting for eight hours per day. Probably the best book on the market right now for strategies for dealing with this is Dr Kelly Starrett's *Deskbound.*

I personally have been using a standing desk for years. My friend Neal Stephenson goes one further and has a treadmill desk, so he walks for miles every day while typing. Neal wrote an article about it entitled "Arsebestos," which is found in his book *Some Remarks*. The critical thing is to avoid long periods of sitting still. Or even standing still. Modern offices are not well adapted for healthy living, especially offices in which "all nighters" are a thing, so I don't know what you personally should do, but there is no negotiating with heart attacks, strokes, or cancer. You should be able to negotiate with your boss.

Flexibility Training

The range of motion you have is determined by the structure of your skeleton (which you can't change, so let's move on), the length of your muscles (which is easily changed), and the flexibility of your soft tissues. Let's take a really simple example and work from there. Stand up on straight legs, reach up to the ceiling with your hands, and – keeping your feet flat on the floor and your knees locked – bend over and touch your toes. For some people, reaching the knees is hard; others find it trivial to put their palms flat on the floor. Note how far you reach today.

Now do a few squats, jump about a bit, swing your arms back and forth, and then repeat the toe-touching exercise. Chances are, you can now reach further. This is only because your muscles are willing to permit more movement. You haven't made any real changes. When a muscle is stretched, it hits a point at which it contracts to prevent the stretch, to protect itself from tearing. This is called the stretch reflex. Increasing range of motion usually begins by resetting the stretch reflex. There are two common ways to do this:

1. You can hold the stretch for 30+ seconds. This lulls the muscle into a sense of security, and it will usually allow a

longer stretch. You can then hold this for another 30+ seconds and get a bit further

2. You can hold the stretch, and then deliberately contract the muscle against the stretch (without allowing the muscle to actually shorten). Hold the contraction for about 10 seconds, and then relax. You will then be able to reach a bit further before the stretch reflex kicks in again.

In any given session, reset the reflex a maximum of three times. After this, the muscle will be weaker and more prone to injury for a bit, so do it *after* any strength or power training.

Dynamic range of motion training is done by repeating an exercise at slightly greater ranges, over and over. For example, to increase the length of your lunge, do a series of lunges with an immediate recovery, making each lunge a bit longer than the one before it, until it becomes uncomfortable. Once you are at the edge of your comfort zone, hold the position for 10–30 seconds to establish your balance and allow the supporting structures to develop. It is simply dangerous to develop unsupported ranges of motion. If you don't have the strength to hold the position, you probably shouldn't go into it. Then repeat the dynamic motions, but keep an inch or so in the pocket: don't go to the maximum range, because the static stretch will have temporarily reduced your strength.

I do my range of motion work in the evening before bed, often while watching TV. I go through all the motions that I want to retain, and spend extra time on any area that is stiffer than usual, or where I am trying to develop more range for some reason.

Strength Training

I am weak. So I study strength. In martial arts, strength has little to do with the usual measures of muscular performance, and everything to do with grounding, structure, power generation and joint maintenance.

Given my choice of profession, my naturally weak skeleton is a blessing. My petite twelve-year-old niece has wrists about the same size as mine; I've had neck issues since I was fourteen; and I will generally get injured at the slightest provocation. This means I have always been looking for ways to win fights that did not rely on robustness, and that I have always been working through health issues of my own. So I am able to help my students, most of whom have some kind of physical imperfection. Indeed, about half my time in private lessons is spent fixing postural issues, knee or wrist problems, or similar.

My wrists, for example, have suffered from tendonitis since the early nineties. It got so bad when I was working as a cabinet-maker that I literally had to choose between swinging a sword and working the next day. Then I met a kung-fu instructor who in twenty agonising minutes did what the combined medical professionals of Edinburgh had failed to do in five years: he fixed my wrists. The treatment involved massage (the agonising bit), very specific exercises with very light weights, and breathing exercises. I had gone a year without touching a sword and five years without push-ups, and then suddenly my wrists worked again. I can now do push-ups on the backs of my hands. So it is no wonder that I place massage, targeted weight training and breathing exercises at the core of the conditioning syllabus. If your body doesn't work, you can't use it. Striking targets and being a target require that your joints can handle the impact of hitting and being hit. You can find my training routines for looking after my arms on my free course, Arm Maintenance, at swordschool.teachable.com.

Simply building up the joints is not enough: we have to minimise the impact they are subjected to. Every action has an equal and opposite reaction: when you hit the target, the target hits back. That energy has to go somewhere. If it is not carefully directed, it may very well go into shocking your joints. So it is necessary to establish a safe route for the kinetic energy coming back from the target. It either moves the weapon (not ideal, usually), or is routed down into the ground through the passive structure of your skeleton. This skill can be refined for decades, but I find that even beginners can generate major improvements if we simply create the position of the moment of impact (the lunge, for instance) and apply very gentle pressure in the reciprocal direction to the strike. The student can feel the place where it takes most effort to hold the position (the lead shoulder, for instance), and create a correction to the position that allows the same pressure to be absorbed with less effort. Then we can apply the pressure at the beginning of the movement and establish that the entire movement is properly grounded. (This is much easier with thrusts than cuts, obviously.) Ultimately, we are looking for a structure which does not need to change at all to route the energy: when we add the pressure, there is no need for any kind of muscular reaction, nor any increase in effort or tension.

This sort of practice leads to all sorts of gains in efficiency: the starting position, the movement, and the end position are all naturally grounded, and so all the muscular effort being made is directly applying force to the strike. Muscles that are not working to hold the position are available for generating power. So, a deeply relaxed guard and a deeply relaxed movement allow for massive increases in power generation. We can see hints of this in Fiore's famous elephant, the only one of the four animals depicted standing on a surface (which is rectangular, suggesting stability), the tower on its back indicating that your back should be straight and balanced.

As the text says:

> *Ellefante son e un castello porto per chargo/ E non mi inzinochio ne perdo vargo*
>
> I am the elephant, and a castle I carry as cargo / And I do not kneel nor lose my stride.

Power is generated by muscular contraction, the difference between the relaxed state of the muscle and the contracted state. It pays to work both ends of the differential. Increasing the raw strength of the muscle is an obvious way to go. Creating more efficient positions and movement is less obvious but generates much faster gains because it doesn't require opening up new nerve channels, nor building muscle mass. Of course, most beginners come to their first class woefully weak and unfit. It is necessary that swordsmen, especially in the early years, develop a decent level of core strength and fitness. This prevents injury, allows sufficient endurance for training sessions that are long enough to actually learn the cool stuff, and makes precise postural adjustments much easier.

As a basic guideline, look at the warm-up shown at this URL: http://www.swordschool.com/wiki/index.php/Sample_warm-up.

If it feels like a warm-up and not a workout, you should have the basic strength and fitness level at which the fastest gains come from the kind of grounding training we are looking at here. Note that, compared to the average competitive boxer or wrestler, we are pathetically unfit. But then the sword is a labour-saving device, not an oddly-shaped dumbbell.

In many students the weak link in the chain between sword-point and ground is their grip on the sword. I don't think I have ever come across a student in any seminar, regardless of experience, whose grip could not be improved. In most cases, the interface between sword and hand does not allow a clean flow of energy from the blade up the arm. The modern tendency to chunky grips on swords exacerbates this; most antiques I have handled have very slim grips, which makes perfect sense when you understand grounding. Indeed, after coming to a seminar on this topic, many students end up having their sword grip modified. The human hand is an incredibly complex and sensitive machine, but all too often folk hold onto their swords like they are carrying a suitcase.

I usually demonstrate the proper interface by hitting a tyre with a longsword with all my fingers open, and by hitting the wall target with my rapier, again with my hand open. You can see a video of me doing that here: https://guywindsor.net/blog/tyre

Simple beer-can-crushing grip strength has almost nothing to do with striking power with the sword. The role of the fingers is to direct the energy in the sword into the lifeline of the palm, and thence up the arm.

Having established a safe and efficient route for the energy to travel down, we can use the same pathway for energy to travel out. With a rapier, for instance, once the lunge position is grounded, we can find the same pathway in the guard position too. Clearly though, while the lunge creates a straight diagonal line from the point of the sword to the ground, in guard that line goes horizontally along the arm and curves into the upper back to go down through the hips and into the (usually) back leg. If you can feel this line clearly, lunging is simply a matter of taking that curve and snapping it straight. A more sophisticated version of this works for cuts too (with any weapon). It is much easier to maintain the groundpath than to break and reform it in motion, so establish it in guard, and let the strike be a resistance-free extension of it.

As you become more efficient so you hit much harder, so there is more energy coming back down into your body, so you need to improve your grounding; so you can hit harder, so there is more energy coming back, and so on. Given that you can break your hand by punching a concrete wall, it is obvious that you can generate far more power than you can withstand the impact of. So gains in power generation come from increases in your ability to handle the power, more than increases in the power itself.

When you practise like this, it swiftly becomes obvious that general carry-a-TV-up-the-stairs real-world strength has little bearing on the outcome of a sword fight once you are highly skilled, but because it helps prevent injuries in training, and it is very useful for life in general, it is necessary to do a bunch of not-sword-training to develop it. Push-ups, kettlebells, and the like are useful here. This is not to help us hit harder, but is more an insurance policy against errors in technique, and for general health and fitness. Likewise, joint strength training and massage should ideally be a matter of maintenance, not cure.

There is a very interesting article by Alen Lovric called "Skill Training vs. Strength Training" on the HROARR website, here: http://hroarr.com/skill-training-vs-strength-training/. It goes into more detail about the benefits of strength training for skills acquisition, which may inspire you to put a bit more effort into your strength training.

So, how do you build strength? It helps to know how strength is developed. As with nutrition, I'll give you the main points, enough to actually get started getting stronger, and a reading list on page 281 if you want to delve deeper.

Assuming you have got the necessary range of motion and the structures you are making with your skeleton are correct, strength comes from two connected systems: your muscles and your fascia. Your muscles burn energy to contract, creating movement. Some of that energy can be stored in the elastic stretching of your fascia (and tendons and ligaments). This creates an elastic recoil, like snapping a rubber band. This is why it's easier to squat down and immediately go back up than it is to get up from a squat you've been holding for a while. The elastic band kind of strength is generally called plyometrics, and the general term for the tendons, fascia and ligaments is "soft tissues."

You increase strength most quickly by increasing the nervous activation of the muscles – in effect waking up more muscle fibres by re-opening the signal pathways. The next fastest way to add strength is to increase the metabolism of the muscles themselves. Adding actual muscle mass is the next but slower method; finally there is the option of increasing the strength of the soft tissues, but it is the slowest method. For most people it takes a couple of weeks to open the nerves, a month or so to get serious metabolic changes, a couple of months to start adding real mass, and at least nine months to make significant improvements to the soft tissues.

Speed Training

Speed, *celeritas*, is one of Fiore's four key virtues that a swordsman must possess. The others, for non-Fioreista readers, are *audatia* (boldness), *forteza* (strength), and *avvisamento* (foresight). There are two key models available to us for developing speed. These are the sporting approach and the musical.

The most obviously applicable is that of sports. High-level sportsmen, in games like tennis and fencing, must be quick. This is trained mostly by repeating explosive movements to task the correct muscles with the desired motion. In this model actions should pretty much only ever be trained at speed. If you do the action slowly too often you end up training to use the wrong muscles, and the maximum speed of the action is diminished. This sort of thing tends to emphasize gross motor movements, such as extending the arm, rather than fine motor movements, such as manipulating with the fingers. As Johan Harmenberg writes on page 28 of his must-read book *Epee 2.0*, "only simple movements are used (even an action like a disengage is not very common in a World Championship final)". He attributes this to the stress that the fencers are experiencing. At this level, "the pressure is so intense it is impossible to describe". (P. 43.) Harmenberg won the Epee World Championship in 1977 and Olympic gold in 1980, so may reasonably be assumed to know his stuff.

In music, though, speed of execution is attained through getting it right at slow speeds first, and then letting the phrase get faster and faster. Wynton Marsalis playing the *Carnival of Venice* by Jean-Baptiste Arban is a good example of astonishing speed of execution (you can find it on YouTube). If music's not your thing, just scroll ahead to 2:40 where he plays the eighth variation so fast it sounds like there are two cornets being blown: one for the tune, and one for the accompaniment. The fine motor control is just dazzling. I have been taught to play this (though I never got close to this level of execution) and can attest that it is simply appallingly difficult to do, and that it's even worse under the stress of the performance. But the advice I was given (and every musician I have ever met would agree) was to get it absolutely accurate slowly first, and then speed it up. As my teacher Mr Foster wrote on my sheet music, "go at the speed of NO mistakes".

We find a remarkable similarity between training to play a musical instrument and combat shooting. All actions in shooting are trained slowly first, to become smooth and efficient first, and are then sped up. I've been shooting pistols since I moved to Finland in 2001 and I have never, ever heard an instructor tell a shooting student to hurry up. This is not only because mistakes can cost lives (just like in a sword fight) but also because shooting requires fine motor control, which becomes inaccurate if sped up too soon. In both areas, music and shooting, the goal is to enable the practitioner to execute complex motor skills under high levels of stress.

I can attest to the stress of performance: I played the trumpet at school and developed an absolute phobia of playing solos, despite being a member of several bands and orchestras. Though I was never under any direct physical threat (there were no beatings for splitting a note, nor would anyone have shot me for fluffing a phrase), I was at times incapacitated by fear when a solo was coming up. I never actually vomited, but it was pretty damn close. Yet I still did solos. While they were never perfect, and I could always play a lot better in practice than during a performance, I was able to produce a passable result. The training worked. The level of stress is probably much higher for a professional musician because not only their ego but also their career rides on the quality of the performance, and is much higher still for a soldier or policeman facing an armed assailant. Yet the process is the same.

In both these areas you'll hear the phrase, "slow is smooth, smooth is fast." In other words, get the action right slowly and let it speed up as you practise. Keeping it smooth will allow it to become fast.

We can summarize then by saying that if you think of swordsmanship as a fine motor control skill then the music/shooting model is best. If you think of it as a gross motor control skill then the sporting approach will work best. In my experience, students training to win tournaments should emphasize the sporting approach; students training to recreate historical duelling arts should emphasize the musical approach.

It is, of course, possible – often desirable – to do both. Swordsmanship for sport and swordsmanship for murder (duelling) have some overlap. Use the slow-smooth approach for those elements of the sporting game that are improved by fine motor control; use the sporting model for those elements of the martial art that involve improving explosive power. If a student is having difficulty lunging with sufficient speed to take advantage of tempi that he ought to be able to strike in, for example, the critical skill for the instructor is to diagnose the problem. Are the mechanics of the lunge at fault? If so then slow it down and smooth it out. If the mechanics are okay then apply drills that develop the raw speed of the lunge. Just don't try this with a disengage; it's so much a fine motor skill that trying to speed it up by making the student go faster will just make it clumsier and slower. Get it smoother and smaller to make it faster.

Speed serves two functions in swordsmanship: damage and timing.

Damage first: the speed of the sword is a major factor in determining how hard it hits. By making it move faster, we hit harder.

I believe that the sword should act as a labour-saving device. Its function is to destroy certain types of target, and it should require less effort to do so with the sword than without. So there is limited virtue in simply making the sword go faster and faster to hit harder and harder; at some point there is sufficient energy to do the desired damage, so additional speed is wasted effort.

Timing: the purpose of speed is to ensure that your strike arrives before your opponent's parry, and your parry arrives before their strike. It is therefore proportional to the motions of your opponent. The key skill here is to be able to adjust the acceleration of the weapon, rather than attain a specific top speed. Refer back to page 63 for a discussion of this.

The easiest way to reduce the time in which an action is done is to make the action shorter. So, a great deal of speed training, training to do an action in less time, is to eliminate any extraneous motion – to pare the movement down to its absolute minimum. There are several ways to do this, from the obvious (select a starting point that is closer to the end point) to the more sophisticated (tuning the path taken between those two points). In general, the sword hand should move in a straight line from A to B. But sometimes it's the middle of the blade that does that, and sometimes it's other parts of the weapon or wielder.

In practice, it is useful to be able to adjust the path and the rate of acceleration at various points on the path for best effect. To simply hit hard, make sure the sword is at maximum velocity at the moment of impact. To make the hit more likely to land, though, adjust the acceleration pattern and the path taken to best fit the tactical circumstances. Easier said than done. It is always slower to lift a heavy weight than a light one. So speed training is also about reducing unnecessary tension, making the action as smooth and efficient as possible, and expending the least possible force to get the job done.

So, as we would expect with a medieval virtue, cultivating speed for its own sake – simply going as fast as possible – is a route to ruin. It takes an essential quality that should exist in equilibrium with others and makes a vice out of it. A common theme in medieval thought (and should be still today) is: that which is virtuous when in balance becomes vicious when done to excess. Excessive courage leads to foolhardiness, excessive strength leads to stiffness and slowness, excessive speed leads to weakness and over-extension, and excessive judgement leads to cowardice.

In the case of speed, emphasizing raw speed over speed in proportion to your opponent's movements leads to getting hit through being over-committed and over-extended. It is also hell on the body because explosive force applied to the joints is only safe when the motion is being done perfectly.

In every discipline there is usually an optimum balance between youthful vigour and the experience of long practice that can only come with age. A sportsman usually peaks between the ages of 20 and 40, a concert soloist peaks somewhere between 35 and 60, and a martial arts instructor normally peaks somewhere between 50 and 70. Fiore said he was about 60 when he wrote his book. So cultivate speed carefully, getting the mechanics absolutely right before you put a lot of force through them, and make sure you develop the muscular support of your joints to absorb any slight errors. Muscles and bones last forever; the weak spot in any mechanical system is the joints. The syllabus wiki has some of the school's joint care curriculum uploaded, including wrist and elbow exercises, knee exercises, and joint massage, here: http://www.swordschool. com/wiki/index.php/Conditioning. I do these a lot because I intend to hit my peak in about fifteen years, and I need to make sure my joints can handle all that force. You should also enrol on my free joint maintenance courses at swordschool.teachable.com.

Ficher's speed training device, "Lunge of the Heart".

In a strictly fencing context, the way we teach speed (other than standard physical training) is to reduce the amount of time the student has to complete the action. This is not a new idea, as you can see from the above plate, which is from Ficher's treatise of 1796 (which we saw on page 174). The fencer holds the string and releases it, causing the heart-shaped target to fall; the fencer is supposed to hit the target before it lands. By restricting the time available to make the strike, the student naturally speeds up.

When giving an individual lesson, or even in class practice, you use exactly the same principle. By restricting the time window for the action to work, the student will naturally change the speed of their action to fit it. A couple of examples might help to illustrate the idea.

In my Armizare classes, the first technique students learn against a dagger attack is the first play of the first master of the dagger (from Fiore).

Initially, the attack is done very slowly, and the scholar has all the time in the world to figure out the technique. But very early on, I have the attacker make the dagger strike and immediately (but not quickly) reach out with their other hand and tap the defender's mask. This denotes the end of the window of opportunity to do the disarm. The defenders change how they do the disarm to avoid getting hit with the second action: either stepping more offline, breaking the attacker's structure earlier, or keeping moving, where previously they froze. Then, bit by bit, the attacker ramps up the speed, and the defender will naturally speed up their actions to stay successful.

With swords, one simple way to get students to strike faster is to offer the same restricted window. Let's say they are working on a parry-riposte defence. In its most basic set-up, the attacker attacks, the defender does their parry-riposte, and the attacker just lets them. To speed up the riposte, have the attacker parry it – slowly at first. The defender's job then is to make the riposte before the attacker can parry it. If the attacker's parry starts out big and slow, it's easy for the defender to get the riposte in. But as the parry gets smaller and faster, the defender will naturally get faster to make their riposte arrive.

The true essence of speed, though, is foresight.

Suggested Reading for Physical Training and Nutrition

This book is not intended as a training guide or a guide to improving your basic health or longevity. But given that it takes a lifetime to truly master the art, a long, healthy life is a pre-requisite. I've found the following books really useful.

Body by Science by Doug McGuff and John Little covers the basics of muscles and how they work, global metabolic conditioning, and the dose-response relationship of exercise – in short all of the necessary science for understanding how to generate fitness changes. I don't follow their training program because it doesn't address my specific requirements, but as a primer on the basics, it's excellent.

Thomas Myers is credited with discovering the power-storing functions of fascia, and connecting Buckminster Fuller's idea of tensegrity with biomechanics. It's one of those lovely moments where modern science confirms what martial arts teachers have been saying for centuries! *Biotensegrity: the Structural Basis Of Life* by Graham Scarr is a good starting point for looking at this.

Tim Ferriss's *The Four Hour Body* is a very useful book, especially on strength training and diet.

Gary Taubes' seminal *Good Calories, Bad Calories* is a critically important book for the study of nutrition.

Waking Up by Sam Harris is a really useful look at the uses of meditation from the perspective of a neuroscientist who meditates. The subject is stripped of the usual metaphysical and cultural baggage.

Pavel Tsatsouline is very good on both strength training (e.g. *The Naked Warrior*) and flexibility (such as his *Relax into Stretch*).

Dr Kelly Starrett's *Becoming a Supple Leopard* has some very useful flexibility and mobility exercises.

For traditional barbell training, you can't beat Mark Rippetoe's classic *Starting Strength*. It's an excellent book, well worth your time even if you never touch a barbell.

TRAINING FOR FORESIGHT

There are few things that all martial artists agree on, but I think this may be one of them: it's easier to fight someone if you know exactly what they are going to do. To predict their actions. To see the future. This skill is one of the aspects that marks an experienced fighter in any discipline. They can read their opponent and see what they are about to do; but also they can create the situation so that the opponent is led into a trap. Fiore dei Liberi knew this perfectly well back in the fourteenth century: it's one of the four virtues he says a swordsman should possess. It's *Avvisamento* (foresight) in the *Getty MS*, and *Prudentia* (prudence) in the *Pisani Dossi MS* and *Paris MS*. For what is prudence if not the ability to foresee danger and avoid it?

> *Meglio de mi lovo cervero non vede creatura*
> *Eaquello mette sempre a sesto e a misura.*

> No creature sees better than I, the lynx
> And this virtue puts everything in its right place and its measure.
> (Translated by Tom Leoni)

Foresight is a virtue and a skill, and it can and should be trained. As you probably guessed, I have a well-developed system for doing exactly that. It relies as always on starting very simple and then gradually increasing complexity, while always focussing precisely on the one thing you're working on. Because the virtue is first discussed in fencing literature in *Il Fior di Battaglia*, it makes sense to use longsword for my example, but you should be able to apply this to any martial art. This is the bare bones of the three step process.

Step One: Establish the Base

1. Set up a basic drill. We'll use first drill as an example: https://guywindsor.net/blog/firstdrill
2. Set up a simple variation, ideally with the defender responding differently, such as a counterattack rather than a parry. (Such as in the *stretto* form of first drill.) https://guywindsor.net/blog/firstdrillstretto
3. The attacker's job is to counter the defence: either parry the counterattack or strike on the other side of the parry (as here in our set drills).

At this stage the attacker is just watching the defender, and the defender is just feeding the attacker one defence and then the other. No variations. Okay, we have established our base.

Step Two: Create Controlled Complexity

1. The defender now varies their defence, so that the attacker doesn't know which one they will pick
2. The attacker's job is to predict the defence. If they counter it, great, that's a bonus. But we're working on the skill of foresight, not the application of that skill. The attacker makes five attacks, and counts how many times they accurately predicted which of the two things the defender would do
3. Change roles. Five attacks, five defences. Try to be as random as possible
4. Use the rule of Cs (see p. 183 if you've forgotten them) to adjust the level of the drill so that the attacker has difficulty predicting the defence.

In a perfect world, you can always predict exactly what your opponent will do and set things up so that if he does anything else, it will fail naturally, and if he does what you expect, he falls onto your prepared counter.

Step Three: Reduce Their Options

1. The attacker adjusts their attack so that the counterattack will naturally fail. In this example, that means aiming the *mandritto fendente* slightly further over to the left, and stepping slightly across the *strada* to the attacker's left. There is no hole to counterattack into. So the defender either parries or their action will fail.

2. The attacker adjusts their attack to invite the counterattack. They do this by swinging the *mandritto fendente* round, offline and a bit to the right. If the invitation is accepted, the attacker parries the counterattack; if it is declined and the defender parries, their parry will be wider than usual, making the attacker's counter much easier.

3. To start with, exaggerate these adjustments to the attack, and co-operate in the responses. Once the idea is clear in both player's minds, they should ramp it up a bit.

4. Once this is going well, the attacker's job becomes simply to predict the defender's actions, and the defender's job is to respond naturally to the attack with one of the two options. As before, use the rule of Cs to adjust the level of difficulty until the attacker is getting it right about four times out of five.

And Finally: Add Complexity

So far so good. We have a drill in which there is only one degree of freedom – the defender's action. Everything else is set: the roles of attacker and defender, the attack, and the two defences. Everything. So now apply the variation engines – who moves first, add a step, and degrees of freedom (you can find them in the "Skill Development" chapter, page 176) – to add complexity to the point where the attacker can only get it right three or four times out of five. This might be as simple as step three above, or as complex as full-on freeplay.

Be very clear about what you are training: if you are working on foresight, success means "I predicted exactly what they would do". It doesn't matter if you got hit or not. Of course, as your foresight improves, not getting hit should be a lot easier than before.

TRAINING FOR BOLDNESS

Boldness is a key virtue in swordsmanship. Perhaps the key virtue. Above the Lion on the famous *segno* page, Fiore wrote *"Piu de mi leone non porta core ardito. Por di bataglia fazo a zaschun invito."* "Nobody has a bolder heart than I, the Lion. I call everyone to battle."

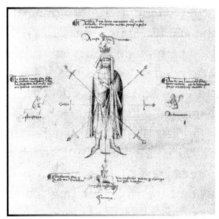

It is a key virtue, and one which can be trained for. I covered it in breadth and depth in my book *Swordfighting*, especially as regards personal fear, but didn't include there the specific exercises we use in class to begin the study of boldness. In a women's class I led in Seattle in April 2016, the participants explicitly requested boldness as a topic, so I took them through the following sequence. This was a longsword class in which most of the participants were relatively inexperienced, so these exercises were done relatively slowly.

The first step, always, is to decide what you're working on. In this case, it's boldness. So the only thing that matters (other than "everyone finishes class healthier than they started it") is whether you are embodying that virtue in the constraints of the drill. It's okay for technique and other things to suffer.

The flinch is the enemy. Your body's instinctive jerking away from threat needs to be brought under control. For many people, simply having their personal space invaded is enough to make them flinch, but to train martial arts effectively, you have to get comfortable with people getting right up in your face. So we began with the standing step drill, in which two players face each other square on in a wide stance, touch wrists, and then try to make the other player take a step. Moving a foot means you lose. You can find the drill here (and on page 215):

https://guywindsor.net/blog/standingstep

This involves pushing and being pushed, and some arm locks. Once the first level is comfortable, you can introduce things like gentle face slaps. Anything that does not threaten your position can be ignored, so it's remarkable how quickly incidental contact that would previously have created a flinch becomes something the players can simply choose not to react to. It also gets everyone playing together in a useful way. The next level is to allow one step, in either attack or defence; you lose when you make a second foot movement.

This drill is all about standing your ground, grounding, tactics, misdirection, wrestling, locks, and throws; it's a very good way to get beginners into the game. It also caused a lot of hilarity in the class, which in the circumstances was a good thing. It broke the ice and made being brave easier. I also covered what to do if you are much bigger and stronger, or more experienced: take it to the very edge of your balance, and play from there.

After this, we did some basic sword handling so I could assess the level of the class as a whole, and then we got started with step one of first drill: defender on guard in *tutta porta di ferro*, and the attacker strikes a *mandritto fendente* (controlled, of course) to the head. The defender does nothing. You can see the drill here: https://guywindsor.net/blog/firstdrill

That is hard. Don't blink. Don't flinch. Don't even change your breathing. Stare over the attacker's shoulder and do absolutely nothing as the blade touches your mask. We also do this exercise with no masks and no contact. It's harder, for most people. The exercise should be done at the rate that maintains the difficulty for the defender, so long as that doesn't take the attacker past the point where they can properly control their strike.

Now we have identified the problem (i.e. flinching), we have to set up exercises in which it will happen naturally, allowing you to practise preventing it in circumstances of ever increasing complexity. Remain calm and dispassionate. It really is better to get hit in training than to practise flinching: every time you flinch, you are ingraining that response in your nervous system.

Once you can remain impassive against the attack, you can defend against it with much better precision. So from here, move on to the second step of the drill: actually defending yourself. Now it's the attacker's turn to be impassive about being struck.

Boldness is also about moving forwards against the threat. In the Lonin loft they have two car tyres hanging from the ceiling, which act as pells and striking targets, so from here we moved on to hitting the tyres: approaching boldly, striking hard and moving away under cover. This was fun and should be trained regularly, not least to make you aware of just how hard you can hit.

We then went back to the pair drills and worked on the attacker's bold entry. I prepped one of the students during this time, and then gave orders for the class to go as hard and fast as they could, with no masks, to really hit each other. A dangerous, stupid, thing to do with a class at this level. But the teacher was telling them to! And there was some trepidation, but they trusted me, so there was no dissent until the student I had prepared beforehand said, quietly but firmly, "no."

I said "what the hell do you mean, no?"

And she replied "no, it's too dangerous."

I then explained what we had done to the class.

It takes boldness to stand up to authority figures when they are not acting in your best interests, and as with all necessary skills, it can and should be trained for. Roleplaying the scenario can really help. So what the class saw was one of their own (boldly) saying no to a dangerous exercise, in defiance of my authority. That was probably much harder – required more boldness – than simply not flinching when a friend gently approached with a sword.

Training for boldness only works if the situation is one in which it is hard to be bold, but you can just manage it. It is especially important to emphasise that success is defined only by whether you manage to act in a way that demonstrates the virtue of boldness according to the scenario of the drill. No other factors are important. This is the key to successful training. In weightlifting, you either lift the weight the prescribed distance, or you don't. Success is easy to define. When training for virtues, success is more difficult to pin down. That's why I like controlling the flinch as the starting point: it's the easiest way to check on physical courage.

We can take this out into the wider world too. Let's say you have difficulty talking to strangers, so you set yourself a task of asking one stranger for directions every day on your way to work. It doesn't matter if you stammer, or if you forget what they tell you, or if they are rude, or any other thing; you did it if you went up to someone you don't know and asked. Success is making the attempt.

Fear Practice

I've borrowed this from my book *Swordfighting*.

One of the many things that martial arts training can teach you is the ability to deal with fear: the ability to control your autonomic responses, the ability to choose all your actions from a position of confidence and strength, rather than just react out of fear and dread. In addition to fear management strategies, it is also useful to actively practise handling fear. For this you will need one irrational fear-inducing activity, ideally one that requires little cash or preparation, and a commitment to daily practice. One easy option is cold showers; not ideal, because most people are not actively afraid of cold water, they just don't like it. But having the nerve to turn the tap all the way to cold and let it hit you is a good start.

I personally have a wildly irrational fear of hanging off things. Especially upside down. I'm okay hanging off a pull-up bar by my hands, but jumping up to catch hold of it in the first place gives me a heart attack. In the back of my mind I am completely certain that if I miss my catch, the contact of my fingers on the bar will flip me upside-down, and I'll fall on my head. Yes, really.

But I know that it isn't so; the forces at work just cannot make that happen. My rational mind overrules my irrational body, in this case. So every day, I jump and catch the bar. And every day, I nearly die of fright. But it is much easier to handle now than it was a year ago. I can feel the dread building as I approach the bar, and steel myself to jump and catch. It's horrible. But useful. And good practice.

Hanging upside down by my knees is another one. For the longest time, I could not do it. In my heart of hearts, I knew that if I let go with my hands, my legs would straighten, and I would fall. As if my legs were not under my control at all. And as if the teeny little muscles in my grip were somehow able to generate more force than the ginormous (in comparison to my forearms at least) muscles in my thighs.

My cousin is a professional aerialist (she organised the Mary Poppins's at the London Olympics opening ceremony in 2012), and way back in 2005 she was performing in Berlin, doing scary-as-hell rope tricks. You can see her in action here: https://guywindsor.net/blog/katharine

I flew over to see her and, while I was there, she invited me along to their training hall, to have a go on ropes and trapezes. It was fantastic good fun. While she was teaching me to get onto a trapeze, I managed to get my legs over the bar, but I could not let go with my hands and hang down. No way. Instant fall onto head. So she shinned up the rope next to me, laid her arm on my shins and said "don't worry, I won't let you fall." (The physics do not work, of course. She was about half my weight, and hanging off a rope. But irrational fears do not require rational solutions.) And so I let go, and after a moment, she could take her arm away, and there I was, hanging by my knees upside down for the first time ever.

Unfortunately, trapezes are quite tricky to find around here, so I didn't do it again until the summer of 2014. We have a climbing frame in our yard, and my eldest daughter and I were playing on it, and I did Katharine's trick of holding her shins (though in this case the reassurance was backed up by physics!); in short order, my seven-year-old turned into a monkey, as regards hanging off stuff at least. So I decided to join her, and had my wife hold my shins, and I let go with my hands. After a few reps of that, I could do it without help. And now it's easy. Scary, but easy. I still know in my bones that I'm about to fall, but I still do it. When that stops being scary enough, I'll have to find something else to be frightened of. Because the benefits of daily overcoming terror are way too great.

Fear Management

Fear management is the key skill underlying all martial arts. If you are not afraid of getting hurt or killed, there's something wrong with you. But if you are frozen in place by that fear, prevented from acting, then your training has failed.

As you now know, I'm a great big fraidy-cat and so am always on the lookout for ways to practise handling fear. And there is *nothing* scarier than the dentist. I have sensitive teeth, which doesn't help; that metal spike thing they use to poke and scratch around your teeth feels to me like sticking splinters under my nails. But in my mouth. In addition, and for no good reason, people prodding about in my mouth has a similar shudder-inducing effect on me as scraping nails down a blackboard. Seriously, if you want information out of me, don't bother with the waterboard; the threat of dental torture would break me in no time.

This irrational fear is of course excellent and very useful, because as a responsible parent I have to set a good example and get a check-up once a year. Not too long ago, I went for the check-up, and was horrified to hear that an old filling was cracked and needed replacing. Which meant THE DRILL. We made the appointment for the following week, and I had seven whole days in which to build up a profound sense of dread.

What can I say about the drill? Except that if it doesn't terrify you with its hideous shriek (happening *inside your head*), and the promise of pain (which never comes; what an improvement in oral anaesthesia since I was a kid!) then there must be something wrong with you. Really. It's just a nightmare made flesh. It's actually worse than the anaesthetic injection, and, to me, a hypodermic syringe is an object of terror. I loathe and fear those things. When someone is giving an injection on TV or in a movie, I close my eyes. It's just wrong on every level. I spend my professional life working on ways to NOT get stabbed, and you want me to let you stick a spike in me? Are you mad? When someone comes at me with a syringe, it takes all my willpower not to disarm them and stick it in their eye. Which is also totally irrational, but there you are. Knives, swords, and guns? Not scary. The tools of modern medicine? Fucking terrifying.

Let me point out here that my dentist is a lovely, kind, and expert woman – gentle and professional. But she's still a DENTIST. Indeed, all my dentists have been good, and gentle, and caused no unnecessary pain. This is a totally irrational fear.

So there I was in the chair, as my dentist started to work, and I was actually quite relaxed. Pulse under 80 the whole time (well above my normal 55 or so, but manageable). Manual dexterity okay. Maintaining full use of my rational faculties despite gibbering terror.

How?

I chose to focus on something else.

I experimented in the chair with several different approaches, and the one that worked best was to place my attention on my breath. After every ten breaths, I went through a manual dexterity drill (finger wiggling, to the uninitiated), and then back to my breath.

The hard part was staying still; every now and then I had to bring my attention up to my neck, because the effort of not moving my head was causing stiffness. Relaxing my neck was harder than keeping my pulse down.

I was hugely pleased at one point when she stopped to ask me something, and I hadn't immediately noticed that the drill had stopped. That was a major success.

So, how do you cultivate the ability to choose your focus to this degree?

The answer is meditation. It is the best and fastest way to develop focus, because it isolates focus and works on that to the exclusion of all else.

MEDITATION

I have been meditating in one form or another for about eighteen years. Of all the things I do to be a better human, and a better martial artist, writer and teacher, I think meditation is perhaps the most important, and the most effective in terms of time spent to results obtained. This is because 95% of training happens in the brain, and you need your brain to do the other 5% too. Meditation can work like defragging your hard drive, installing a better CPU, quadrupling your RAM, and upgrading your operating system. Only better. There are dozens of studies that suggest that meditation is good for you. And there are a bagillion pages of hippy crap out there claiming it will make you fly, or infinitely wise, or good in bed, or whatever other nonsense.

Here are two articles, both from major government health organisations, which seem to conclude that it's healthy: one from the UK National Health Service – www.nhs.uk/news/2015/04April/Pages/Mindfulness-as-good-as-drugs-for-preventing-depression-relapse.aspx – and one from the US NCCIH – https://nccih.nih.gov/health/meditation/overview.htm.

Tim Ferriss has an interesting podcast in which he interviews overachievers of every kind, and one thing that they all seem to have in common is that they meditate.

There are lots of different ways to meditate, with lots of different effects, and of course every system claims wonders for its own special style. But really, meditation is about two things: focus and awareness. The easiest place to start, I think, is with "mindfulness of breathing." It goes like this:

- Set a timer. I recommend perhaps three minutes if this is your first ever go.
- Sit comfortably, or lie down. I like sitting cross-legged on a kicking pad, at the salle, or on my pillows in bed if I've just woken up, or on the floor in my study if I don't want to wake my wife.
- Close your eyes, and notice your breathing. Don't interfere with it, just pay attention. if that's a bit vague, try noticing the feeling of the breath coming in through your nostrils, and out of your mouth.
- Start counting your breaths: one in, out; two in, out; three in, out; and so on.
- When (not if) your mind wanders, just notice that it has wandered, and bring it gently back, starting the count at one.
- If you get to ten without distraction, go back to one anyway.
- Keep doing this until the timer goes off.
- Repeat this every day. First thing in the morning is probably best, but any time will do. I do it on waking.

I usually set my timer for about ten minutes, or twenty. No more, because I'm not a Buddhist monk. On a good day, I get up to about six breaths, sometimes even ten without distraction, but quite often it goes *one, one, one, one, one, one, one two Yay I got past one! oops, now I'm distracted again one, one, one.* That's okay. *The practice is the process of gently returning your attention to the breath.* Nobody cares that you did ten rounds of ten breaths without your mind wandering even once. Any computer will do that for you, and better. This meditation teaches you a relaxed, gentle focus. If the timer going off feels like a surprise, that's great. Try adding a minute or two to the time on your next session. Or not. If you can't wait for the damn thing to beep already, that's okay too. Be gentle. And set your morning alarm three minutes earlier. You can manage that, right?

The next stage is to apply that focus to something beyond your breath, such as the feelings in your body. The idea is that by making space for the feelings and being aware of them, they cease to control you and fade away. It's also generally useful in that it teaches mindfulness as a specific skill unconnected to your daily tasks. I have recently come across Tara Brach's guided meditations, which seem pretty good. You can find her beginner-level meditations here: https://www.tarabrach.com/guided-meditation-basic-meditations/. I have also used the "Calm" and "Headspace" apps, which both have useful free introductions for complete beginners to the practice.

Give it five minutes per day, every day. After ten days, if it's doing nothing for you, stop. But I'm confident you'll already be giving it seven minutes. Or ten. Because it's wonderful. As is breathing . . .

BREATHING

Breathing exercises of various kinds are fundamental to most traditional martial arts, and are increasingly widely used in modern military and police training. In this chapter I will cover how breathing works, the main kinds of breathing exercises and what they are for, and how to train your breathing to achieve the goals you want. This is one area of martial arts that is especially prone to woo-woo bullshit, so let me be clear; no matter how much you train your breathing, you will not learn to fly, stop bullets, or kill without touching. Sorry.

That said, breathing exercises are a kind of magic. I've always been drawn to the more indirect, even spiritual, aspects of martial arts training, and breathing exercises are perhaps the most obvious example of that. What possible use is gently waving your arms about and breathing deeply in a fight?

Well, none. But training is not fighting. Push-ups don't help much when boxing either. But have you ever met a boxer who didn't do push-ups?

The primary benefits of breathing practice can be summed up as fitness and calmness. By learning to breathe better, we are automatically fitter because we can get more air for less work. By learning to use breathing to control our nervous systems (at least up to a point) we become better able to manage stress and control fear.

Most people think of me as a swordsman, and I suppose that's true enough. Something all my regular students know, but maybe you don't, is that I might go for a month, or even three, without touching a sword. But hell will freeze over before I spend even a week without doing some kind of breathing practice. It's the foundation of my skill at arms, and the rock upon which I build my physical and mental practice.

In this chapter I'll take you through my go-to breathing exercises, explaining exactly what they are for and how they are supposed to work. You can read this for an academic understanding of the topic, if you like, but that's not what this is for. I intend this for people who want to at least try breathing exercises. I would like you to set aside five or ten minutes every day to try one or more of these exercises, and see if you get any benefit from them.

You are probably expecting a whole lot of black and white photos demonstrating the exercises. This seems very last-century to me, so instead I have videoed all the exercises, and added links into the text so you can find them.

I have also put together a six-week breathing course, which is based on this chapter but expands on it in all sorts of ways. This includes audio files of the instructions, a load more exercises, and tutorial videos. The key difference is that in the course I will take you step by step through a training program. Each week there is a class in which I teach you the exercises for that week, and a separate, shorter practice session for you to follow once you know the exercises. In the final week I teach you how to create your own practice routines of different lengths, so you can always find time to practise.

Traditionally I should insert a bunch of testimonials here from students who have used the breathing exercises I've taught them to improve their health, cure their asthma, control panic attacks, and so on. I've taught breathing exercises to hundreds, maybe thousands, of students by now, so there's no way for you to know whether these stories are representative, or correctly ascribe the cause of the improvement to the exercises; it could easily be that some other factor (like, say, medicine) was actually responsible. We didn't run proper scientific controlled experiments, so I make no claims. Just because they worked for someone else doesn't guarantee they'll work for you. But I do challenge you to try these exercises for yourself, and see what benefit you get out of them.

In this chapter I'll first explain what breathing is for and how it works, and then describe the different kinds of breathing exercises that I tend to use. Some of them are similar to meditation, and indeed there is a lot of crossover. Before you take a step further, a safety warning . . .

Do these exercises in a safe space: never when driving or swimming, or in any situation where blacking out is especially dangerous. Never push yourself hard when doing them. Take it slow and easy. Always. These are dangerous forces, and must be treated with respect.

If you hold your breath long enough, you will pass out. This is not dangerous if you're lying down somewhere safe. Your body will resume breathing for you. But under water? You could die.

If you have any kind of heart condition, hypertension, or risk of stroke, check with your doctor before doing any of these, and be especially careful if you choose to do any of the breath-holding exercises.

What is Breathing For?

The core purpose of breathing is gas exchange. You burn the oxygen in the air you breathe, and produce carbon dioxide. You breathe out to expel the carbon dioxide, and breathe in to get more oxygen.

The process of breathing takes some energy, because it requires muscular effort. One of the benefits of breathing training is you will learn to breathe more efficiently, getting more gas exchange for less effort, and so improve your overall efficiency. Energy that is not needed for breathing can be used for running, jumping, hitting things, and so on.

The Process of Breathing

The best summary of the process of breathing that I know of was written by Jaana Wessman, a doctor and long-time rapier student of mine, in a PDF called "What every swordsman should know about breathing." I'm borrowing from it liberally here. You can download the PDF from here: https://guywindsor.net/blog/breathingjw (I have her permission to share this).

When your lungs expand, air flows in. When they compress, air is expelled. The process of breathing, the process of expanding and compressing your lungs, is done mostly by your diaphragm (a muscular sheet between your lungs and your guts), and goes like this:

- The in-breath: Your diaphragm contracts, pushing your guts down, and pulling your lungs down, making them expand. The muscles round your waist must relax to allow the guts to move down, making room for the lungs to expand.
- The out-breath: The diaphragm relaxes; the guts push it back up, and so compress the lungs, pushing the air back out. You can increase the exhalation by using your abdominal muscles to push the guts even further up, forcing more air out.

The secondary system for getting air in and out is to use the intercostal muscles (between your ribs) to pull your ribs up and out, expanding your lungs. Relaxing them allows the ribcage to fall, pushing the air back out.

To get a clear sense of your breathing, try this exercise:

- Lie on the floor, and relax everything as much as you can
- Breathe out, contracting your stomach muscles a little to push the air out
- Now just relax, and notice how your stomach rises, your ribs expand, and air comes in. This is the passive phase of the in-breath. Do nothing to interfere or change it

- After a while, you will naturally breathe out again, which will probably feel like your belly dropping down towards the floor
- Just lie still, do nothing, and notice this process for a short while

Now we are going to interfere a little:

- Stay lying down, and as the next passive in-breath reaches its end, suck more air in. You will notice that this happens by expanding your stomach. That's your diaphragm pushing your guts out of the way
- When the diaphragm reaches full contraction, keep sucking the air in. Your chest will rise, as the effort transfers from your diaphragm to your ribcage. Hold the breath in for a moment
- Now relax; your ribcage will fall, then your belly, and air will flow out. Once you have come to the end of the passive out-breath, start squeezing the air out with your belly
- When you can't get any more out with your belly, keep pushing it out with your ribs. This is a complete out breath
- Now relax completely, and let nature take over. Just breathe naturally and without effort. Notice how much movement is involved.

As Dr Wessman points out, most of the time your breathing should be passive, with just the diaphragm contracting to pull air in, and relaxing to push it out. For this to work, your chest and belly should be relaxed. One of the things you will learn from breathing exercises is how to remain relaxed in order to allow your breathing to work more efficiently.

Breathing and Stress

Your nervous system is made up of three elements. The somatic nervous system is the stuff you control directly. Waving hello to a friend, for example. The sensory nervous system is the stuff your body senses: seeing your friend and hearing their cheery reply. The autonomic nervous system is the stuff you don't control directly, such as the way your pupils just dilated a bit when you saw your friend. Stress is an autonomic response. When your friend turns out to be a lunatic and pulls a gun on you, and your heart-rate suddenly hits the roof – that's another autonomic response.

Breathing is normally governed by your autonomic nervous system. This means that even if you never think about breathing, it will still get done. It's automatic, and your brain will generally do an excellent job of making sure you get enough oxygen.

But breathing is the one autonomic process that is easily brought under conscious control. Anyone can hold their breath at will. This means that breathing exercises form a bridge between the somatic and autonomic systems. One of the more common applications of breathing exercises is to reduce or control the autonomic response to stressful situations, such as remaining calm while at the dentist or in a sword fight. (Guess which one I find more scary.)

Breathing and Fitness

There are lots of ways to measure fitness, and all have their drawbacks. I think we can agree on the following as generally "good things":

- Being able to do an activity like running or fencing for longer without getting out of breath. This requires that we can either move more efficiently, or be able to use oxygen more efficiently
- Recovering more quickly from being out of breath. This requires that we have a good level of metabolic fitness.

The primary way that you train for endurance in any field is to make your body burn oxygen faster than normal, until you are really struggling to keep up the pace. In other words, we create an oxygen debt. This lack of oxygen basically teaches your body how to use the oxygen it does have more efficiently, and how to get more oxygen into the system by breathing better. Traditional exercise works the "oxygen out" end of that equation by making you burn more (by running further or faster). That is good, excellent, don't stop. But you can also work the other side of the equation by deliberately reducing the amount of oxygen you bring in, while keeping the level of exercise the same. Some of the more advanced breathing exercises do this. You can experiment with it easily by taking an exercise you already know (such as a push-up) and seeing how many you can do after breathing out completely and holding your breath empty.

What is Oxygen For?

Your body uses oxygen to generate energy. Basically, you get energy by burning large molecules, breaking them down into carbon dioxide and water.

Your cells use a molecule called ATP (adenosine triphosphate) like a battery. ATP releases energy when a phosphate group is removed; that energy can be used to make a muscle cell twitch. The molecule, now called ADP (adenosine diphosphate), can be recharged by adding a phosphate group. In other words, ATP converts into ADP and releases energy; ADP can then be recharged to create ATP again.

ATP is created when blood glucose is converted into pyruvate (a chemical) in a process called glycolysis (literally, "glucose splitting"). One molecule of glucose makes two molecules of pyruvate and two ATP molecules. This is called anaerobic respiration because it doesn't require oxygen.

If oxygen is available, little structures in your cells called mitochondria combine the pyruvate molecules with oxygen. This is done in a chemical reaction that produces carbon dioxide, water, and enough energy to make about 30 molecules of ATP. So, being able to use oxygen lets you get about fifteen times more usable energy from a molecule of glucose.

If pyruvate is not oxidized, it is converted to lactic acid, which has to be removed from the cell eventually.

When you burn more energy than you have oxygen for, you have an oxygen debt. This is only possible because you have stores of energy in your cells, and can also generate energy (in the form of ATP) anaerobically. Anaerobic respiration is fast, but it is inefficient. Aerobic respiration is slower, but much more efficient.

Breathing and Strength

Unlike most traditional strength training programs (of which I am a fan – breathing exercises should not replace "normal" exercise), breathing exercises tend to emphasise conditioning your tendons and ligaments, and most especially your fascia. Fascia is the elastic sheath that keeps your muscles in place, and for a long time in conventional medicine it was basically ignored as simply "connective tissue." As it so often does, medicine is now catching up with traditional martial arts training by recognising that fascia is actually vital to generating power. It stores energy when it is stretched in one direction, and that energy is released when the movement reverses. This is why it's easier to drop into a squat and bounce immediately back up, rather than squat down, wait, and then come back up. Fascia is critical to springy, explosive power. The most recent "revelation" of this power is in Christopher McDougall's excellent book *Natural Born Heroes*, which is about the Cretan resistance to the Nazis during the Second World War. Many "internal" or "soft" martial arts, like T'ai Chi, get their explosive power from fascia training. When you are lifting heavy weights, you should tense up to support and create the movement. But when doing breathing exercises, we are trying to emphasise and develop the fascia, and so we try to do the movements with the absolute minimum of muscular tension. These systems, muscles and fascia, are deeply intertwined, and the separation is therefore a matter of focus and emphasis.

I should also point out that all serious weight lifters in every style – including power-lifting, Olympic lifting, kettlebells, and the rest – pay close attention to how they breathe when doing a lift. They don't all necessarily agree on the best breathing pattern for a given lift, but they all agree that how you breathe matters.

Breathing and Power Generation

It is common in most martial arts to teach beginners to breathe in a particular way when doing an action; usually, breathe out as you strike. This is often accompanied with a vocalisation of some kind, such as a "kiai." This is no different to weight lifters breathing in a particular way when doing a lift. Advanced practitioners also use breathing, especially the out breath, when doing feats of power, like breaking boards. Back in the eighties, my Korean karate teacher in Gaborone used to break paving slabs with a single blow of his hand, and he had a special grunt we only ever heard when he was doing it. But, and this is a big "but", if you are conditioned to strike at a particular point in your breathing cycle, the chances of that coinciding with the opportunity to strike a resistant opponent are very, very small. The opportunity to strike, and so the timing of the strike, is determined by your opponent's actions. The need to breathe, and its timing, is determined by your metabolism. It is suicide to give your breathing pattern into your opponent's keeping.

The best instruction I ever got about how to breathe in a fight was this: "don't stop". It's worth practising your strikes and other actions to be timed with every part of your breathing cycle. You'll see that some are better than others, but your strikes should be sufficiently powerful for your combat purposes (whatever they may be) at every stage in the cycle. One of the main purposes of using a sword is that it doesn't require so much power to do lethal damage.

What about Ch'i?

Ch'i, prana, ki, lifeforce, The Force, call it what you will, is a major part of many martial arts and of most breathing practices.

The Chinese word for breathing exercises is indeed *qigong*, or "life-energy-practice." In Europe, the closest equivalent idea is probably *pneuma*, which is essentially the same thing. Breath, spirit, life force.

However, this concept is never explicitly mentioned in the sources for the arts that I teach and it is very rare to find any source dealing with it in a practical way, so I don't tend to mention it. At best it's a really useful graphical user interface for the body. By visualising the energy flowing in certain ways, you can create movement in a more accurate and natural way. When you learn to feel it flowing, and perceive blocks in your natural flow in energy terms, clearing those blocks is much easier.

But it is a very slippery slope from a useful way of thinking about things to all sorts of ghastly delusions, such as no-touch takedowns. There are lots of videos on the web of deluded martial arts "masters" getting the crap kicked out of them by people who can actually fight because their "no touch" ch'i mastery has failed to protect them. By all means, interpret the exercises I will describe in terms of ch'i, and feel free to visualise it. But please don't start thinking that you'll be able to shoot lightning from your hands, no matter how much you practise.

For visualisation purposes, you will need to imagine three centres in your body. The body centre is your centre of gravity, about three fingers below your navel, and a few inches in. The heart centre is in the centre of your chest behind your sternum. The mind centre is in the middle of your forehead, and a couple of inches in. In every exercise, you can visualise the energy moving. As you breathe in, the energy rises up your spine from the body centre, through the heart centre, and up to the mind centre; and as you breath out it descends back down through the heart to the body centre. If this makes no sense to you, just skip it. If you are experienced at breathing exercises and have an existing ch'i visualisation method, feel free to apply it to any of these exercises.

How to Breathe

Your nose is a filter that cleans and warms the air you breathe, sampling it for good and bad smells, and it does a pretty good job of keeping dust out of your delicate lungs. The simplest way to breathe is just in and out of your nose.

Because your nose is a filter, it does slow down the rate at which you can move air in and out. This is why if you are really out of breath, you will automatically switch to breathing in and out of your mouth. I play the trumpet occasionally, and was taught to always breathe in through my mouth when taking in air between passages, because it's much faster.

If you think about it for a minute, it would seem that the most perfect breathing would be in through your nose and out through your mouth: the air is cleaned and warmed going in, but it would leave through the exhaust, not the filter. When possible, that's how we do it while doing breathing exercises. It does require a bit more work though, because you have to change the structures at the back of your mouth to switch channels. When using the exercises in this book, unless I say otherwise, please do breathe in through your nose and out through your mouth.

It is also important to have your tongue in the right place. This is especially true for active martial artists, as anyone who has bitten through their own tongue when they got hit can attest. The tip of your tongue should rest on the hard palate, the bony ridge just behind the top front teeth. This not only keeps your tongue out of the way, it also activates some of the stabiliser muscles in your neck. In the ch'i paradigm, it is said to connect one of the major meridians.

To sum up then: tongue behind your teeth, and breathe in through your nose and out through your mouth.

Strict versus Relaxed

There are several kinds of breathing exercise in this section. Some are linked to specific body movements; others are done sitting still, or while walking, or in whatever situation you find yourself in. The ones that are done with specific movements fall into two types: strict or relaxed.

"Relaxed" exercises have a general form, but no very exact choreography. You can adjust the stance and the movements to suit yourself.

"Strict" exercises are very, very precise. The position of every bone in your body is absolutely defined, and the motions are very strictly controlled. Most of my students over the years have found that these give the best results, but they are much more difficult to learn. We will start with a couple of relaxed exercises, but spend most of our time on the stricter ones.

Follow or Control?

There are fundamentally two different ways to do breathing exercises. You either control the rate and type of your breathing, making your breath conform to your movements or some other external factor (such as time) – we can call this "control the breath"; or you breathe naturally and make your actions conform to your breath – we can call this "follow the breath".

Generally speaking, most of the basic-level breathing exercises we do that include specific body movements will be done by "following the breath". Most of the seated exercises will be done by "controlling the breath". Some advanced exercises include both.

What we are trying to establish is the habit of being in control of your physiology, at least up to a point. You don't really want conscious control of most of your autonomic systems, even it it were possible. But being able to bring your heart rate down after a fright, or regaining conscious control of your actions when panicked – those are useful skills. So is a deep level of fitness, so you can keep going longer when the air supply is cut off.

Think of stage fright. We've all experienced it in some form – that gut-wrenching terror that chokes performance, and is a horribly self-fulfilling prophecy. When performing, the optimal level of arousal is somewhere between the extremes of being completely blasé and completely terrified. In martial arts, we don't ever worry about bringing your level of arousal up; that happens naturally because the situations we deal with are inherently scary. Bringing it down is the key skill. How is it done?

In modern combat training, the most common approach is "combat breathing". Let's start with that.

THE EXERCISES
Combat Breathing
I learned this from Col. David Grossman's seminal book, *On Killing*.

- Breathe in for a count of four beats
- Hold your breath for four beats
- Breathe out for four beats
- Hold your breath empty for four beats
- Repeat.

Practise this for a few rounds. It feels odd to start with, especially holding the breath empty. That's okay. The trick now is to associate switching to that breathing pattern when you are stressed. I'm not going to suggest popping down to gangland and insulting someone to get a gun shoved in your face to generate stress. Instead, just imagine the sort of situations in which you might get frightened, and picture yourself switching to this breathing exercise when it happens. Try it the next time somebody almost crashes into your car, or you are startled by the cat jumping on you.

If you've read my book *Swordfighting*, you may remember the spider story. I'll recap it here just in case:

"The thing about Australia is that all of the most poisonous animals in the world live there. It's remote for a reason: you're not supposed to go there! Take the funnel-web spider. It looks like it can kill you, and it can. I was staying at my friend Paul Wagner's house, and he calmly informed me that there are certainly funnel-webs in his garden (so where's the napalm, Paul?). Later that day we visited the National Museum, and in the gift shop he picked up a plastic model of one to show me what they look like. Walking home from the pub after a seminar the following day, just strolling down the pavement, I walked between someone's garden hedge and a tree, and got a faceful of spiderweb. "Oh shit," I thought. Then I looked down, and there was a fucking funnel-web on my shoulder! A moment later, I realised I was running like hell, and screaming in terror. Running away from the spider on my shoulder. Not a carefully-thought-out strategy. A part of my mind was taken by the irony of being one of the very very few tourists who die from Australian wildlife. So I started unzipping my jacket, but my hands were shaking too much. My legs carried on running, and I started combat-breathing (in for 4, hold for 4, out for 4, hold for 4) to get my heart rate down, and in a moment I could get the zip open, and the jacket off. After about another 50 yards, my legs were mine again, and I stopped.

Paul was doubled up in paroxysms of hysterical laughter. Rational thought was returning. I explained about the spider, how a funnel-web was on my shoulder, and I knew I was going to die stupidly. "Oh, don't worry, funnel-webs live in the ground. That was probably a little huntsman. Very unlikely to kill you. Unless you happen to be allergic."

"No, Paul, it was a fucking great ozzy spider and I was going to die."

Paul kindly picked up my jacket and shook it out. I refused to put it on until he had gone through all the pockets. By this time my heart rate was back below 100 and I had full use of my faculties. Just the occasional full-body shudder."

So, I've tested this in conditions of extreme mortal terror, and can confirm that it works!

Walking and Breathing

You can do two things at once, right? Walking AND breathing? Sure you can.

This is the exercise I usually start people off with when I teach breathing seminars. Simply walk. Inside, outside, doesn't matter. On your next in breath, breathe in for four steps, then hold for four steps, breathe out for four steps, and then hold empty for four steps. Keep this going. After a round or two you'll probably find it quite hard to keep your next in breath slow and calm, in time with your steps. Use your walking pace to determine the pace of your breathing.

If a four-step pattern is quite easy, try extending it to six steps (in for six, hold for six, out for six, hold empty for six, repeat), or eight, or ten. I find that it's a real challenge to maintain a ten-step pattern for more than a couple of rounds.

If you practice this regularly (say, every time you walk to work, or indeed anywhere), you will start playing games with it, and you can interval your way up to a pretty good standard of aerobic fitness by just doing this. You know you're really training when you have to fight hard to keep that desperate in breath long and slow, when every cell in your body is screaming at you to suck air in hard and fast.

And that's the point. Depriving yourself of enough oxygen establishes a level of physiological distress that taps into some pretty deep biological processes. Any ancestor of yours who didn't fight for air would have died very young and their genes would not be passed on. Air is more immediately vital than water, food, shelter or sex. Trigger this distress, and then maintain your calm, slow movements and your absolute control over your behaviour, and you are practising the ability to maintain composure under pressure. You are also learning to breathe more deeply, and more efficiently.

Posture Exercise

Posture is very important for your overall sense of wellbeing. It works in both directions: if you feel happy and confident, you'll tend to stand upright, and if you feel miserable and insecure, you'll tend to hunch. But you can generate a better mood by modelling the physical behaviour of someone in a better mood. Smiling, for instance, is well known to increase happiness. So learning to have better posture is good for your mind and heart as well as for your body.

Posture is balance. Think of your spine as a set of toy bricks, piled one on the other. Ideally, gravity should keep them all in place, and keep the tower tall. Good posture allows the muscles around the spine to relax, because they are not needed for keeping you upright. Of course, you do need some muscular activity to maintain your posture, but it's probably much less than you're using right now. This is directly related to martial arts. Muscles that are working to keep you upright are not available for generating power. The less tension you need to hold your position, the harder and faster you can strike.

Given that I am usually surrounded by swords, I often illustrate this exercise with one. Any long thin object will do – a long-handled broom is perfect. Balance the (blunt!) sword with the point on your palm or fingertip. Notice what you need to do to keep it upright. Try to minimise movement. When you can hold it steady, choose a direction to walk in, and go in that direction without losing the balance of the sword.

The pommel or broom head is your head; the blade or broomstick is your spine; and your hand is your pelvis. What we will do is balance your head on your spine, to allow as much relaxation as possible.

You will need a ball to sit on. Anything as big as a basketball, or bigger, will do. I've used my wife's Pilates exercise ball, and my own basketball and medicine balls for this. If you are using a basketball, kneel on the ground, put it between your feet and

313

sit on it. If you're using an exercise ball, sit on it and place your feet flat on the floor. Rest your hands on your knees.

Now shut your eyes and focus on your breathing. Let each breath expand your belly and rise in your chest. Relax completely. Think of balancing your head on your spine like a rock on a willow wand. Wherever you feel yourself holding, gently instruct the muscles to let go. As the breath comes in, you expand; as it leaves, you contract. It moves your whole body.

As you practise this, you will find that the breath moves you more and more, and there is less and less tension holding you in place. You know you are really getting it when it feels like the beat of your heart affects your overall posture, because it is so carefully balanced, and is held in place by nothing at all.

You should probably set a timer for this. I suggest three minutes for the first session. Add to it as you wish.

When it is time to stop, open your eyes and rise up with your spine balanced on your pelvis like the sword was on your hand. It's useful to cultivate the habit of checking your posture regularly. It can almost always be improved.

Autumn Leaves

This is perhaps the most widely practised breathing exercise of all (though I've renamed it to avoid confusion with other styles and uses. You can find versions of it called "pulling down the heavens", "Lift ch'i up and pour ch'i down", and many others). Whatever you call it, it's relaxed, slow and lovely. Your hands make big circles, more or less in the plane of your body. Imagine, as you raise your arms, that you are standing with your back against a wall, and your hands almost run along it on the way up, until they almost meet over your head. Then let your hands fall naturally in front of you; if it helps, imagine the wall is now a foot or so in front of you. Your hands should remain level with each other and not touch the wall. Let your hands finish their natural arcs and come to rest again at your sides.

1. Stand with your feet about shoulder width apart, knees slightly bent, and with hands by your sides. Exhale
2. When you're ready to breathe in, do so, and let your relaxed arms gently rise in a big circle until they are above your head
3. As your breath leaves, allow your arms to bend and the hands to gently fall, like autumn leaves
4. Repeat about eight times, or more if you like.

Points to bear in mind:

• Be gentle
• The hands don't touch
• Let the breath lead the exercise
• Stop if you get dizzy.

You can see the video here: https://guywindsor.net/blog/ breathingautumnleaves

Two Bowls of Whisky

The traditional Scottish drinking vessel for whisky is a quaich, which is a shallow bowl with two small handles. In this exercise, you'll take two imaginary quaichs, one on each palm, and offer them in front of you, behind you, and to the angels overhead.

Let's start with just the movement.

1. Stand with your feet shoulder width apart, or a bit wider
2. Place your hands palm up in front of you, as if resting on a chest-high table
3. Bring your elbows back, keeping your palms level
4. Turn your hands round under your armpits, so your fingers point behind you. Don't spill the whisky!
5. Reach as far behind you as you can, bending forward at the waist

6. Bring your arms round, still palm up, leading with your little fingers, until your hands are in front of you

7. Keep the motion going, leaning back, until your arms cross over your head, palms still up

8. Keep the circle going until you return to the start position.

Got that? Pass it behind you, pass it in front, and then pass it overhead.

As you do this, keep your back rather straight, and make space for the motion by hinging at the hips and bending your knees.

Now the breathing:

• As you pass your hands back and hinge forwards, breathe out

• As your hands cross and you pass your hands overhead, leaning back, breathe in

• Experiment with leading with the breath, and with controlling the breath.

You can see the video here: https://guywindsor.net/blog/breathingquaichs

How to Stand: Horse Stance

If we consider the range of martial arts and related practices, we have a huge range of breathing exercises and styles to choose from. I've practised t'ai chi ch'üan, kung fu, aikido and karate quite a bit, and picked up a lot of breathing exercises from all of them. The most famous kind of breathing practice is probably chi kung (qi gong), of which there are hundreds of styles and thousands of exercises. I'll introduce you to a couple here. We should start by establishing a standing position in which your back can relax, and your weight is carried by the fascia of your legs. You'll notice that the instructions from here on are a lot more detailed. This is the beginning of the "strict" exercises.

Most breathing exercise systems have some variation of the horse stance. I'll take you through the version I find most repeatable – it tends to give the most consistent starting point for your exercises.

1. Begin with your feet together
2. Stretch your arms out in front of you at shoulder height, palms down. Your thumbs touch
3. Breathe in through your nose while pulling your hands back into tight fists, tight under your armpits. Your elbows go as far behind you as possible
4. Holding your breath, pivot your heels out 30°, turning on the balls of your feet (your body stays still)
5. Pivot your toes out by about 30°, then your heels, then your toes, and then your heels. This broadens your stance by a consistent amount. Your heels will be turned out a bit, toes in
6. Relax your legs, letting your knees bend, and breathe out
7. Tuck your tailbone slightly, tilting your pelvis
8. Push your hands down in front of you, open and flat. At the end of the out breath, your hands are about at your hips.

By setting your stance in this way, you have activated the muscles of your shoulders, hands, and belly; established a broad stance that relies on the fascia of your legs; and found a stable, balanced position from which to begin every breathing exercise. Some people find the pigeon-toed stance unhealthily uncomfortable – by all means adjust the turns to leave the feet parallel at the end if that's better for you.

Also, please note that this is not a "fighting stance." It's optimised for breathing exercises, not hitting things or making rapid movement out of it.

You can see the video here: https://guywindsor.net/blog/breathinghowtostand

Separate Clouds

This is a really useful exercise. It will teach you how to breathe deeply and efficiently, and establish better posture and more precise movements.

- Establish your start position, as described in "How to Stand"
- As you relax your belly, the in breath starts and your hands turn palm up
- As the breath comes in, the hands rise up your body. They are open and flat, and do not touch
- Allow your elbows to rise
- As your hands pass your face, they turn, so your palms keep facing up
- Your hands continue until your arms are stretched out over your head, palms up
- Pause your breath as the hands descend down towards your shoulders; your arms are in a straight line with each other, palms out to the sides
- As your hands pass your shoulders, you breathe out slowly.
- As you come to the end of the out breath, your hands are relaxed and down by your hips.

You might notice that I'm using a very passive way of describing the action: not "raise your hands," but "your hands rise." This is to convey the feeling that what your hands do is sort of automatic and determined by the breath. That said, keep the following points in mind.

- Your hands should be open and flat, with the fingers together and the thumb tucked in to the side of the hand
- Your hands never touch
- In the top position, it's as if your hands are holding up the ceiling

- As your hands fall, if you were to do this exercise with your back against a wall, your little fingers would be in contact with the wall from the top position until near the end of the out breath
- Breathe as deeply and slowly as you can, and your hands follow the breath.

Do at least eight cycles (breathe in; pause; and breathe out) per session. You can do more. Stop if you feel dizzy. Don't push it. Be gentle.

You can find the video here: https://guywindsor.net/blog/breathingseparateclouds

In the videos you will notice that I often finish an exercise by bringing my feet together and breathing in as my hands rise to chest height, and then throwing my hands up with a sharp exhalation. I often grunt a bit on that exhalation. This is a habit I picked up a long time ago when doing breathing exercises in kung fu; feel free to use it, but be aware that strictly speaking it's not part of the exercise.

The Crane: Part One
This is perhaps my favourite breathing exercise of them all. It works so many things all at once: core strength, mobility, balance, and breathing – the lot. I was taught it by Num, my kung fu instructor friend, all in one go, but I'll break it down for you a bit.

What you're going to do in part one is "Separate Clouds", but as your hands fall, you sink onto one leg; as they rise, you come up on that leg, lifting the other knee as high as it will go. As the hands fall, you sink onto the same foot, and are basically doing a kind of one-legged squat with the "Separate Clouds" hand movements and breathing pattern.

1. Get into horse stance as described earlier and, as you let go with your breath, your hands fall. Sink onto your right foot, as low as you can go. Ideally your hands almost touch the ground
2. Your left foot comes off the ground. Bring your left knee up to your chest
3. As the breath comes in, the hands rise and the body follows, up and up, until your right leg is straight and your hands are above your head, palms up. Stretch up. Your left knee is as high as possible, your toes pointed to the ground
4. Hold your breath as your hands fall, until they pass your shoulders. Sink down onto your right foot, bending the knee. Follow the breath down, until you are at the starting point for the in breath
5. Repeat twice more for a total of three breaths on your right foot (do not reset with horse stance in between the breaths)
6. Change sides and repeat three times on your left foot.
7. Repeat on the right, left, right, and left, for a total of nine breaths on each foot.

Most people find this really hard to start with. You should have seen me wobbling about all over the place when I was learning it! The key points to remember are:

- Your hands are flat like spades, the fingers together and the thumbs tucked in against the sides of your index fingers
- Your hands do not touch
- Keep your unweighted knee as high as possible and the toes pointed
- Fix your gaze on a single spot, to help with balance
- The movement follows the breath
- If you get out of breath, stop for a bit
- If you feel dizzy, stop
- Aim for slow, perfectly controlled movements.

- Imagine you are scooping water with your hands up from the ground, up your leg, up your body, and up into the clouds.

You can see the video here: https://guywindsor.net/blog/breathingcrane1

The Crane: Part Two

When part one is reasonably comfortable and you're not falling over too much, start working on part two. Start crouched on your right foot, as if you were about to do one of the three breaths in part one. Lungs are empty. As you breathe in, straighten your supporting (right) leg as before, but stay crouched over. On the out breath, push your arms out to either side and extend your unweighted (left) leg behind you, so you look like a crane spreading its wings.

As you breathe in, straighten up, bring your hands to your chest and lift your unweighted (left) knee to your chest, and then lower it to the ground. As you breathe out, sink again onto your weighted (right) leg, and let your unweighted (left) leg extend forward. Reach down your extended leg, stretching the hamstrings. Breathe in as you scoop your hands up your body and return to a normal standing position.

It's quite a lot to remember, especially when you see it written down. So let's step it out:

1. Start on the right foot, lungs empty, as if you were about to do an in breath in Part One
2. During the in-breath, straighten your right leg but stay crouched over, and bring your hands to your chest, palms towards each other, fingers pointing straight down
3. During the out-breath, extend your arms out to the sides, like Samson pushing down the pillars of the temple. Extend your left foot back, pointing with the toes
4. At the end of the in-breath, your arms and leg should be fully extended.

5. Your head, hands, and foot all about level with your hips or a little higher
6. As you breathe in, bring your body upright and lift your left knee to your chest. Your hands are coming round and rising, palm up, a little higher than your sternum
7. Place your left foot on the ground, extending the leg, keeping your weight back on your right foot
8. As you breathe out, keep your fingertips pointing towards each other, and turn your hands palm down
9. Sink your weight on your right foot
10. Pass your hands down your left leg, as far as you can reach in a gentle stretch
11. Reach the end of the stretch as you reach the end of the out-breath.

You can do the whooshy-breath finish here if you like:

1. Breathe in, scooping your hands up your body, coming to a normal standing position
2. Your hands come to the top of the chest at the end of the in-breath
3. Turn your hands up as usual, but breathe out hard and fast with a *whooosh*, throwing your hands up and out.

Practice the sequence on both sides, at least three times each.

Points to remember are:

- Keep this slow and steady
- You can practise the Crane position separately, using a friend to spot you. Are your head, hands and foot at the same level? Is your back arched a bit? Are you tipping over sideways?
- You can also video yourself and compare your video with mine
- Imagine you are scooping water up your leg, then squirting it out through your hands, head and foot, and then swooshing

it down into the ground through your extended unweighted leg at the end.

The Crane: Complete

Once you have parts one and two reasonably solid, you can put them together.

1. Start on the right foot
2. Do three breath cycles, rising up each time, as in part one
3. On the fourth in-breath, begin part two: bring your hands to your chest
4. Breathe out into the Crane
5. Breathe in, hands to chest
6. Breathe out down your leg
7. Finish with the in-breath to stand, out with a *whoosh*
8. Repeat on the other side.

Well done! That's one repetition of the Crane (five breaths on each side is one rep).

You can see the video here: https://guywindsor.net/blog/breathingcrane2

I was taught that the optimum dose of the Crane is three repetitions, three times per day: before breakfast, before lunch, and before dinner. The most important set is the first one, of course.

Wim Hof Breathing

There is a man in Holland who has run a marathon in Arctic conditions, wearing only a pair of shorts; spent hours in the death zone in the Himalayas, wearing only a pair of shorts; and run a marathon in the Namib desert, with no water or rest – and, you guessed it, wearing only a pair of shorts.

I don't think it's the shorts we should be focussing on. The question is, how does he do it?

More impressive, to me at least, were the tests that were run in the Radboud University Medical Center in Nijmegen, Holland, in 2014. In these tests Wim Hof was injected with deactivated bacteria, which causes an immune reaction with fever and flu-like symptoms but is not actually dangerous. He stopped his immune system from over-reacting, and had no symptoms. Impressive. But vastly more impressive (to me at least) was the follow-up. The researchers took 24 people, and split them into two groups of 12. One group was taught how to control their immune systems with ten days of training. The other group, the control, was not. Then both groups were given the same deactivated bacteria shot. The control group were sick as dogs; meanwhile, all of the trained subjects managed to control their reaction and were fine. It was written up in Nature magazine here: https://www.nature.com/news/behavioural-training-reduces-inflammation-1.15156

You've got to admit, that's pretty cool.

His skills come from breathing exercises he has adapted from Tummo yoga, and gradually increasing exposure to the cold. I signed up to his online course and found it interesting – a combination of breathing exercises, yoga poses, and cold exposure. It didn't teach me the immune system stuff, but I have incorporated the breathing element and cold exposure into my daily practice for some years now.

I'll introduce you to the breathing. If you find it useful and interesting, by all means go and try his course for yourself.

What I've said before about safety goes double for this kind of breathing. The risk of passing out is much higher, so do not do this in or near water, or when driving.

You'll need a stopwatch and a place to sit (on cushions on the floor is best). What you will do is hyperventilate to over-oxygenate your blood, then hold your lungs empty for as long as you can, and then breathe in, and hold that for at least fifteen seconds before breathing out.

1. Take 30 full deep breaths, in through the nose and out through the mouth, quite fast. Really suck the air in
2. On the last out-breath, breathe out as fully as you can, and hold
3. Start your timer. Don't look at it, just keep still
4. Wait until you really need to breathe in. You might feel a kind of body-panic set in. That's okay
5. When you need to breathe in, do so, and hold the breath
6. Check the timer, make a mental note of the time you held your breath empty, and hold it full for at least fifteen seconds
7. Breathe out.

That's one cycle. I suggest doing at least three. Begin the hyperventilation immediately after that last out breath, unless you really need a break.

One very interesting aspect of this is how your body learns to adapt. If you do this daily, you will probably find (as I did) that to start with you can hold your breath empty for about 45 seconds to a minute; but after a few weeks or months, you can easily hold for 90 seconds, or even two minutes or more.

Once you are comfortable with this, you can add what Wim calls a "bonus round", in which you do push-ups while you hold your lungs empty. When you max out and have to breathe in, hold the breath for fifteen seconds or more as usual. Again, with practice, you can build up the push-ups. I started with having to breathe in at about fifteen push-ups. I can now usually do 30 on one breath, and occasionally have got to over 40.

One of the advantages of this method is you can quantify it quite easily. I do recommend writing down your times and keeping track of your progress.

You can see the video here: https://guywindsor.net/blog/breathingwimhof

Create a Practice Routine

Your habits define you. If you find a way to incorporate breathing exercises into your everyday life, I've no doubt you'll become fitter and healthier, and start to see benefits in all aspects of your life. But the trick is creating the habit. I believe in putting first things first, so I usually do my breathing exercises first thing on waking up. Probably the easiest approach is to set your alarm ten minutes earlier, and just do the exercises.

Alternatively, you can link your new habit of breathing practice to another existing habit. Do you break for lunch? Then add your breathing practice in as the first thing you do on breaking. It's best to do them on a not-full stomach, so after lunch isn't optimal.

A good system that you actually follow is better than a perfect system that you skip, so go easy on yourself. Ten minutes. Every day. Find a way to build it into your schedule, and into everyone else's expectations of you. Ten minutes is not a lot, but it is way more effective than a beautiful hour-long regime that you get to maybe once per week at best.

It may also help to set a reminder – put your new ten minute breathing practice slot into your calendar.

It's often helpful to commit to a specific period, such as 10 minutes per day for 30 days. It's less scary, easier to commit to. I'd be astonished if when you get to day 30, you don't decide to go on for another 30 days. And another, and another. But don't try to commit to a lifelong practice at first, because it's too easy to fail.

And you will fail. There will be days when you don't get any breathing practice done. That's okay. Get back to it tomorrow. But be strict with yourself: I didn't make it yesterday, so I must do it today.

What Next?

I hope that this chapter has sparked an interest in breathing training for you. By themselves the exercises here are enough to keep you busy and improving your health for a long time, but if you want more, I recommend the following ideas.

- Keep an eye out for chi kung (qi gong) classes near you. Not every chi kung teacher is any good so be a little wary of extreme claims, but try it out with an open and sceptical mind
- Play with the exercises and practices. Simply being aware of your breathing will probably improve it
- You might also like my breathing course, which you can find here: https://swordschool.teachable.com/p/breathing-basics

Mine is a six week program, which includes more instruction on all of these exercises, with video and audio. It also has a broader range of exercises, and training routines of varying lengths and difficulty. If you've enjoyed this chapter, you'll probably love the course. You can use this coupon code to get 25% off the course: TTPHMAREADERS25

I look forward to seeing you on the course!

Safety Reminder

Do these exercises in a safe space: never when driving, swimming, or in any situation where blacking out is especially dangerous. Never push yourself hard when doing them. Take it slow and easy. Always. These are dangerous forces, and must be treated with respect.

If you hold your breath long enough, you will pass out. This is not dangerous if you're lying down somewhere safe. Your body will resume breathing for you. But under water? You could die.

If you have any kind of heart condition, hypertension, or risk of stroke, check with your doctor before doing any of these, and be especially careful if you choose to do any of the breath-holding exercises.

WHY DO WE DO THIS?

Historical Martial Arts can be the hook that brings people out of mediocrity . . .

For many of us, there is no need to even think about why we would train in the Art. It is simply an irreducible desire, like the way many people want to have kids. But we all know someone for whom our passion for the sword is inexplicable, just as we all know someone who does not want to be a parent. I thought I would write this so that you know why I have chosen the path of the sword. If it resonates with you, you can direct the baffled in your life here for enlightenment.

Let us begin with a wide focus: why martial arts at all? Some have practical uses, sure: those living on meaner streets will have use for self-defence skills. But most martial arts, if they convey those skills at all, are very inefficient at it. Some martial arts, or combat sports at least, offer a career path that includes fame and riches. An Olympic gold medal, perhaps. But that is not true of ours.

I train martial arts because they can offer moments of utter transcendence. The ineffable made manifest. This is traditionally described as "beyond words" or "indescribable", but as a martial artist and a writer, that would feel like a cop out. I will take this feeling and wrestle it down onto the page, or at least give it my best shot.

It is a moment when every atom in your body is exactly where it should be. Every step you have taken on life's path makes sense, is part of a coherent story. The pain of every mistake is made worthwhile by the lessons contained therein.

There is a feeling of physical power without limit; strength without stiffness; flow without randomness; precision without pedantry; focus without blinkers; breadth and depth; massive destructive capability but utter gentleness; self awareness without self consciousness; and force without fury. Your body alive as it has never been, all fear and pain burned away in a moment of absolute clarity; certainty without dogma; and an overpowering love, even for your enemies, that enables you to destroy them without degrading them. It is, for a religious person, the breath of God within you. For an atheist, it is a moment of attaining perfection as a human being.

And I can, in theory at least, get that feeling every time I pick up a sword. In practice, I've been there a dozen times. And I've had a lesser version of it, a breath or a hint of it, almost daily.

It is, of course, an illusion. Even in that moment of grace, you are not perfect or invulnerable. And this is where the discipline of a serious art saves you from the wishy-washy hippy shit of some other "spiritual paths". It is so easy to slip, to believe your own hype, and simply essential that the moment you do so, reality comes crashing in like a sword to the head. The rigour of a true martial art contains at its heart a continual examining of your skills. This can come in all sorts of forms. I tend to use pressure drills and freeplay, but the critical component is the existence of an objective external test: "Does this work?" with a clear yes/no feedback mechanism in place. In many ways, the books from which we draw our art are that mechanism: the benchmark against which you measure the correctness of what you do. This academic aspect is I think unique to historical martial arts, and it requires that we are able to articulate in reasoned argument why we do anything a particular way. This adds a mental dimension, a way of thinking clearly and logically – of making arguments supported by evidence – which is the antithesis of the "feel that energy, man" hippy shit I refer to above.

There is also the question of morality. The moral dimension

to swordsmanship comes from the lethal nature of the art. It is, originally, for killing people. Some systems emphasise self defence, but the knightly arts were for professional warriors. You kill people because that's your job – much like a modern soldier, who must only distinguish between legal and illegal orders. If the order is legal, and obeying it means killing people, well, that's what they train for. I'm not suggesting that any part of that is easy, especially distinguishing legal orders from illegal ones, but at its base, it is simple. Do, or do not. But for us, training exists in an artificial space that allows us to deeply examine the morality of the martial arts. (I've written elsewhere about training as a holodeck for the philosophy of ethics.) We are training a killing art, so we must ask ourselves this question: in what circumstances, if any, is it acceptable to take life? This is why I have no interest in non-lethal arts. They simply lack this moral aspect. Especially combat sports, where your opponent has chosen to compete with you in a fair fight, and so long as you both follow the rules, there is no question of right or wrong at all.

Bodily health is also an issue. We have no choice but to live in this carcase until it stops working. There is just no way round the fact that you either figure out how yours works and get the best out of it (it is a stunningly fabulous machine), or you ignore it until it fails. I don't train to stay healthy – I stay healthy so I can train. All of my students know that I put maintenance and conditioning at the heart of our training, and I spend about 90% of my own training time, and about 40% of my teaching time, working on mechanics. Most of my students come to me a bit broken in the beginning. Poor posture, bad wrists, a dodgy knee, excessive weight, or whatever. We work together to develop good habits, mostly by paying attention to posture, breathing, joint strength training, and – of course – diet. This has a way of both preparing the student for the physical training and keeping them grounded when the magic starts to happen. For many students, the sword has hooked them out of physical lassitude and ill health and into a more active, healthier life. It is certainly part of the core mission of the School. Our training is healthy – our one golden rule is everyone must finish class healthier than they started it. And because we are interested in process, not outcome, it is literally irrelevant how fit a student is when they start. Only the attitude they bring to training matters.

(And this is another reason why I am not interested in combat sports. They have a pretty high threshold for physical fitness, which means that you have to start quite fit (and young!) if you wish to get really good at them. There is a genetic lottery (every sport has an ideal body type), and luck plays a huge part too. Read *Bounce*, by Matthew Syed, for more on this. Combat sports also have a very high risk of injury. So the students who need hooking off the couch and into a healthy life are barred from admission. The ones who need it least are the only ones who can have it.)

So why the sword? All of these spiritual, mental, moral and physical benefits can be accomplished with other weapons, or with no weapons at all. There is no good reason, though I could rationalise it at length. We could talk about flow states, à la Mihaly Csikszentmihalyi: swordsmanship practice is most certainly a way to bring "order to consciousness" (as opposed to entropic chaos). We could talk about the social aspect: how good it is to find, coming to the salle, that you are not the only sword-obsessed loony out there. But fundamentally, some people are just drawn to the magic of steel. It resonates in them. Many students remember the first time they heard the clash of blade on blade, and how their heart leapt.

I train because I feel it. Oh Lord, I feel it in my very bones. But how I train is utterly rational. Together, the martial and academic truth-testing keep me from flying away with the fairies. The physical training keeps my body strong and agile. The mental training keeps my mind clear and focussed. The moral aspect leads me to consider the meaning and value of every part of my life.

So when someone asks you "Why practise Swordsmanship?", perhaps the best answer is "how the hell do you manage without it?"

So, that's my reason. What's yours?

BIBLIOGRAPHY

Primary Fencing Sources

Please note, this only includes fencing sources I refer to in the main text of the book; it does not include everything on the list of popular sources, on pages 75–83.

Capoferro, Ridolfo. 1610. *Gran Simulacro dell'Arte e dell'Uso della Scherma*. Siena, Italy: Silvestro Marchetti and Camillo Turi.

Codex Döbringer. MS. 3227a. Germanisches Nationalmuseum, Nuremberg, Germany.

Kal, Paulus. (No title). Cgm 1507. Bayerische Staatsbibliothek, Munich, Germany. Reproduced in Tobler.

Fiore dei Liberi. *Il Fior di Battaglia (MS Ludwig XV13)*. J. P. Getty Museum, Los Angeles.

Fiore dei Liberi. *Flos Duellatorum*. Pisani-Dossi Library, Corbetta, Italy.

Fiore dei Liberi. *Il Fior di Battaglia. (Morgan MS M 383)*. Pierpont Morgan Museum, New York.

Fiore dei Liberi. *Florius de Arte Luctandi (MSS Latin 11269)*. Bibliothèque Nationale Française, Paris.

Ficher, Baltazar. 1796. L'art de l'Escrime. St. Petersburg.

Giganti, Nicoletto. 1606. *Schola overo Teatro*. Venice. Giovanni Antonio and Giacomo de' Franceschi.

Marozzo, Achille. 1536. *Opera Nova*. Modena.

Meyer, Joachim. 2006. *The Art of Combat: A German Martial Arts Treatise of 1570*. Translated by Jeffrey Forgeng. New York. Palgrave Macmillan.

Codex Ringeck. *MS Dresden C.487*. Sächsische Landesbibliothek, Dresden, Germany.

Royal Armouries Ms. I.33. Royal Armouries Museum, Leeds.

Vadi, Philippo. *De Arte Gladiatoria Dimicandi*. Biblioteca Nazionale, Rome.

Vadi, Philippo. 2005. L'arte cavalleresca del combattimento. Ed. Marco Rubboli and Luca Cesari. Rimini. Il Cerchio

Viggiani, Angelo. 1575. *Lo Schermo*. Venice. Giorgio Angelieri.

Secondary Sources (and modern sources)

Aviroop, Biswas et al. 2015. *Sedentary Time and Its Association With Risk for Disease Incidence, Mortality, and Hospitalization in Adults: A Systematic Review and Meta-analysis*. http://annals.org/aim/article/2091327/sedentary-time-its-association-risk-disease-incidence-mortality-hospitalization-adults

Bernstein, Peter. 1998. *Against the Gods, the Remarkable Story of Risk*. Wiley.

Brown, Terry. 1997. *English Martial Arts*. London. Anglo Saxon Press.

Capwell, Tobias. 2012. *The Noble Art of the Sword*. London. The Wallace Collection.

Castle, Egerton. 1892. *Schools and Masters of Fence*. London. George Bell and Sons.

Charrette, Robert N. 2011. *Fiore dei Liberi's Armizare, The Chivalric Martial Arts System of Il Fior di Battaglia*. Wheaton, IL. Freelance Academy Press.

Clements, John. 1998. *Medieval Swordsmanship*. Boulder, CO. Paladin Press.

Dweck, Carol. 2006. *Mindset: The New Psychology of Success*. New York. Random House.

Ekirch, Roger. 2006. *At Day's Close: A History of Nighttime*. W&N.

Epstein, David. 2013. *The Sports Gene*. London. Yellow Jersey Press.

Fallows, Noel. 2010. *Jousting in Medieval and Renaissance Iberia*. Ipswich. Boydell and Brewer Ltd.

Ferriss, Tim. 2011. *The Four Hour Body*. New York. Vermilion.

Ferriss, Tim. 2012. *The Four Hour Chef*. New York. Houghton Mifflin.

Gallwey, Timothy. 1997. *The Inner Game of Tennis*. Random House Trade Paperbacks.

Gaugler, William M. 1998. *The History of Fencing*. Bangor, Maine. Laureate Press.

Gilbert, Daniel. 2007. *Stumbling Upon Happiness*. Vintage.

Goldacre, Ben. 2009. *Bad Science*. HarperCollins. London.

Harmenberg, Johan and Björne Väggö. 2007. *Epee 2.0*. SKA Swordplay Books.

Harris, Sam. 2015. *Waking Up*. New York. Bantam Press.

Hegarty, Stephanie. 2012. "The myth of the eight-hour sleep" (article). BBC. http://www.bbc.co.uk/news/magazine-16964783

Heffernan, Margaret. 2012. *Willful Blindness: Why We Ignore the Obvious at Our Peril*. London. Simon and Schuster.

Hodgkinson, Tom. 2012. *Brave Old World*. London. Penguin.

Hutton, Alfred. 1901. *The Sword and the Centuries*. London. Grant Richards.

Johnsson, Peter. 2012. "Righteousness is Quadrangular: A Hypothesis on Geometric Proportions of Medieval Swords." Park Lane Arms Fair Catalogue, Spring 2012. London Arms Fair. London. 14–27.

Kaeuper, Richard and Elspeth Kennedy. 1996. *The Book of Chivalry of Geoffroi de Charny: Text, Context, and Translation*. Philadelphia. University of Pennsylvania Press.

Kahneman, Daniel. 2012. *Thinking, Fast and Slow*. Penguin.

Leoni, Tom. 2010. *Venetian Rapier: Nicoletto Giganti's 1606 Rapier Fencing Curriculum*. Wheaton, IL. Freelance Academy Press.

Leoni, Tom. 2011. *The Art and Practice of Fencing*. Wheaton, IL. Freelance Academy Press. (Translation of Capoferro's *Gran Simulacro*.)

Leoni, Tom. 2012. *Fiore dei Liberi Fior di Battaglia*, Second English Edition. Wheaton, IL. Freelance Academy Press.

Malipiero, Massimo. 2006. *Il Fior di battaglia di Fiore dei Liberi da*

Cividale (Il Codice Ludwig XV 13 del J. Paul Getty Museum). Udine, Italy. Ribis.

McBane, Donald. 1728. *The Expert Sword-man's Companion.* Glasgow. James Duncan.

McDougall, Christopher. 2016. *Natural Born Heroes: The Lost Secrets of Strength and Endurance.* Profile Books

McGuff, Doug, and John Little. 2009. *Body by Science.* New York. McGraw-Hill.

Morgan, Forrest E. 1992. *Living the Martial Way.* Barricade Books.

Muhlberger, S. 2014. *Charny's Men at Arms: Questions Concerning the Joust, Tournament and War.* Wheaton, IL. Freelance Academy Press.

Norman, A.V. B. 1980. *The Rapier and Small-sword: 1460-1820.* Ayer Co Pub.

Novati, Francesco. 1902. *Flos Duellatorum in Armis, Sine Armis, Equester, Pedester. Il Fior di Battaglia di Maestro Fiore dei Liberi da Premariacco.* Bergamo. Istituto Italiano d'Arte Grafiche.

Oakeshott, Ewart. 1991. *Records of the Medieval Sword.* Boydell Press.

Pinker, Stephen. 2011. *The Better Angels of Our Nature.* Penguin.

Pollan, Michael. 2007. *The Omnivore's Dilemma.* London. Penguin.

Porzio, Luca and Gregory Mele. 2003. *Arte Gladiatoria Dimicandi: 15th Century Swordsmanship of Master Filippo Vadi.* Union City, California. Chivalry Bookshelf.

Richardson, Brian. 2009. *Manuscript Culture in Renaissance Italy.* Cambridge. Cambridge University Press. Paperback edition 2014.

Rippetoe, Mark. 2011. *Starting Strength (3rd edition).* Wichita Falls. The Aasgaard Company.

Scarr, Graham. 2014. *Biotensegrity: The Structural Basis Of Life.* Fountainhall, UK. Handspring Publishing Limited.

Silver, George. 1599. *Paradoxes of Defence.* London. Edward Blount.

Silver, George. 1898. *The Works of George Silver.* Ed. Cyril G.R. Matthey. London. George Bell and Sons.

Starrett, Dr Kelly. 2013. *Becoming a Supple Leopard.* Las Vegas. Victory Belt Publishing.

Starrett, Dr Kelly. 2016. *Deskbound: Standing Up to a Sitting World.* Las Vegas. Victory Belt Publishing.

Stephenson, Neal. 2012. *Some Remarks.* New York. William Morrow.

Szabo, Laszlo. 1998. *Fencing and the Master.* SKA Swordplay Books

Taubes, Gary. 2008. *Good Calories, Bad Calories.* New York. Anchor Books.

Tobler, Christian. 2002. *Secrets of German Medieval Swordsmanship.* Benecia, CA. Chivalry Bookshelf.

Tobler, Christian. 2004. *Fighting with the German Longsword.* Highland Village, TX. Chivalry Bookshelf.

Tobler, Christian Henry. 2006. *In Service of the Duke: The 15th Century Fighting Treatise of Paulus Kal.* Highland Village, Texas. Chivalry Bookshelf. (Reproduction and translation of Kal's *Cgm 1507.*)

Tsatsouline, Pavel. 2001. *Relax Into Stretch.* Saint Paul. Dragon Door Publications.

Tsatsouline, Pavel. 2003. *The Naked Warrior.* Saint Paul. Dragon Door Publications.

Turner, Craig and Tony Soper. 1990. *Methods and Practice of Elizabethan Swordplay.* Carbonsdale and Edwardsville, IL. Southern Illinois University Press.

Viggiani, Angelo. 1575. *Lo Schermo.* Trans Jherek Swanger. Published online at http://mac9.ucc.nau.edu/manuscripts/LoSchermo.pdf

Walker, Matthew. 2017. *Why We Sleep: The New Science Of Sleep And Dreams.* London, Allen Lane.

Waitzkin, Josh. 2008. *The Art of Learning.* Free Press.

Whymper, Edward. 1871. *Scrambles Amongst the Alps in the years 1860-1869.* London. John Murray.

Wilson, William. 2002. *The Arte of Defence.* Benecia, CA. Chivalry Bookshelf.

Windsor, Guy. 2012. *Mastering the Art of Arms, volume 1: The Medieval Dagger.* Wheaton, IL. Freelance Academy Press.

Windsor, Guy. 2014. *Mastering the Art of Arms, volume 2: The Medieval Longsword*. Helsinki. The School of European Swordsmanship.

Windsor, Guy. 2016. *Mastering the Art of Arms, volume 3: Advanced Longsword: Form and Function*. Helsinki. The School of European Swordsmanship.

ACKNOWLEDGEMENTS

This chunky volume has benefitted enormously from the help, advice, suggestions and criticism of many people, both in its incarnations as instalments of *The Swordsman's Quick Guide* and in its current form. These kind and helpful souls deserve my thanks; and if you like this book, yours too!

Beta readers for instalments of the *Swordsman's Quick Guide*. These kind souls read and commented on the earliest drafts of some of the chapters in this book:

Andrew Lawrence-King, José Luis Zamarripa, Chris Halpin-Durband, Alan Gee, Fuller November, Amy Peare, Mariusz Wesolowski, Gregorio Manzanera, Jeremy Bornstein, Robert Elm, Peter Jaimez, Carlos Loscertales, Tom Outwin, Juha Pitkänen, Michael Bernstein, Tero Alanko, Richard Cullinan, Ilkka Hartikainen, Jake Priddy, Jordan Hinckley, James Wran, Sascha VonSachsen, Christian Stickel, Alex Hanning, Reinier van Noort, Eduan Slabbert, Teemu Kari, Kelley Costigan, James Wran, Tuomas Tähtinen, Erkan Mete, Michael Beardwood, Juuso-Matias Maijanen, Enrico Tomasi, and Haden Parkes.

Beta readers for this book had a thorough look at the first draft and quite rightly tore it to shreds. Most notably, I expanded the section on tournaments, and added a lot of the physical training material thanks to their suggestions. My focus has always been on books I can actually read, and as I can only read European languages (English, Italian, French, Spanish and some Finnish), that made me blind to sources from outside Europe (such as the Persian and Korean sources available). My beta readers pointed out that Historical Martial Arts exist outside of Europe too. Those beta readers are:

William Jost del Solar, David Tehan, Lee Marshall, Russell Weisfield, Liam P. Boyle, Jason Palumbo, Sean M. Barton, Martin Schol, Pete Diggins, Lindoret of Byrn Myrddin (Linda Ramsbottom), Tom Karnuta, Théodore Bray Laverdure, Tyson Wright, Mike Prendergast, Gindi Wauchope.

I would also like to thank Dr. Manouchehr Moshtagh Khorasani, whom I met in New Zealand in October 2017. It was this meeting that convinced me that Historical Martial Arts are indeed a global phenomenon, and not confined to Europe.

Writing a book is one thing, publishing it is something else. I rely entirely on my team of freelancers: Becca Judd, editor of outstanding pernicketyness, Bek Pickard, layout expert and cover designer, and Kate Tilton my assistant, who does the boring stuff so I can get on with the writing. My mum also did an amazing job of proofreading the book. My friends Dierk Hagedorn and Curtis Fee helped greatly with the cover design.

It takes a village to raise a child, and it takes a team to create a book worth reading. It's my name on the cover so I take full responsibility for the content, but the credit should be shared. Thank you all.

ABOUT THE AUTHOR

Dr Guy Windsor is one of the founders of the Historical Martial Arts movement, and began reconstructing swordsmanship styles from historical sources in the early nineties. He was one of the founders of the Dawn Duellists Society in Edinburgh, and of the British Federation for Historical Swordplay. Both these organisations are still running. In 2001 he moved to Finland to found The School of European Swordsmanship, which soon expanded across Finland, and now has branches and study groups worldwide. Guy has been a guest instructor at dozens of other schools and events, and is one of the most highly renowned teachers, writers, and practitioners in the field. In 2018 Edinburgh University awarded him a PhD by Research Publications for his work recreating HMA.

His other books include *The Swordsman's Companion, The Duellist's Companion, The Armizare Vade Mecum, The Medieval Dagger, The Medieval Longsword, Advanced Longsword,* and *Swordfighting,* in addition to a host of articles and blog posts.

You can find him online at guywindsor.com

Remember to visit
https://guywindsor.net/blog/theoryandpractice
for free books, videos, and other resources.